Praise for
The Sharper Your Knife, the Less You Cry

"I can never get enough of true stories about people who stop in the middle of their life's journey to ask, 'What do I really want?' and then have the guts to actually go get it. Kathleen Flinn's tale of chasing her ultimate dream makes for a really lovely book— engaging, intelligent and surprisingly suspenseful."

—Elizabeth Gilbert, author of *Eat, Pray, Love*

"*The Sharper Your Knife, the Less You Cry* is an engaging story about a fantasy fulfilled. It's *Under the Tuscan Sun* goes to cooking school."

—Michael Ruhlman, author of *The Soul of a Chef*

"Although I can't cook my way out of a *sac de papier*, I found this book a joy to read. It's a compelling story about learning to cook and learning to love at the same time, told with humility, humor, and passion."

—Bill Radke, host of NPR's *Weekend America*

"Kat Flinn's vivid story of her adventures at Le Cordon Bleu Paris had me smiling page after page. It's about what you should always think about in the pressure behind a hot stove—the pure romance of cooking."

—Jerry Traunfeld, author of *The Herbfarm Cookbook*
and *The Herbal Kitchen*

ABOUT THE AUTHOR

Kathleen Flinn has been a writer and journalist for twenty years. Her work has appeared in the *Chicago Sun-Times, USA Weekend, Smithsonian, Men's Fitness,* and *The Globe and Mail* (Toronto), among many other publications. She divides her time between Seattle, Washington, and Anna Maria Island, Florida.

THE
SHARPER YOUR KNIFE,
THE LESS YOU CRY

LOVE, LAUGHTER, AND TEARS IN PARIS AT THE
WORLD'S MOST FAMOUS COOKING SCHOOL

Kathleen Flinn

PENGUIN BOOKS

PENGUIN BOOKS

Published by the Penguin Group

Penguin Group (USA) Inc., 375 Hudson Street, New York, New York 10014, U.S.A.
Penguin Group (Canada), 90 Eglinton Avenue East, Suite 700, Toronto,
Ontario, Canada M4P 2Y3 (a division of Pearson Penguin Canada Inc.)
Penguin Books Ltd, 80 Strand, London WC2R 0RL, England
Penguin Ireland, 25 St Stephen's Green, Dublin 2, Ireland (a division of Penguin Books Ltd)
Penguin Group (Australia), 250 Camberwell Road, Camberwell,
Victoria 3124, Australia (a division of Pearson Australia Group Pty Ltd)
Penguin Books India Pvt Ltd, 11 Community Centre, Panchsheel Park, New Delhi – 110 017, India
Penguin Group (NZ), 67 Apollo Drive, Rosedale, North Shore 0632,
New Zealand (a division of Pearson New Zealand Ltd)
Penguin Books (South Africa) (Pty) Ltd, 24 Sturdee Avenue,
Rosebank, Johannesburg 2196, South Africa

Penguin Books Ltd, Registered Offices:
80 Strand, London WC2R 0RL, England

First published in the United States of America by Viking Penguin,
a member of Penguin Group (USA) Inc. 2007
Published in Penguin Books 2008

1   3   5   7   9   10   8   6   4   2

Names and identifying characteristics have been changed
to protect the privacy of certain individuals.

THE LIBRARY OF CONGRESS HAS CATALOGED THE HARDCOVER EDITION AS FOLLOWS:
Flinn, Kathleen.
The sharper your knife, the less you cry : love, laughter, and tears at the world's
most famous cooking school / by Kathleen Flinn.
p. cm.
ISBN 978-0-670-01822-2 (hc.)
ISBN 978-0-14-311413-0 (pbk.)
1. Cordon bleu (School : Paris, France)   2. Flinn, Kathleen—Knowledge and learning.
3. Cookery—Study and teaching—France.   I. Cordon bleu (School : Paris, France)   II. Title.
TX669.F8F585   2007
641.07—dc22   2006102084

Printed in the United States of America
Set in Bembo
Designed by Daniel Lagin

For Mike

There are not enough words in any language to say how much I love you.

CONTENTS

AUTHOR'S NOTE

This book is drawn from my personal experiences while studying at Le Cordon Bleu in Paris in 2004 and 2005. Although every character in this book is based on a real person, most of the names have been changed, including those of all the chefs. In a handful of cases, I've altered identifying details to protect privacy. In a few instances, time has been compressed and events rearranged for the purpose of story and narrative.

Readers should know that I paid my own tuition and that I waited to tell Le Cordon Bleu about this book until I had written and sold the manuscript. Drawing on my background as a journalist, I wanted to be treated like any other student so that I could tell an objective story. During school, I kept a journal that ran more than 600 pages, recorded about 120 hours of audio from demonstration classes, and took detailed notes on the 300-plus recipes in the curriculum. That material, along with interviews of students, school staff, and alumni, form the basis of this book.

This account is not meant to describe what every student experiences while attending the world's most famous cooking school—only what I did.

The Sharper Your Knife, the Less You Cry

THIS IS NOT FOR PRETEND

"Cooking is like love. It should be entered into with abandon, or not at all."

— Harriet Van Horne, *Vogue* (1956)

As a little girl, while other children played house, I played restaurant. In our basement, I set up two sets of child-sized chairs and tables topped with fabric remnants and plastic flowers. I scrawled menus in crayon, featuring the likes of licorice soup, Pez casserole, and cotton-candy pie. I pretended to prepare everything for my guests—often imaginary—on a broken-down Easy-Bake oven. My parents viewed it all as an overzealous game of tea.

I think of that now, as I stand here in ill-fitting kitchen whites in the middle of a cramped training kitchen in Paris. My handwritten notes from the day's demonstration, sheathed in a protective plastic liner, sit crowded within the twenty-two inches I'm allotted on the nine-foot-long marble worktable. My blue-handled knives lie neatly along the edges of a scarred plastic cutting board. I feel the heat from the electric stove at my back. A chef who has headed a legendary Paris restaurant now prowls this kitchen, barking out orders in French.

This is not for pretend.

As we've done three or four times a week since January, my Basic Cuisine class gathered this morning en masse, on time and in uniform. We first watch a chef move through a three-hour demonstration; we anxiously take notes, as we must repeat his lesson in a training kitchen later. This afternoon, I'm searing thick *magrets de canard* for a classic preparation of duck à l'orange. *Magrets* are the breasts of Moulard ducks force-fed corn to fatten their livers for foie gras, a process that fattens everything on the duck. We must take care with the sauce, a slightly complicated preparation that requires cautious reduction of veal stock and orange juice, the sweetness tempered with vinegar. Our potatoes and carrots must be "turned"—a cut that transforms an otherwise unremarkable vegetable into a precise seven-sided torpedo shape.

This is my life now. I am no longer a corporate refugee, sitting in my cubicle with photos of Paris tacked to the wall, dreaming about learning to cook at the world's most famous culinary school. Three months ago, I walked out of my office for the last time, in my hands a heavy cardboard box filled with what felt like my entire life. A knot hit my throat in the elevator on my way down. It's hard to know how to feel when you leave a job; it's even harder when a job leaves you.

I've traded that life for days spent soaking up heat in the kitchen or absorbing knowledge from the chefs. I chop, braise, grill, roast, and sauté. Every session in the kitchen feels like an exercise in stress loading. We must complete our recipes within two and a half hours, shifting raw, whole ingredients into a finished, attractive dish presented to the chef on a warmed plate. The food must be hot, it must demonstrate technique, and, above all, its flavor must appeal to the meticulous taste buds of the French chefs.

Some of my classmates have cooked professionally. About half plan to go on to work as chefs. I fit into neither category. I just want to learn to cook. Some days it goes well, sometimes it doesn't.

Today, the chef is not in good humor. His mercurial moods have earned him a nickname from me, the Gray Chef, not only for his graying hair but also for the clouds that sometimes follow him into the kitchen.

I take care as I arrange and finish my dish and present my plate to the chef for my daily grade. He does not smile as I put it down in front of him. Chef takes a quick taste with a spoon, and his dour face darkens. Suddenly, a wrath is unleashed. My offense, ostensibly minor: a too-sweet sauce. But to the Gray Chef, this symbolizes a shameful culinary trespass—he believes I have not followed his mantra, to *taste, taste, taste* while cooking.

"C'EST HORRIBLE!" he shouts at me. With that, he begins a rant. "Ça n'est pas difficile! . . . Pourquoi présenteriez-vous ce plat?! . . . Vous ne pourriez pas servir ceci!"

I snatch at words, trying to comprehend. "You," "serve," "no," and "this."

He slams a meaty fist against the counter, inadvertently tipping the edge of the plate I'd just presented. It spins hard on the marble worktable. The tense kitchen halts as the students freeze midmotion. Chef's face grows visibly red as he escalates his fierce attack on me in rapid-fire French.

My head sinks as his voice rises, and I try to fight back the tears—not just from his diatribe but from the humiliation of being unable to defend myself. In the nine weeks since classes began, my college French has proved wretchedly inadequate.

Everyone waits. The chef stares at me.

They expect me to say something, *anything* in French to my defense. But I can't think of a single word. He sighs. Like most chefs at the school, he speaks little English. Disappointed that I haven't grasped his insulting wrath *en français,* he waves me away and turns to the next student, a Taiwanese girl with thick glasses. As she apprehensively extends her plate, he volleys over one last assault, the coup de grâce:

"Vous perdez votre temps!"

My mind races to translate. *Perdez?* To misplace? To be lost? To waste. I move to the other words. "You." "Time." "Your."

Then comes the dawn.

"You're wasting your time."

That's it. I turn back to my oven. As the kitchen resumes its buzz, I start to cry. Robotically, I rush to pack up my knives and flee down the three flights of stairs to the cramped basement locker rooms, where I escape into a pocket-sized staff bathroom and lock the door. I cannot stop the tears now. I have not sobbed like this in years. Then, I catch my reflection in the mirror.

Under a buzzing fluorescent light, I see my smeared mascara and stained kitchen whites. I am thirty-six, unemployed, and I've spent the last of my savings to pursue a dream of studying at Le Cordon Bleu only to be reduced to tears by a chef I hardly know in a language I barely understand.

What am I doing here? Maybe this is all a big mistake.

PART I

BASIC CUISINE

"This isn't cooking, it's like learning a complicated sport!"
—Kim, a student in Basic Cuisine

CHAPTER 1

LIFE IS NOT A DRESS REHEARSAL

"I didn't start cooking until I was thirty-two. Until then, I just ate."
—Julia Child

After a few moments of small talk and tea, my boss leaned over, clasped her hands, and dropped her smile. "This is going to be a very difficult conversation," she began.

I should have known. It's never a good sign when the boss tells you to avoid the office when you come back from vacation. Worse, she insisted we meet in a hotel lobby two hours after my plane had landed. I nodded, kept my composure, and declined an offer of more tea. I stood up, smoothed my skirt, and walked out.

With that, I lost a job that I was desperate to quit. I felt relieved yet rejected to the point of being crushed, not unlike when a boyfriend has the gall to break up with you before you break up with him.

I pushed open the door of the hotel, my head held high, pleased that I did not break down at the news. I was tough, I told myself, and this was not such a big deal. Twenty minutes ago, I was an executive with a major software company, the manager of twenty-four people, and a member of a team that ran a hundred-million-dollar division.

Now who am I? As an American living in London, without my job I can't stay in the United Kingdom. In one fell swoop, I felt dismissed from both the company and the country.

I stopped abruptly on the street, blinking in the bright afternoon sun. Where was I going? People swarmed around me on the sidewalk, each with a purpose. It was 2:23 on a Monday afternoon, and I had no idea where to go or what to do next. I had never been unemployed a single day since I had turned sixteen.

Since then, I'd done what so many of us think we're supposed to do: work hard and be successful. I went to college and then I worked, first as a newspaper journalist, trying to prove myself with every story, sometimes two or three a day. Almost by accident, I wound up on the corporate ladder for nearly eight years. I fought tenaciously for every rung with sixty to seventy hours a week, weekends spent working, relationships left in a heap. All along, I'd been rewarded, Pavlov style, with incremental rewards of a raise here, a promotion there. It had been enough, until a year ago when I'd been promoted to a grown-up middle-management position.

"There's no career path for writers at this company," a human-resources woman with overplucked eyebrows counseled me. "Of course you want this promotion, don't you?"

I'm a woman; in so many ways, I've been programmed to please. I took the job and spent time hunkered over figures, budgets, charts, and fiscal-year projections. I tried, but I hated it.

"Working at a job you don't like is the same as going to prison every day," my father used to say. He was right. I felt imprisoned by an impressive title, travel, perks, and a good salary. On the inside, I was miserable and lonely, and I felt as if I was losing myself. I spent weekends working on reports no one read, and I gave presentations that I didn't care about. It made me feel like a sellout and, worse, a fraud.

Now set free, like any inmate I had to figure out what to do with the rest of my life. I turned down a side street to avoid walking past my office building and took a long way home to my flat near Covent Garden.

As I do in any moment of trauma, I phoned my mother. A former human-resources manager, she responded to the news with sheer panic. "You have to get another job immediately," she urged on the phone. "Or you'll never get hired anywhere ever again."

Unsettled, I headed upstairs for another opinion—not to God but to my neighbor Jeff. "Nah, just live off your severance for a while," he suggested. He himself was unemployed and therefore capable of pouring me a glass of pinot grigio at three in the afternoon as I sat in his kitchen watching him make a cranberry tart.

I finished my wine and went to my own apartment to call my best friend, Laura, who alternated between doling out pragmatic advice and corralling her two children. "You should try to get a job back at the main office in Seattle. NATALIE! PUT THAT DOWN! I mean it! . . . They'll pay to move your stuff back to the U.S., and besides—NATALIE! Give that G.I. Joe back to your brother! I don't care that you put a dress on him! . . . You'll be in Seattle with Mike. Isn't that what you want?"

As I'd just learned on vacation, Mike *was* what I wanted.

Mike and I had become friends about three years earlier, when I'd left Seattle after he'd helped me get a job in my company's London office, where he was working as a senior manager at the time. Strong chemistry bonded us from the start. We flirted, we danced, we once kissed but resisted more, fearing it could damage our friendship. That is, until three months ago when we found ourselves alone on a weekend trip in Milan. Our short romance was going so well that I invited him home to meet my family in Florida—something I hadn't done with a boyfriend since college.

I rented a romantic, odd, little brick house near the beach, distinguished by a round tower meant to evoke a small castle in Normandy. I picked Mike up at the airport in Tampa, giddy with excitement as I greeted him at the gate. We drove to the bungalow with plans to change for dinner, but we never made it to the restaurant.

Instead, we broke the bed in the master bedroom—in three places.

The next morning, Mike awoke early to mend the shattered bed frame before my family arrived. But, eager to meet him, they showed up early—two hours early, just as Mike began clamping and gluing key pieces back together. The pieces lay scattered on the living-room floor, and the seven members of my family offered to help, making the whole situation worse.

My stepdad, Eddie, is an old-fashioned type who had not been keen on me and Mike "sharing quarters" from the beginning. A few days earlier, he had counseled me on why I was still unmarried. "Why would a man buy the cow when he can get the eggs for free?" He cast a suspicious eye on the whole situation as he thoughtfully chewed on a toothpick.

He broke the conversation with a loud cough.

"That bed's made out of solid mahogany, isn't it? How'd it get broken there anyway, Mike?" He rolled the toothpick around, looking at Mike hard, waiting for an answer.

"Hey, I forgot, I brought bagels," my mother said brightly, attempting to divert the conversation.

Eddie picked up a piece of wood. "Is it broken here, too?"

My mother grabbed him. "Honey, you *need* a bagel" and shoved him into the small kitchen. My brother-in-law helped Mike move the pieces outside. The next day, my mother pulled me aside. "Broke the bed? I'm impressed," she said, winking. "If that happened how I think it happened, I'd say *he's* a keeper."

The rest of the week was bliss. No one mentioned the bed again. We ate burgers at a favorite beach shack, we made sand castles with my niece, and we walked the beach at sunset, hand in hand, almost every night. I cooked dinners that I served by candlelight in the vaguely gothic dining room of the "castle."

On the last morning of our trip, wrapped up together warmly in the sun-filled room in the now-fixed bed, I looked at him sleeping. A startling revelation hit me: *I could wake up next to this man every day for the rest of my life.*

By that evening, we were apart once again. He got on a plane for Seattle, and I caught the red-eye back to London, only to get sacked two hours after my plane touched the ground.

"So what do you think?" I asked Mike, deciding it was finally late enough to call him. The eight-hour time difference had been a detriment to our blossoming romance. I was making a case to join him in Seattle. I could only hope that he wanted me as much as I wanted to be with him.

"I've got work-permit hell to go through to get another job in the UK. But I could probably get a job in Seattle, and we'd at least be in the same city. I mean, if you *want* me to be in the same city."

He thought for a long moment. "No, you shouldn't come to Seattle."

My heart fell.

"Because what I really think," he said slowly, "is that you should put your stuff in storage, go to Paris, and study at Le Cordon Bleu."

"*What?* Where did that come from?"

He reminded me of an evening I'd almost forgotten. It was a brisk, full-moon night in October 1999. I'd flown to London for my final job interview, and afterward Mike invited me to a dinner party at a friend's house. We arrived before the other guests, and his flustered friend handed us a list and sent us straight back out to a neighborhood store. "Go through the park, it's faster," she said, and turned around, apron strings flying. We talked as we walked, the night lit almost as bright as day from the brilliant moon. He was fishing, asking questions, the kind that you ask to really get to know a person.

"If you could do anything, anything at all with your life, what would it be?" he asked. I had a ready answer, but I debated whether to tell him. We barely knew each other; this was the first time we had ever been alone together. But something about him was reassuring. My secret dream, I told him, would be to work in London for a couple of years and then quit to go live in Paris and study French cuisine at Le Cordon Bleu. He mused on it.

"I like it," he said. "How about if I quit my job then, too, and I'll go with you. Is it a deal?" We shook on it and then held hands as we walked back through the park to his friend's flat.

Back on the phone, I told him that that was just a dream. This was reality. "My mother says I'll never get another job if I don't get one right away."

"Sure you will, just go do this first. Why not? You're not married, you don't have kids, and now you don't have a job." He knew one way to get to me. "Do you want to be on your deathbed, wondering why you never went?"

I can't afford it, I argued.

"They're going to give you a severance. You've got some savings," he replied. "And if you have to, you can cash in your 401(k)."

I don't speak French well enough, I said.

"You know enough to get started, and besides there's no better place to learn."

I won't know anyone in Paris.

He paused.

"You'll know me," he said gently. "If you want me to, I'll go with you."

It turns out that you can sign up for Le Cordon Bleu online in a process that appears dangerously simple. Prerequisites are few. After hanging up with Mike, I go online and take a look. "Je regarde, tout simplement," I think, *I'm just looking.*

To earn a diploma from Le Cordon Bleu, a student must successfully complete three parts of what it calls its "classic cycle": Basic, Intermediate, and Superior Cuisine. A student can study cuisine, pâtisserie, or both at the same time. The cost for Basic Cuisine was €6,750, or $8,842 with the unfavorable exchange rate. For the full cuisine diploma, the tuition was more than $26,500.

I got up and walked around my flat, shaking my hands as I do at these times when I long for a cigarette even though I've never been a smoker. I looked out the window at the busy London street below, where people—employed people—were scurrying home from work. How much would it cost to live in Paris? What if things didn't work out with Mike? What if I didn't get another job? I had never been unemployed. What if . . .

It won't hurt for me to just read through the application, I thought.

Did I have a high school diploma? Yes. Did I have a college diploma? Yes. Could I tell them about my work experience and attach a résumé? No problem.

Then I came to the five-hundred-word "Statement of Motivation," the key component of the application. Why did I want to study at Le Cordon Bleu? Ugh. I wasn't sure how to answer that. I sat back and looked at the screen.

It started with my sister, but an obituary clenched it.

Eight years my senior, Sandy got her Francophile tendencies from I don't know where, living as we did on a ten-acre farm in semirural Michigan. By the time I was four, the rose-colored walls of the bedroom we shared were thoroughly plastered with posters and photos of Paris. I literally dreamed about it—a glimpse of the Eiffel Tower was often the last thing I saw before falling asleep. After reigning for two years as president of her high school French club, she mailed away for an application to the Sorbonne in Paris. The heavy packet arrived *par avion* the day after our father was diagnosed with terminal cancer.

It was twenty-five years before my sister could bring herself to visit Paris for the first time.

When I was thirteen years old, my father died. I found myself alone with my mother, and it was hard. I was in a new school in a new state, with no friends. We'd recently escaped the Michigan winters, hoping the milder climate of southwest Florida would benefit Dad's fragile health. My mother was beyond devastated. Married for twenty-six years, my parents were always in love, the kind of couple who still got dressed up and went out on Saturday-night dates even after they had five kids. I was the youngest, a daddy's girl. I had worshipped him. For both of us, grief was exhausting. My mother would lie in bed for an hour or two when she came home from work just to get the strength to make us dinner.

On days that I didn't have ballet lessons, I came home three hours earlier than Mom. So, one afternoon, I went ahead and made *boeuf bourguignon* for dinner. I'd made it a year earlier for a Girl Scout badge, using Julia Child's recipe. Mom was thrilled. The next night, I tried trout almondine, and then leek and potato soup the night after that.

Feeding my grieving mother gave me a purpose, and this brought me out of my own depression. No more make-believe food but real food that simmered, smelled, and sizzled, and someone destined to eat it, and whose appreciation fed me in return.

Shortly afterward, Mom went back to college. She agreed to hand over the reins of our meager food budget; with Dad gone, we had to rely on her $5.50 hourly income. I clipped coupons and pored over the weekly food sections, my mother's *Joy of Cooking,* and my sister's copy of *Mastering the Art of French Cooking*. Sometimes Mom took me to the grocery store, sometimes I took the bus.

This made me unlike other kids. Most teenagers don't ask for a good sauté pan for Christmas. While other high school kids threw keg parties, I organized formal dinners for my friends. On my sixteenth birthday, I got both my driver's license and a job in a yacht-club restaurant. It wasn't much of a yacht club, as it had berths for only four small boats. But it was a pretty good restaurant despite a kitchen managed by the horrible Chef Randy. After starting on the buffet table, I was promoted to salads and stealthily shifted to plating desserts. I quit after Chef Randy dropped his false teeth into a chafing pan of bread pudding, fished them out, and insisted that I put it on the buffet anyway.

Despite that, I came to an important conclusion. I wanted to be a chef.

Or a ballerina, I couldn't decide.

My mother, by then a college graduate herself, nixed both ideas. She insisted that I get a "real degree." I didn't know where to do that, either. I threw a dart at a map on my wall, and it ended up on Gary, Indiana. Since no one would willingly move to Gary, I packed up my car and headed to Chicago, with vague plans for law school.

I returned to Florida five years later with a journalism degree. Times were tough in the print world, so despite internships at *Playboy* and *Adweek* magazines I found myself writing obituaries under a despotic editor at my hometown newspaper. Taking a break from death, I flipped through a *Gourmet* magazine. An ad caught my eye: "Study French cuisine in Paris," read the headline. The walls of my childhood bedroom flashed through my mind. In the ad, a proud student smiled in her white chef's jacket. I cut out the ad and taped it to the wall of my cubicle. When my editor agitated or the work became painfully dull, I'd look at that ad and imagine myself crafting a soufflé in the school's kitchen. It surely had to be more glamorous than the obits desk in Sarasota.

Then, one day, I typed in the shortest obituary I'd ever seen.

It read simply: "Gladys Smith, 82, died Saturday at home. She was the wife of the late Harold Smith. She left no survivors."* No services. No

---

* Not her real name.

directions for flowers or donations as a clue to any interests or hobbies. Apparently no college education, no profession, no personal *accomplishments*. What had this woman done with her life? I wondered. Did she ever wonder that? I cut that out and tacked it up, too, as a reminder of my parents' constant phrase: "Life is not a dress rehearsal." Right then, I resolved that I wanted my own obituary to read, "She also earned a degree from Le Cordon Bleu in Paris." The ad and the obit followed me to later desks I occupied as my career shifted from newspaper reporter to magazine editor to restaurant critic to corporate executive with the company that had just let me go.

But how do you sum all that up, explain that in five hundred words or less?

I wrote:

I have wanted to attend Le Cordon Bleu for at least 10 years. No, that's not true. I think I've always wanted to go to Le Cordon Bleu, even before I knew that's what I wanted. I have been passionate about food and cooking since I was a little girl. Professionally, I have worked as a journalist for more than a decade. I once figured out that by age 30, I'd written a thousand stories. I've worked as a restaurant critic and a food writer, and I believe this training will give me greater understanding and perspective in that aspect of my career. It is my dream to write books about food, about cooking, about nourishing people, heart, soul and stomach. . . . I don't know that I want to be a chef, or that I particularly want to work in the food industry when I am done with my training. . . . I just know that going to Le Cordon Bleu is something that I have to do.

I sat back and looked at the bright screen. The room had grown dark. *This is crazy, I can't do this,* I thought, and moved forward to hit DELETE. But something stopped me. My hand hovering above the keyboard, I thought of my sister, who never got to study at the Sorbonne. I thought of my dad, who died at age fifty. My mind ran back to that short obit. Mike was right. I could go now or spend my life wondering why I didn't.

"Life is not a dress rehearsal," I whispered to myself.

Instead of DELETE, I hit ENTER.

Three days later, I got a response by email. I had been assigned one of the last places in Basic Cuisine for January 2004. Classes started in just twenty-four days.

CHAPTER 2

LOST IN TRANSLATION

LESSON HIGHLIGHTS: INTRODUCTION TO THE RULES,
UNIFORMS, AND A TOUR OF THE SCHOOL

As a building, Le Cordon Bleu is not immediately impressive. Nestled on a nondescript residential street in southwest Paris, the four-story beige structure was formerly a medical clinic, the larger examination rooms now converted into kitchens. On orientation day, I walk right past the entrance before I spot the blue logos stenciled on the windows. Inside, I find a compact reception area stuffed with staffers and students.

An elegant French woman with a dark chignon, draped in a purple pashmina, claps her hands twice amid the crowd.

"*Vous tous,* everyone, they're starting, come with me," she says, herding us around the corner to a vaulted room where some seventy students sit arranged toward a trio of women at the far end. I slide into an open seat directly in front of a graceful Asian woman clad in a black Chanel suit.

My French culinary training begins—in Japanese.

"Ohayou gozaimasu!" belts the woman in Chanel. My hands fly to cover my ears. I've inadvertently sat among two dozen Japanese students. For the next hour, she continues a strident, concurrent translation for their benefit, drowning out both the French presenter and the English translator.

Still, it's impossible not to get the drift. They start with the vaguely draconian school rules: uniforms must be immaculate; no jewelry can be worn except wedding rings; no tardiness; and only four permitted absences—no exceptions. Well, there's one. For a resident visa, the French government requires a medical exam. Impossible to reschedule, the school allows an absence should it cause a conflict. So students may be excused for the sake of French bureaucracy but not for contracting the Ebola virus.

Leading the presentation is a freckled fifty-something woman with a distinct American accent, the lead academic administrator for the school. She motions to a soft-faced girl to show off the uniform: an apron worn over a crisp white jacket, houndstooth trousers, and a white necker-chief. Under her cap, the girl's nut-brown hair is held back by butterfly barrettes.

Madame introduces two chefs wearing tall toques. They nod politely, and one begins to talk in a quiet French monotone, his voice no competition with the staccato Japanese translation. I give up trying to hear and look around the room.

Known as the Jardin d'Hiver, or the Winter Garden, this airy loft provides the school's sole communal gathering spot. A peaked glass ceiling offers ample light for a few live trees to grow in huge planters. For orienta-tion, blue-and-white caned bistro chairs are arranged in rows, their match-ing tables pushed to the side. High on a wall, there's an official-looking plaque commemorating the opening of this latest physical incarnation of the school in 1988. It feels like an institution: practical, yet furnished on a budget.

The audience skews young, with most students in their twenties. About three quarters are women, and one third or more appear Asian. It's a cold January day, and many cradle Styrofoam cups of coffee gathered from a nearby table. They're all paying rapt attention—except for a strik-ing brunette in the back row, scanning the crowd. She reminds me of someone famous for being beautiful. Catching my gaze, she flashes a radi-ant, practiced smile. I smile back. The crowd shifts as the chefs organize everyone into groups to tour the school.

The curious brunette is in my group. As we shake hands, she says in a posh British accent, "Hello, I'm Katrina."

It hits me. "You look just like—"

"I know, I know, Elizabeth Hurley," she says, rolling her eyes.

It's true, she's a dead ringer.

"My friends even call me Liz," she says. "It's sort of embarrassing."

She appears as unpretentious about being confused with an internationally famous beautiful person as possible. "But my friends call me Kat," she says, as she shifts a black coat trimmed with plush, silky fur from one arm to the other.

On hearing my nickname is also Kat, she assures me that I can call her Liz. "To avoid confusion, you know." Before we can settle this Liz vs. Kat situation, an imposing-looking chef shushes us. He and a female translator corral our group together, and we follow like children behind a pair of pipers.

In her biography of Julia Child, *An Appetite for Life,* Noël Riley Fitch notes that during the 1940s and 1950s Le Cordon Bleu "had only one sink, and did not have electrical equipment other than stoves (and some of them did not work)." This was in one of the school's former facilities, a warren of seven rooms on rue du Faubourg St.-Honoré in central Paris. In the 1980s, André Cointreau, heir to his family's orange liqueur and Rémy Martin cognac fortune, bought the school and moved it here. By comparison, the modern Le Cordon Bleu brims with technology, even if there are only a handful of food processors on the premises.

As we descend the winding beige tile stairs to the basement, known as the *sous-sol* in French, the sharp smell of simmering meat stock hits me. We turn the corner into a cramped preparation area dominated by a massive built-in cauldron gurgling with gallons of silky brown liquid. Cutting boards and boxes of produce are everywhere. A corkboard holds the week's lessons for all levels of cuisine and pâtisserie, listing required ingredients, delivery schedules, and so on.

"This is the nerve center of the school. Everything comes in or out of here," the translator says.

Chef shows off the two large walk-in coolers as he explains that each of us will need to take turns acting as assistant for our hands-on class at least one week per semester. Class assistants fetch the ingredients assembled by the *sous-sol* crew for the practical sessions, transporting them upstairs via an electric dumbwaiter system. The dumbwaiters work only if the two safety doors are closed at both destination and departure. Already, LizKat and I can tell this is an imperfect system as we hear an urgent plea to close the basement dumbwaiter door over the intercom. "Fermez la porte, s'il vous plaît!" bleats a thin female voice. "S'il vous plaît, fermez la porte!"

Nevertheless, the dumbwaiters are a smart move. With an average of two hundred students cooking daily, Le Cordon Bleu receives enormous shipments of ingredients from morning to night. One chef, a lean, mustached gentleman referred to as Le Maestro, controls the inventory. Scraps from each practical are sent down to the *sous-sol* for reuse, typically in the preparation of stocks. Butter, cream, and eggs are among other unused items returned. As little as possible is wasted, we're told, because that's how real kitchens should work.

Next, we're led to the main demonstration room on the ground floor, just off the Winter Garden. Plastic chairs with collapsible white writing desks are arranged in tiered rows, auditorium style, to assure everyone a view of the workstation where the chefs teach. A massive mirror tilted at an angle above allows students to watch the chef's handiwork. One floor up, there's a second demonstration area with a similarly organized workstation. Although smaller, this room is flanked by French windows. "Basic Cuisine rarely meets here," the translator says dismissively.

Next, we hit the kitchens. Four in total, they're all the same and surprisingly small. The largest, the *grand salon,* accommodates just fourteen students, the others just ten. On the top floor, there's a large, bright, and airy kitchen that smells warmly of freshly baked apples. For pâtisserie only, the chef says. A pity—I've signed up only for Cuisine.

A long, central marble work area, set atop waist-high stainless fridges, anchors each kitchen. Rows of electric stoves line the walls.

"Electric?" I whisper to LizKat. "Surely not at Le Cordon Bleu."

They are there for two reasons. Le Cordon Bleu's first classes in 1895 were taught on electric stoves, then a radical invention. Also, electric stoves are safer—less worry of gas leaks and hapless students catching fire.

We're told that although a dishwasher will wash our cookware, students are responsible for keeping knives, personal cooking utensils, and the work areas spotless. On this note, Chef warns us "Ce n'est pas un détail." A student who leaves a work area less than immaculate receives no credit for the day.

The chef bows, tips his hat, and bids adieu.

For a nonoptional €450, all students purchase a set of gear along with their education, whether they need it or not. My set includes Mundial-brand knives with blue handles, a sharpening steel, and a whole load of utensils that slide cozily into the pockets of a dark blue canvas holder that wraps and folds into a lean, heavy meter-long purse. Added to this are a piece of cake-sized Tupperware, a digital scale, aprons, side towels, and other accoutrements. Last, we receive three-inch-thick blue binders, our text for the course, neatly organized with all information provided in both English and French. Arms full, we teeter down to the main women's locker room in the basement.

"You've got to be kidding," LizKat says as we arrive. About ninety lockers are crammed into a space the size of my mother's living room. At least LizKat gets a top locker; mine is on the bottom near the door. Already, our gear almost fills the locker. We leave the chaos and head to the Winter Garden.

Just twenty-two, LizKat comes from a different social echelon than I. She just spent three months in Barcelona, "To work on my Spanish," she says. Before that, she spent six months in Rome, to work on her Italian. She speaks fluent French. She came to Paris because her mother thought it might be good for her to learn the basics of French cooking.

"No diploma?" I say.

"Oh, no," she says with a laugh. "Who wants to work *that* hard? I'm going into PR."

Just then, the well-dressed woman in the pashmina corrals us into a small room where racks of chef's jackets and piles of houndstooth trousers await. It feels like trying on clothes at a basement clearance sale. A thrill runs up my spine as I slip on a white chef's jacket emblazoned with the Le

Cordon Bleu logo—that is, until I see how it fits. The "small" chef's jacket fit too snugly at my hips and tents high on my shoulders. The sleeves droop over my hands by a good half inch. "Man-tailored," I'm told. "It's tradition." I look for an extra-small and push up the sleeves.

"Those look bad on you," says a monotone voice behind me as I slip on a pair of trousers. I turn to face an expressionless Asian woman. "You should get a size larger. It will help hide your stomach."

Hello? Who *is* this person?

"It's the buttons," she explains. "Get the larger size. You'll be more comfortable, and the buttons will lie flatter." Oh, all right. We begin chatting, and when she says nothing further that I find offensive, we decide to head out to a late lunch at a brasserie. Her Chinese name is complicated, she says. "Just call me L.P." Does it date me that I think of her name as a record?

L.P. is not a big talker. She says only what's needed, to the point, and offers sometimes harsh opinions. Hers is not a ready smile, her face as mute as a poker player's. I learn she's in her thirties, from China by way of England, an intellectual property lawyer, though she stopped enjoying it a few years ago. An avid cook, she took time off to investigate whether she might want to swap the law trade for life in a kitchen. She left two dogs and her husband in the UK. She doesn't say, but they may rank in that order.

By the time we finish lunch around four o'clock, it's almost dark. An icy wind kicks up. She lives close to the school, so we say good-bye, and I head to the Vaugirard Métro around the corner.

Our apartment on rue de Richelieu is so close to the Louvre that when I take the wrong exit, I end up in the entryway of the museum, where tourists are buying their tickets. I find my way out, cross rue de Rivoli, and navigate past the Comédie Française to our street. As I turn the corner, I bump into a pair of American tourists intently studying a paperback copy of *The Da Vinci Code,* presumably trying to follow in the steps of the book's main character. This has the feel of a side street, even though it's busy with traffic hoping to avoid the often congested avenue de l'Opéra nearby.

Passing a flower store, a sushi-on–conveyor-belt restaurant, and the mysterious dark entrance to what's rumored to be a wife-swapping bar, I stop at an *alimentation*. That's the name for the small convenience stores selling overpriced wares found in most Parisian neighborhoods. I've not yet located a nearby supermarket, so I stop in to purchase some coffee, milk, soft cheese, and a bottle of white wine. Behind the counter, the cashier hums along to the remake of "La Vie en Rose" by Tony Bennett. A French classic sung by an American man hummed by a genial Moroccan, all in my little corner store.

Balancing the heavy binder and a shopping bag in one hand, I enter the security code and lean with a shoulder to push open the ornate blue entry door. From there, it's huff and puff up the six flights of stairs, pausing outside the door on the fourth floor to catch my breath. I overhear a couple arguing in French inside. Does it count as eavesdropping if you can't understand what they're saying?

Breathless, I open the door to the apartment. You would never know this used to be the servants' quarters. The seven-hundred-square-foot loft is utterly modern, resembling an art gallery with stark white walls, modern skylights, and polished wooden floors. Almost medieval exposed beams lend contrast, making it feel both aged and industrial. The open kitchen— an unusual fixture in France—crafted from burlwood and featuring metal drawers without handles, is a sleek design. Lean dangerously out the front-room window and you can see the Sacré Coeur to the north. The building dates from the mid-1700s, its major claim to fame being that Napoléon's hatmaker once operated here.

Paris is rich with short-term rental flats, and online sites and agencies manage them at widely varying rates. Mike and I had settled on a starkly furnished one-bedroom near the Luxembourg Gardens, but three days before my arrival in Paris the agency called with an urgent message: that apartment's owner changed her mind about renting it. To make amends, they offered us this apartment for three months at a steep discount. We take it, despite one major concern: we'll have to find another apartment in just three months.

Arriving "home," I call Mike. As I had to do in London, I check my math. If it's 5:00 p.m. in Paris, it's 8:00 a.m. in Seattle. I text his mobile phone, and wait for him to return my call using a cheap international calling card from his home.

"Good morning, sexy," he says, his voice thick with sleep.

"Good evening, handsome," I say, and with that we talk for two hours. I tell him about my first day at school, about meeting LizKat and L.P., about the Métro, about everything. His days are busy, too, preparing to join me.

To come to Paris, Mike has to leave his new consulting business, find someone to rent his house and manage his tenants in his rental property, finish his studies to become a private pilot, and generally put his entire life on hold for the rest of the year. If all goes well, he will join me in two or three weeks, to make what we both know will be the largest leap of faith he's ever made for love.

After I hang up, I pour a glass of wine. I sit by the window, contemplating the French rooftops, reflecting on the whirlwind day. For the first time in weeks, I feel as if I can breathe. I am alone in Paris, the eve of my first full day at Le Cordon Bleu. I flip open my binder, reading the rules, the chef bios, the explanation of cuts of meat and conversion charts, and finally the ingredient lists for the recipes. As I close the cover, I marvel at what's printed there: "Kathleen Flinn, Cuisine de Base, Hiver 2004."

I'm really here.

CHAPTER 3

CULINARY BOOT CAMP

LESSON HIGHLIGHTS: HOW TO USE KNIVES, INTRODUCTION TO
COOKWARE, RUSTIC VEGETABLE SOUP

As my mother always warned me about men in the service, you can
never underestimate the power of a uniform.

Entering the windowless ground-floor room for our first demonstration, I marvel at the sight. Freshly stripped of street clothes, the Basic Cuisine students are a wave of white, sitting in tight, cramped rows, nervously chatting, expectant. Although the fifty students represent seventeen countries, the group looks impressively identical.

That morning, as I'd slid on my own chef's jacket, my stomach constricted nervously with anticipation. Is this what a soldier feels the first time in fatigues? Or medical students, their first time in scrubs? In a uniform, some part of your individual identity inevitably gets lost, given over so you can become part of something larger than yourself.

Or, in my case, into clothing that simply makes yourself look larger.

Like many of the female students, I appear as if I'm wearing culinary pajamas one size too large, effectively adding twenty pounds to my five-foot-four frame. Even the willowy LizKat looks like a dark-haired Barbie dressed in Ken's clothes. She waves at me from the front row, where she and L.P. have saved me the last seat on the left. It's ten minutes until class begins, and the room is already packed.

"Where is your necktie?" asks L.P., frowning.

I hold up the stiff, white triangle of fabric. "I tried, but it looked like I was attempting to cover a neck wound." She rolls her eyes, snatches the triangle, and efficiently pulls it into a taut knot around my throat. "Thank you," I wheeze. With a satisfied look, she turns to talk to LizKat.

Along the right wall there's a second, smaller work area for the *sous-sol* assistants. In exchange for a small stipend and a discount on tuition, they prepare the ingredients for these demonstrations and assist the chefs through class. They prepare all our ingredients for the resulting practical classes as well. Today, the assistant is Bernadette, the soft-faced uniform model from orientation.

Wearing a tall paper toque, Chef Jean-Yves Bertrand busies himself behind the workstation, giving hushed orders to Bernadette as she bounces around in preparation for class. A kind-faced man with nervous eyes, Chef Bertrand reminds me a bit of a worried puppy. He glances up through his thin-rimmed glasses to survey the new troops as we file into the room. Typical of most of the chefs here, the Bayonne-born Chef Bertrand never went to culinary school. Like many in his profession in France, he started as a teen, laboring long hours in lowly positions. Over the years, he worked his way up, shifting from one Michelin-rated restaurant to another. In his late thirties, he took over the kitchen at a legendary Paris restaurant. When the restaurant decided to set up outposts in Shanghai and Bangkok, Chef Bertrand was their man. A few years ago, he gave all that up to teach beginning students at Le Cordon Bleu.

At precisely 12:28, the day's translator arrives, a soft-spoken British woman named Anne. Somewhere in her early forties, with ivory skin and a swoop of coarse red hair, she has a gentle nature about her. Clad in a chef's jacket and black trousers, Anne perches on a stool near the worktable. In a calm yet projected voice, she starts with roll call, to which I am to answer *"oui"* or *"présente."* This seems simple, but it proves a true tongue-twister event, starting with Yoshimin Amharined from Israel through Ouyang Xiurong from China. An especially challenging one proves entertaining.

"Hor-han-zee . . .," Anne begins.

"Non," says a giggling young woman, holding her hand over her mouth. "You may caw me 'Hor,' " she offers.

Anne, pausing only a moment, says, "How about we call you Horhan?"

Roll complete, cue Chef Bertrand. He straightens his toque and clears his throat.

"Bonjour, bienvenue au Cordon Bleu," he begins in a pleasant, soothing voice. "Comment allez-vous cet après-midi?" He waits, while Anne translates into English. Chef continues, his French rhythmic, evenly paced.

"Chef says that you must respect those with whom you work. It's not exactly the army, but we do expect you to say *'Oui, chef'* or *'Non, chef.' "* Together, they reprise the rules, adding that wearing our uniforms outside of school is "frowned upon." Food, coffee, sodas, or anything other than water in the demonstration rooms is not allowed, as a courtesy to the chef.

After the demonstration of three recipes, we will break into small groups to prepare one of the dishes in a kitchen upstairs. In the practical class, we will be graded daily on five areas: organization, sanitation, technique, and the arrangement and taste of our daily dish, presented to the chef at the end of each class. Afterward, what we prepare is ours to keep or give away.

At this, Anne adds, "Please don't just throw your food away. It's such a terrible waste. If you don't want what you've made, please do try to find someone to give it to. The dishwashers are often happy to take home food."

L.P. and I exchange glances, marveling. Why would anyone ever throw out Le Cordon Bleu food? we wonder.

Chef Bertrand then begins to go through each item in our kit, starting with the role for each *couteau,* or knife:

- *Office,* or small paring knife—good for cutting small items, such as your fingers
- *Éminceur,* a chef's knife—good for many things. Curl your fingers as you cut, or you'll lose the tips

- *Désosseur,* the boning knife—the rigid blade allows you to take meat off bones, including the meat on your fingers
- The heavy cleaver, a *couperet*—used for cutting bones or carcasses for stock or soup, and it can take off an entire finger
- Finally, a *filet de sole,* or fish-filleting knife—the flexible blade allows you to do a close fillet of the fish and also of your fingers.

"Chef tells you all this for a reason," Anne says. "In the first couple weeks, at least a couple of students will cut themselves badly, so do be careful."

Finished with knives, he selects items from the assistant's kit as if choosing chocolates from a box. With each, he explains its purpose, offers insight, and returns the item to its place. For instance: "Roasting forks are useful for positioning meat," Anne translates. "But never pierce meat until you're sure it's cooked through, or you'll release the juices and dry out the meat." And so on with a trussing needle, kitchen shears, scraper, whisk, pastry brush, melon baller, and citrus zester.

This methodical guide to the kitchen continues with cookware. We must learn to use their French names: a *casserole* is a saucepan, a *passoire* is a strainer. The cone-shaped sieve used for straining liquids gets its name, *chinois,* from the flat, triangular sun hats worn in Asia.

"Any questions?" Anne asks the crowd, scanning for hands. Chef Bertrand straightens his glasses. "No?" With that, as thousands of Le Cordon Bleu students have done before us, we officially start with the first recipe, *potage cultivateur,* or rustic vegetable soup.

Le Cordon Bleu began life in the late 1800s as a cooking magazine started by French journalist Marthe Distel. *La cuisinière Cordon-bleu* centered on classic recipes and tips for entertaining, a nineteenth-century version of *Gourmet.* To boost circulation, Distel offered free cooking classes to subscribers. After the first was held in 1895, the lessons proved more popular than the magazine. Le Cordon Bleu now has twenty-seven schools in fifteen countries; the magazine closed in the 1960s.

"Et bien sûr, nous commençons avec la mirepoix," the chef continues.

"And of course," Anne translates, "we will begin with mirepoix."

Recipes drive Le Cordon Bleu's curriculum, with the intent that each one will teach required techniques. Dishes increase in complexity as the course progresses. So it makes sense we start with mirepoix, a base seasoning used to flavor dishes—traditionally, raw carrot, onion, and celery cut into a small dice. Later, I consult *The Oxford Companion to Food* and find that the mix is named after the duc de Lévis-Mirepoix, a field marshal for Louis XV. Renowned French publisher Pierre Larousse didn't think much of him. "Mirepoix was an incompetent and mediocre individual," Larousse wrote at the end of the nineteenth century, "who owed his vast fortune to the affection Louis XV felt toward his wife." *Ouch.*

Then, Chef Bertrand moves on to the best trick of the morning as he turns a simple task into a moment of beauty: he chops an onion.

With a chef's knife, he cuts a peeled onion in half at the root. He places one half cut-side down on the board and cuts thin vertical slices toward the root but not through it, keeping the onion intact, as if on a hinge. Twisting the blade flat, he cuts thin slices across, parallel to his cutting board, again stopping each slice before the root end. Then, he slices across the top of the onion down, and perfect tiny cubes tumble onto the cutting board. It's quick and precise. Even L.P. raises her eyebrows, impressed.

"Ne jamais couper comme ça," he says, and chops the onion the way I normally have, rocking the center of the knife back and forth to make smaller cuts.

Anne offers a reason. "Chef says don't cut this way as it will make you cry."

Moving on at an intimidating pace, he demonstrates other cuts. French cuisine employs precise vegetable cuts that we must master. He demonstrates *brunoise* (a tiny dice) and julienne (matchsticks). He shows how to "turn" vegetables. Using a paring knife, he trims a quarter of a potato into a little football shape with six equal sides. This provides an elegant presentation and encourages even cooking. Chef puts a sample of the vegetables on a small plastic plate and passes it around. Inspecting his *brunoise,* I can see that it looks as if the vegetables were diced by a machine.

"Chef says that all your vegetables are to be the same size," Anne says. "Anything less is unacceptable."

The class continues. He wraps a bay leaf, thyme, and parsley with the dark green portion of a leek and secures it with a string. Voilà, a bouquet garni. Chef demonstrates how to blanch green vegetables ("to keep their color"), how to make lardons from salt pork ("boil to get out impurities"), and how to peel garlic by banging it with the flat part of a chef's knife ("remove the green shoot, it's hard to digest").

The soup seems painfully laborious. Most vegetables are cooked separately and then brought together in the end. To make the soup, Chef uses no fewer than eleven pans, five *passoires,* three *chinois,* and a dozen stainless bowls, each swooped away by Bernadette and deposited in a dishwashing area out of sight of the students.

"If this seems very complicated, don't worry," Anne advises, translating. "Chef says he won't be going over all these details again. The hope is that we show you once and then it will go into your head."

There's an audible groan at this statement. My notes on the soup cover three full pages. The many steps seem both simple yet needlessly complex at the same time. How am I supposed to remember it all?

With that, Chef ladles the soup into a large white tureen and places it onto a plate topped with a doily on a table in the front of his workstation.

"If you'd like to take a photo of the dishes each day, you may do so," Anne advises. It could not be a more unremarkable-looking bowl of soup. A dozen Asian girls, armed with the latest miniature Japanese camera technology, rush to take photos of the tureen from all angles.

Bernadette ladles soup into small plastic drinking cups. At the end of each demonstration, the chef provides a taste of whatever's been prepared. It's an important part of our education, part of developing what James Beard called "taste memory." We are to focus on the flavor, the seasonings, and the texture, as our guide for how the food should taste.

Excited, LizKat, L.P., and I stand together and try it.

Huh. It's remarkably bland. Not unpleasant, but disappointing after all that work. L.P. has just one small sip and throws the rest away.

★   ★   ★

We rush from Chef Bertrand's practical to the locker room, retrieve our knives and other gear, and head to the kitchen. It's showtime. Now we must reproduce the soup we just watched the chef create.

I'm one of eight women in the ten-member-strong Basic Group Four, or B4. We represent Taiwan, China, Israel, Mexico, Spain, Canada, England, and the United States. We file into the windowless *petit salon* on the first floor and take places at the long communal worktable. I take a corner near the dishwasher. Across from me is a pretty woman named Anna-Clare. To my right, there's twenty-year-old Amit, who reminds me of a young prince from an exotic country. He smiles at me, bright teeth against smooth dark skin, the tip of his chin covered in a tiny goatee. "I'm from Israel, but my father is French. He runs a French restaurant in Hadera," he says.

Chef Bertrand enters to supervise. Metal bowls heaped with bright vegetables get slapped on the counter. Someone distributes thick white cutting boards. I wet a paper towel and nestle it under mine to keep it from slipping, as Chef advised in demonstration. Then Chef Bertrand says something about *"quatre légumes."* That's all I understand.

I realize three critical things I should have considered earlier:

1. There's no translator in the kitchen.
2. Like most chefs, this one doesn't speak any English, and
3. My French is shit. Or, as the French say, *merde.*

There's nothing to be done about it now, so I dive in.

I plop the new digital scale and my notes onto the marble surface and start to weigh. There's not an obvious place in the kitchen for our stuff, so most people stow their knife kits and cake-sized Tupperware in one of the fridges. Ingredients in Le Cordon Bleu recipes are given by weight, rather than by cup or similar measure. So it's 200 grams of carrots, 150 grams of celery, and so on. By the time I am done weighing, Amit has finished chopping, his vegetables a colorful mosaic in his side pan. The ten-inch chef's knife from my kit feels heavy and awkward in my hand; I have an eight-inch knife at home. I attempt to chop everything perfectly, as instructed, yet it feels as though I've never cut anything before. Not to mention I'm intimidated by the pace set by Amit.

As Chef Bertrand wanders the kitchen, stopping to praise or correct, no one talks. The kitchen is heavy with quiet concentration. Amit finishes within an hour. The rest of us finish in two and ladle the soup into tureens. Chef goes around the room, taking a taste of each, the moment of truth.

Of mine, he makes a brief comment. I recognize only the word *"sel,"* or salt, but have I added too much? Or too little? He flicks my vegetables with a small plastic spoon and smiles. "Très bien." That, I understand. *Very good.*

"Merci beaucoup," the chef says, and looks at my name tag. "Meeze Fleen," rhyming my last name with "spleen."

In all my life, I never thought that praise for cutting vegetables especially small could make me so thoroughly happy. But I taste my soup again, and I find it quite bland—just like the demonstration. Is this what I'm learning to cook? Bland food? With that, I set it aside and brutally scrub my still-hot stainless-steel stove and wonder what the chefs would make of my idea of rustic vegetable soup, my mother's "minestrone."

Mom could never bear to throw away food. With five kids on a Michigan farm, she couldn't afford to. So she saved leftovers in a lime-green covered plastic container in the freezer. After dinner, if she had anything left over—say, a cup of corn, a bit of meatloaf, or a fistful of green beans—it went into the bowl. For years, she spent each Wednesday blending the leftovers into soup, which changed with the seasons. In summer, she added vegetables from the garden, such as crisp zucchini and weighty Best Boy tomatoes. Squash made an appearance in autumn.

Although the end result was invariably scrumptious, it was never the same from one time to the next. That's the way that I cook at home and the exact opposite of what I am here to learn.

That night, I go over the day with Mike on the phone. It's not what I expected, I tell him. I suppose I had visions of being greeted with a flute of champagne to celebrate my immediate entry into a glamorous world of soufflés and foie gras, led by handsome chefs with Maurice Chevalier accents. ("With *zee* whisk, you must use *zee* wrist, like *zeeze*.") Instead, it's a world of rules, uniforms, and efficient chefs whom I can't quite understand. He listens, amused that reality has so quickly shattered my alluring ideas.

Mike has a talent for woodworking and a penchant for power tools. "Of course they expect you to work with precision, and they have rules for how everything is done," he says. "You are being trained to be interchangeable, so that you can step into a role and just get done whatever is needed. It's like a craftsman working in a shop. He might be creative, but he better know how to do a mortice."

I've held a variety of restaurant gigs, always on the periphery in the kitchens, so I know firsthand that the rush of dinner can appear chaotic. Cooking is a physical job; it requires strength, endurance, and the ability to do what you're told without complaint, even if you disagree.

From that view, I glimpse the larger lessons we're being taught.

To be good foot soldiers in the kitchen, we must be trained to follow orders, to produce consistent results. That's why we are drilled to cut our vegetables with the same military precision, to hit the same basic notes of flavor.

Chefs in a kitchen must be able to rely on one another, the way soldiers do in the heat of battle. But will we students be able to stand the heat of the kitchen? Will I?

Potage "Minestrone" à la Façon de Ma Mère

"MINESTRONE" SOUP LIKE MY MOTHER'S

Serves eight to ten

This isn't true minestrone, hence the quotation marks. I keep most of these ingredients in my pantry or freezer. I use canned fire-roasted tomatoes for this along with white beans. You can also use red kidney or navy beans. For a good stock recipe, see my friend Ted's version on pages 44–45. You can use the tomato sauce from the grilled-pizza recipe on pages 156–157 in place of the spaghetti sauce. This soup also freezes well.

1½ pounds (750 g) lean stew beef, cut into bite-sized cubes
2 tablespoons olive oil
1 medium onion, chopped
1 large carrot, chopped

2 celery ribs, chopped

2 quarts (2 l) beef stock

1 cup (250 ml) spaghetti sauce

4 cloves garlic, minced

1 14-ounce (400 g) can beans, drained, rinsed

1 28-ounce (800 g) can tomatoes, undrained

1 tablespoon dried mixed Italian herbs

1 bay leaf

2 cups frozen mixed vegetables, thawed

1 cup (250 g) elbow macaroni

1 tablespoon butter *(optional)*

Tabasco, salt, and pepper to taste

¼ cup (60 ml) grated Parmesan cheese

In an eight-quart or larger Dutch oven or stockpot, sear the meat in oil over high heat until very brown. Remove beef from pan; pour off excess fat and oil. Add onions, carrots, and celery and cook until tender, stirring around the bottom and edges of the pan. Add the stock, browned meat, spaghetti sauce, garlic, beans, tomatoes, herbs, and a few grinds of fresh pepper. Bring to a boil, skim, then cover and reduce heat to simmer for about two hours. Skim and stir occasionally. Add more water, if needed, during cooking. Add the vegetables and the macaroni and cook another half hour. If desired, finish the soup with some butter and stir through until melted. Check the seasonings, adding Tabasco, salt, and pepper, to taste. Sprinkle a bit of Parmesan atop each bowl when served.

CHAPTER 4

TAKING STOCK

In the 1954 film *Sabrina,* a lovesick Audrey Hepburn is sent by her chauffeur father to Paris to attend "the world's most famous cooking school," its name never mentioned but assumed to be Le Cordon Bleu. In a classroom kitchen with views of the Eiffel Tower, she learns to boil water the first day and how to crack an egg the next.

Our learning curve feels a bit steeper.

For each of the more than one hundred recipes in our binder, we are given only the ingredient list. That's it. The rest of the recipe we learn from watching the chef. On days two and three, the chefs instruct us on how to prepare veal, chicken, and fish stocks, fillet fish, truss and poach whole chickens, and craft two types of white sauces. We're introduced to *"les liaisons courantes,"* common thickening agents such as roux. It is not possible to see the Eiffel Tower from the kitchens on rue Léon Delhomme. The kitchen in which my group works has no windows at all.

"Chef hopes you enjoyed your first practical class," says Anne on day two, back again as our translator. Chef Bertrand peers over his glasses at the crowd and smiles. "Today, we begin with the process to make stocks. In French, these are known as *fonds de cuisine,* or foundations of cuisine."

Like mirepoix, stock is fundamental. Many sauces, most soups, and dishes as diverse as braised meat and risotto rely on it. "Life without stock is barely worth living," writes Anthony Bourdain in *Kitchen Confidential.* I agree. Working in restaurants at an impressionable age taught me its value early. For my twenty-third birthday, I bought myself a twenty-quart industrial stockpot from a restaurant-supply store.

Chef explains that we must understand the basics, although for efficiency the *sous-sol* crew will craft the stock required for our classes, using the huge cauldron downstairs. Quality stocks take time, and by making *fonds* the basement crew can constantly recycle the scraps from our practical classes.

Fond de veau, or brown veal stock, starts life as knobby sawed-off bones roasted for nearly an hour. Peeled and quartered vegetables are added to roast with the bones for forty minutes. Then, into a pot of water they go with a bay leaf, some thyme, perhaps a few peppercorns. "Just remember the theory," Anne translates for the chef. "Use a three-to-one ratio of bones to vegetables. Don't add too many carrots, or your stock will be too sweet, or too many peppercorns or garlic, as it will be too spicy. You want a rich yet neutral flavor."

Chef has other commands on stock:

- Keep it clear; don't stir it, and never let it boil—it will cloud
- Avoid adding salt—it may become unpleasantly brackish
- If refrigerated or frozen, heat to a near boil to kill lurking bacteria.

"Always smell stock to see if it's fresh, and taste it to check the flavor," Anne translates. "If it is poor, anything made with it will suffer."

After he puts his veal stock on to simmer, Chef turns his attention to a mess of fish.

"For round fish, the procedure is always the same," Anne says.

With his left hand, Chef Bertrand gently cradles a fish. With his right, he scissor-clips the fins and tail, brutally grabs at the gills and rips them out, then offers us two options to remove the eyes: cut them out with a paring knife, or dig them out with a vegetable peeler. He puts the extracted fish eyes on the ends of his fingers and holds them up to the crowd like a puppet as he smiles and singsongs, "Allo, allo, Monsieur Poisson."

He sharpens his fillet knife and slices through the soft belly. We can see this clearly in the mirror, yet he lifts the fish up and wiggles his fingers around inside to remove its guts, a glistening slippery mess that drops in gooey clumps from the stomach onto his cutting board. He picks them up and offers them to an Asian student in the first row. She shakes her head, covering her mouth as she emits a high-pitched giggle. "Non?" he asks, feigning surprise. "Mais, c'est très bien pour un sandwich."

Chef rinses the fish, lays it down on the clean part of his cutting board, and gently persuades his fillet knife along its skeleton, removing one long piece of white flesh. He repeats the operation on the other side. Then, he wedges his knife between the skin and the flesh, rocking it back and forth, and the skin peels right off.

"Chef says that it's important you learn to extract as much flesh as possible," Anne says. "There's already a lot of waste in fish, so an additional loss of even ten percent can be very expensive to a restaurant."

An American woman raises her hand to ask a question. "But they have someone at the market that will do filleting, so why do we have to do it?"

The chef puts his knife down and stares at the woman who asked the question, obviously annoyed. After a long response of rapid-fire French, Anne consolidates his message. "Chef asks, Why are you at school? Why don't you have the butcher roast your meat for you, too?" The student shrinks back in her jacket.

Today's recipe, *filets de merlan Bercy,* or whiting in white-wine sauce, has several teaching points in addition to filleting. One is to make a *fumet,* or fish stock, which Chef begins by heating the bones in the bottom of the pot until they get hot and begin to release their internal juices, or "sweat." Then we add mirepoix and water. It needs to simmer only twenty minutes, Chef advises, lest it taste "too fishy."

In a buttered sauté pan, he sprinkles thinly sliced shallots, then adds the fish and equal parts of white wine and the still hot fumet. After the fish poaches, Chef transforms the liquid into sauce by reducing it and then whisking in a half cup of butter.

"Hot food always goes on a hot plate, and cold food goes on a cold plate," Anne says as Chef takes a blue-rimmed dinner plate out of the oven and sets the fish on top with some sauce and perfectly chopped parsley. With that, he bows, the class applauds, and students crowd around the chef's plate to take copious photos.

We taste. The sweet fish couples nicely with the sting of the shallots, muted by the softness of the butter sauce. This is more like it, I think.

He makes it all look easy, but then chefs are like that. They're magicians in white, accomplished at sleight of hand.

Without discussion, in a curious nod to human habit, the members of B4 assemble in exactly the same spots at the communal marble table in the kitchen, where we will work for the rest of Basic Cuisine.

This week's class assistants, Kim and Tai Xing, empty out the dumbwaiters, heavy with fish. Kim, whose husband works at the American embassy, is an attractive, wholesome brunette from Maryland with two kids, a trim figure, and shoes that always match her handbag. Her vague ambitions focus on catering.

By contrast, Tai Xing from Taiwan seems stuck in her awkward teenage phase. Tai Xing's look is a study in practicality: industrial barrettes hold back her otherwise tousled black hair; she wears a thick man's watch on her slim left wrist. "Cruise ships or fancy hotels, that's where I want to work," she says, when I ask her later why she's at school.

Kim artfully arranges the vegetables for our practical in bowls while Tai Xing slaps two lukewarm fish onto our cutting boards. Amit goes right to work, filleting the luckless fish in a few minutes.

I sharpen my knives and review my notes. At thirty-six, I've managed never to fillet a fish.

Although my father often took us fishing on weekends when I was a kid, this messy duty fell to my older brothers. They went outside with fish, newspapers, and my dad's sinister-looking knives and returned with fillets.

I never asked questions. Now I stand, knife in hand, staring at the eyes that I must gouge right out of a poor fish's head.

I take my vegetable peeler, sink it into the edge, and twist. It doesn't budge. I twist harder, tunneling around the cavity of the crunchy eye and through the firm, gooey tendons holding it in. I tug and *whack!* it flies across the marble table and sticks to Kim's forearm. "Ew! Ew! Ew!" she cries, jumping up and down. "Get it off! Get it off!" I pick it off with my snowy-white side towel. She washes her arm a dozen times before she returns to her own fish, poking at it tentatively, as if it might reanimate and attack.

Back at my cutting board, I get on with it, production-line style. Two tails, clipped. Fins, clipped. I cut into the stomach of the first and, using a paper towel, remove the guts. *Ugh.* Even through the paper towel, I can feel them, squishy and slimy. On the second fish, something goes wrong. I cut into its tender belly, and blood gushes out onto my pristine apron. The scales, scraped off with my paring knife, fly everywhere, not unlike iridescent confetti. I somehow manage four awkward fillets, chunks of white flesh still glistening on the skeleton. The skin, which came off so easily for Chef Bertrand, seems adhered by Super Glue, and my fillets fall apart under my clumsy attempts to remove it.

Happy to be done, I throw the bones into a bowl of water to draw out some of the blood, turn over my cutting board, and move on to the vegetables.

"Hmmm, a bit messy," I hear behind me. I turn to see the raised eyebrow of Chef Gaston Dufour. He's one of the few chefs who can speak English, although curiously he has a slight German accent. A veteran of Michelin restaurants, Chef Dufour's most noteworthy job was head chef to the royal family of an Arabic principality the size of New Jersey. Chef Dufour's dominating physical characteristic is a long, black handlebar mustache. He habitually strokes the ends, turning them upward into tight points, reminding me of a shady turn-of-the-century circus barker.

"I've never filleted a fish before—" I start to explain.

"I can tell. You should practice—at home," he says flatly. Still stroking his mustache, he walks over to Kim, who has just finished her first fillet.

"No, no, that is wrong," he chides, exasperated. Taking the fillet knife from her hand, he snaps, "Didn't you watch the chef at all today? A child could do better than this. You are also too slow."

Amit presents his plate and leaves. I aim to follow the chef's instruction exactly for the rest of the recipe, constantly looking at my notes, now soggy and stained with fish guts and blood. After another hour I'm done. I take my plate to Chef Dufour, standing at the end of the counter.

With a plastic spoon, he scoops up some sauce for a taste, then cuts into my fish. "The fillet is not even, your fish is overcooked, your sauce is too thin, it needs more salt, and your parsley isn't chopped finely enough. Thank you," he looks at my name tag, "Miss Flinn." With a bored tone, he calls, "Next?"

That's it. After three hours, two fish, some three thousand calories in wine and butter, and ruined notes, I clean up, put my tiny fillets in my enormous Tupperware, and wearily head downstairs with Kim, L.P., LizKat, and Anna-Clare, the woman who works across from me.

The Winter Garden is back to its usual setup, with bistro tables and chairs in clusters around the room, now buzzing with activity. Most students have finished for the day. The sweet smell of Basic Pastry's *babas au rhum* competes with a lamb dish prepared in the Intermediate Cuisine. We're tired and sweaty, and we smell of fish.

Kim drops her knives on the floor. "This isn't cooking, it's like learning some complicated sport," she says wearily, tugging off her necktie.

"Why am I so flustered in the kitchen?" Anna-Clare wonders aloud. Like me, she had long dreamed of coming to Le Cordon Bleu and finally convinced her advertising agency to give her a three-month sabbatical so that she could. "It's just bizarre. In my job, I have to make presentations to marketing directors and corporate chiefs all the time, and I can do *that* without being nervous. I mean, I knew this would be kind of stressful, but I'm surprised at how the scrutiny of the chefs completely unsettles me."

"But you're probably not as emotionally tied to those presentations," I tell her.

"Well, that's true," she says. "I like my job, don't get me wrong, but cooking is my passion."

I know how they both feel, especially Anna-Clare. In my own kitchen, I'm usually sipping a glass of wine while I cook. Now I'm exhausted, and it's only the second day. I look at my bloodstained apron, gray bits still clinging to parts of it. This isn't like *Sabrina* at all.

Audrey Hepburn would never have ended up covered in fish guts.

On Thursday, a chicken becomes Chef Bertrand's comedic prop. Chef uses his fingers to animate the wings of the plump roaster with feet intact and wiggles it around in a dance. "Aujourd'hui, mesdames et messieurs, vous apprendrez tout du poulet."

Today, our translator is John, a dry-witted Brit with a boyish face. He takes each opportunity to translate as a chance to work on an ongoing stand-up routine.

"Today, the chef will teach you all about chickens, specifically how to hold them up and pretend to make them dance," John says. "It's a wonderful skill that you'll find endlessly useful in the kitchen."

Chef slides his eyes toward John. He doesn't speak English, but he knows that's far too many words for his simple sentence. He moves on.

He begins with a small slit in each ankle and then, with a curved end of a soup ladle, tugs hard. Voilà, the tough white tendons, which resemble thick white strands of silk, come out in one swift tug.

"Chef says that he can guarantee that the chicken didn't feel a thing," says John. "This technique is also useful on turkeys and guinea fowl and people whom you really don't like." A male Asian student has fallen asleep in the front row. John gives him a gentle punch to wake him up. "Hey, now pay attention, the information you're about to learn must be used every time you prepare a whole chicken. It's riveting stuff."

Chef extracts hard, yellowish glands found within the flabby button leading to the chicken's former tail. The wishbone and the excess fat and skin around the neck go next. Then he trusses, skewering the chicken with a long needle threaded with kitchen string, passing it diagonally through the cavity of the chicken, back and forth until it becomes a tight, dense package.

"You can also use this in place of a football," observes John.

The chicken is destined for poaching as part of *poularde pochée sauce suprème avec riz au gras,* a classic Le Cordon Bleu teaching recipe. The whole chicken gets poached in stock, and we cover the pan not with a lid but with a clean towel to keep in moisture. The rice sounds undemanding, baked for twenty minutes with some stock and finished with a few knobs of butter. The simple white sauce begins with a roux, made from melted butter and flour whisked together and set aside to cool.

"Roux must be cold and your liquid hot—or vice versa," John translates. To the cooled roux, we add a ladle of hot chicken stock and boiled cream, then whisk quickly. It's finished by whisking in about a half cup of butter. My thighs are getting bigger just hearing this.

"This should be easy," whispers L.P. to me.

Of course, it isn't.

Half our class turns out inedible, dry rice; the other half seems to have cooked it not enough. I boil over my cream—twice—and once strained, it's too thick. I add more stock, and it's too thin. While trying to fix my sauce, my small poached chicken goes stone-cold. When Chef Dufour isn't paying attention, I dump the chicken into the bubbling, hot sauce. I look up, and he's staring right at me. Busted.

Today we are to plate not a portion but the entire chicken on a platter, atop all of our rice, the sauce spooned over the top. The result: a dull beige chicken, topped by a dull beige sauce, sitting on a bed of dull white rice. It's not a feast for the eyes. I add a bit of parsley, for color.

Chef Dufour cuts into my chicken in three places. "Your chicken is cooked all right, and it's hot." He tastes the sauce and the rice. "Your sauce has too much liquid, it's too thin, and it needs more salt." I explained it was too thick, and I overcorrected. "I know, I saw you," he says dismissively. "And your rice is good, but it needs salt. Thank you," he looks at my name tag, "Miss Flinn."

From class, I rush to Gare du Nord with my chicken to catch the 7:40 p.m. Eurostar to London; on the train ride, I devour half of it. I could not arrange movers before Christmas, so I have returned to finish packing up my flat and put my life as I know it into boxes—indefinitely.

I walk up the three floors on Litchfield Street, in central London. It's a cold, dark state of chaos, with a bookshelf half emptied, clothes in piles, and the rest of my life in various stages of being sorted and packed. I sit down on my red velvet couch in the darkness. I've lived in this apartment for four years, longer than I have lived anywhere in my adult life. I have no idea where I will eventually unpack the things that I look at now. It's as if I am getting on another train, this one to a destination unknown.

I've been in Paris for only a week; it feels like I've been away for months.

Did I act too quickly that night when I signed up for Le Cordon Bleu? Almost on a whim, I decided to empty my savings account and move to another country with my new boyfriend, a place where he doesn't speak the language and I barely can communicate. Why didn't I leave my job earlier and find something else? By fouling up my career, I've also lost the chance to live in London, an opportunity few Americans ever get to experience. I move through my flat slowly, picking up things here and there, taking a mental inventory. There's much power to a place that you know you're about to abandon.

Surveying my closet, I realize I have no use in my present life for all those skirted suits, that corporate attire. Will I ever have a need for them again? I wander into the dining room and sit at the table, contemplating the ghosts of dinner parties past. On a high shelf in the kitchen sits the stockpot that I bought more than a decade ago, now worn by regular use.

Finally, I walk to the window overlooking the street below. London feels so busy and loud to me now, compared to the reserved hush of central Paris. Below my flat, the music from the French wine bar shakes the floor.

"Living is like driving," my grandmother used to say. "You have to pick a lane." Have I chosen the right lane? It feels like this place, this moment in time, lies exactly halfway between my past and my future.

It's too late to change back. When I return to Paris on Monday, I must really start *living there*. So far, I've barely ventured outside my apartment, except to go to school.

I find a bottle of white wine in my tiny fridge, pour a glass, and eat the rest of the chicken. Then, I start to pack.

Fond de Cuisine de Mon Ami Ted

MY FRIEND TED'S STOCK RECIPE

Makes four quarts

My chef friend Ted developed a two-thousand-word missive on the perfect stock. This simplified version captures key points of his *méthode*. A good stockpot is critical. Get a sturdy pan with a thick bottom, preferably stainless steel, which is nonreactive and easy to clean. Pure, clean water is essential, as the long simmering process concentrates all flavors, the good and the bad. This recipe is for a ten- to twelve-quart stockpot. Adjust the recipe as needed to fit your stockpot.

1 pound (1 or 2 large) onions
½ pound (about 3 ribs) celery
½ pound (about 2 large) carrots *(for brown stock only)*
Parsley stems from one bunch
About 8 pounds (3.5 kg) chicken or beef and veal bones
8 quarts (8 l) pure, clean, cold water

Rinse vegetables and chop coarsely. If bones are frozen, remove from freezer with plenty of time to thaw in fridge; this could take twenty-four hours. Place thawed and/or fresh bones in stockpot or bowl and cover with water. Let stand for fifteen minutes and then drain, discarding the water. This helps to remove salt, freezer frost, blood, and other undesirables. If making a white chicken stock, skip the browning step and put the bones into the pot with fresh water.

To make a brown beef or chicken stock, roast the bones in a 375°F/190°C oven for 40 minutes, then add the vegetables. Continue to roast until the bones have a rich brown color, for a total of about sixty to ninety minutes. Transfer the browned bones and vegetables to the stockpot and then cover with water. Pour the fat out of the roasting pan, add water, and gently loosen the pan drippings. Pour this into the stockpot.

In either case, the water level should be at least three inches above the bones. Apply high heat until the stock comes to a slow simmer. Then reduce the heat as necessary to maintain a gentle simmer. For the next couple of hours, use a ladle to regularly skim the foam and fat from the surface of the stock. Don't let the stock boil; it will become cloudy. Simmer the uncovered stock for a minimum of four hours for chicken and at least eight hours for beef, skimming every ninety minutes. Add water as needed to keep the bones submerged.

Straining the stock: first, use a long pair of tongs to remove most of the bones and discard. Ladle or pour the remaining stock and vegetables through a colander into a clean bowl or bowls. Take care to avoid burning yourself.

Strain it again, this time through a colander lined with cheesecloth or a coffee filter. Either use the stock immediately or cool the stock as quickly as possible. To cool, pour the stock into several bowls. Place these bowls over others filled with ice, or, after the stock has cooled to below 175°F/80°C, plop freezer bags filled with ice into bowls. Ladle into freezer-proof containers and freeze.

CHAPTER 5

MEMOIRS OF A QUICHE

LESSON HIGHLIGHTS: BASIC PASTRY DOUGH, ONION TART,
QUICHE LORRAINE, THE RIGORS OF PUFF PASTRY

Chef Pierre Savard has the sexual presence of a celebrity. In his smooth hands, the simple task of peeling a tomato turns into a sensual event. It doesn't matter that he's closing in on sixty, he will always be sexy, sort of the Patrick Stewart or Sean Connery of French cooking. Chef Savard casts a special spell over the female Asian students, of which he is aware. Every so often, he offers an aside, murmured in Japanese.

Even stoic L.P. is not immune to his charms. "He's very handsome," she admits matter-of-factly.

This week, we're studying *les pâtes de cuisine,* common savory pastry doughs. Chef starts with *pâte levée salée,* a basic rising salted dough. Our first culinary task this week is *pissaladière Niçoise,* essentially a personal pizza with flavors typical of the south of France: gently roasted tomatoes, caramelized onions, hairy anchovies, and dark olives. Anchovies are essential, chef says, or it's not a *pissaladière,* as it derives its name from *pissala,* a fish paste made from anchovies. Half the class groans at the mention of anchovies. He treats the crowd to his boyish half-grin.

"Chef says, anchovies are noble. Where would French cuisine be without them?" Anne translates. Chef winks at a Japanese student in the front row. She nearly faints.

Chef Savard finishes the demonstration by making fresh pasta, running it through a stainless-steel pasta machine clamped to the edge of the workstation. Behind me, I overhear another student articulate what the other women in the room are probably thinking. "I wish I were that piece of dough," she sighs.

Then, Chef Savard takes his knife and, holding the tip horizontally, he rhythmically chops a pile of already chopped onions to even smaller bits.

L.P. raises her hand. "Chef, we've been told not to cut onions that way," she tells Anne. Anne nods; she remembers that. As she asks the chef, I hear *larmes,* the French word for tears. Chef stops his knife midmotion. Then, he explains to Anne, who translates.

"Chef says that with a dull knife, it's true, you end up pressing too hard on the onion. This crushes the cells, causing volatile oils from the onion to be released, and it's the oil that makes you cry."

Chef holds up his knife. "Mais avec un couteau très pointu . . ." he says.

"But with a very sharp knife . . .," Anne translates.

"Vous n'êtes pas obligés de pousser si fort avec vôtre couteau, et comme ça l'huile ne s'échappe pas."

"You do not have to push so hard with your knife, and that way less oil releases," translates Anne.

Chef looks around to see if the students seem satisfied with his answer. In English, he says, "So, the sharper your knife, the less you cry."

The next day, my first free one since starting school a week ago, begins with a croissant and a café au lait at a drafty café on the corner of avenue de l'Opéra and rue de Richelieu. I've yet to see inside the Louvre, even though it's just around the corner. I head to the Egyptian hall, wandering among mummies, amulets, and hieroglyphics. It's impressive but overwhelming after a couple of hours.

For me, the Louvre has nothing on the Grande Épicerie, the famous grocery at the Bon Marché department store on the Left Bank. Thinking it will just be a quick break from the Louvre, I end up spending the rest of the afternoon there.

On past trips to Paris, my purchases were limited to food that could be carted home without peril of perishing. Now, I have a refrigerator, thus I am without limits in a French supermarket. The numbers alone are impressive. I count the following: 26 varieties of poultry, 81 brands of olive oil, 214 types of cheese, and 53 options in bottled water. In the seafood display, exotic-looking whole fish rest on piles of clear ice that shimmer like diamonds under the halogen lights. I try to restrain myself. It doesn't work.

I teeter out with four plastic bags plus a stuffed foldable canvas shopping cart on wheels, branded with the store's name. I rationalize my purchases with the thought that since Mike arrives next week, I must stock up.

I attempt to walk to Métro Sèvres-Babylone. The plastic bags do not cooperate and instead fall in all directions. I flag a cab and pop the bags in the trunk.

"Vingt rue de Richelieu," I say, prouncing it "reesh-a-loo."

"Huh?" the cab driver turns to look at me, flabbergasted. What have I said?

"Un moment," I say and dig a paper and pen out of my bag. I write the address down. Aha! The driver seems relieved.

"Reesh-ah-lyuh," he says slowly and makes me repeat it after him. "Oui, bien." Satisfied, he drives me home, and I remember the six, no seven, flights of stairs. What have I done?

It takes three trips to get it all from the cab into the entranceway. A French gentleman checking his mail watches me with interest. "Quel étage?" he asks. Which floor? The top, I reply. I expect a clucked tongue, a look of sympathy. Instead, he puts his mail into the pocket of his worn wool coat, picks up the heaviest plastic bag and the bursting shopping cart, and starts to climb. I follow with the remaining bags. He climbs all the way to the top and drops them by my door.

"Bonsoir, mademoiselle," he says breathlessly and turns to walk downstairs. I begin a flurry of *"merci beaucoups,"* but he waves them off. He says simply *"de rien,"* it's nothing. I go to the staircase and listen for his door to close, somewhere on the second or third floor.

So much for the rude French, I think. But then, the word "chivalry" originates with the French word for knight.

Although quiche seems like the quintessential French dish, it originated in a medieval kingdom under German rule, a place later renamed Lorraine by the French. *"Quiche"* comes from *"kuchen,"* the German word for cake.

Chef Bertrand begins his demonstration for quiche Lorraine with *pâte brisée salée,* or short-crust pastry, made from softened butter, water, flour, and a pinch of salt. "You're trying to smooth it, but don't work it too much," he instructs, working it with his hands in a bowl. "You just want to bring the ingredients together." Once it's a small, firmish ball, he dusts it with some flour, pulls it from the bowl, wraps it in plastic, and puts it into the fridge to rest.

Chef pauses for a moment, resting his knuckles on the worktable. "La pâtisserie, c'est comme les gens," he says.

"Pastry is like people," says Anne, who translates the rest. Some dough needs a lot of kneading, some requires much less. Some dough is satisfied to rise just a little, while other dough needs to double in size. All dough needs warmth to rise.

His words are still on my mind during our practical that afternoon as Chef Savard enters our kitchen to oversee the quiche. I learn that he speaks excellent English.

"This is quite a class," he says when he walks in, talking to Amit, who nods.

Le Cordon Bleu attracts beautiful women from all over the globe, but as a group B4 has particularly blessed genes. Originally from Toronto, Anna-Clare possesses the rare face that can take having the hair pulled back from it in a tight bun without appearing severe. On her, the style is elegant, a simple method to show off her perfect chocolate skin, high cheekbones, and marvelous smile.

Next to her is Kim, who on reflection reminds me of Ashley Judd. Beside her is the stunning LizKat. Even L.P. has a natural, calm beauty to her.

Across from L.P. works Antia from Madrid. I hear that she commutes each week from Belgium, where she lives with her boyfriend. With long amber-colored hair and eyes the color of topaz, Antia doesn't look Spanish at all. She wants to be a private chef to wealthy clients, but she could be a runway model if she were just a little taller.

Next to Antia there's Ramona. She hails from a wealthy family in Mexico City. Her mother went to the Le Cordon Bleu in the late 1950s as a sort of "finishing school," a common practice then and now, especially after the success of *Sabrina*. Without discussion, she sent both her daughters to her alma mater. Chefs still talk about her older sister, an excellent student who spoke flawless French. But stormy-eyed Ramona has little natural talent in the kitchen. When we smell something burn, it's usually followed by her wails of "Ch-ef! Ch——eefff!" with a hard "ch" as in "church."

Diego, one of only two males in B4, also hails from Mexico. He's in the habit of coming to school late, and he attends demonstrations wearing his white jacket and jeans, a violation no one's called him on yet. It's not by accident that he stands directly across from LizKat in the kitchen. When he thinks no one else is listening, I hear him offer her quiet compliments. "Your *brunoise* looks beautiful" or "You're very good at trussing."

Today, Chef Savard hears him praise her quiche as he walks behind Diego. He stops in his tracks and hugs Diego around the shoulder. "You're a lucky man," Chef says. "This class has more beautiful women in it than any other."

When I present my quiche to the chef, he's quite chatty.

"So where are you from?" His blue-eyed gaze pierces through his wire-rimmed glasses to the back of my soul.

"Um, well, London, but, well, really Seattle, or, well, I grew up in Michigan, and later Florida." I'm an idiot. I can't even answer a simple question.

"But you're an American," he says, and smiles. Oh, yes, I agree.

My quiche is fine, but my knees are weak.

I always imagine Paris in the spring, with its well-manicured parks overflowing with flowers. But this is January, and in midwinter the city offers only gray skies, freezing rain, and strong, unpredictable winds that sweep in unexpectedly off the Seine. Then it snows, with large, wafting flakes that remind me of fake Hollywood snow. I decide to take a different route to school, and walk through the Tuileries Gardens. All of Paris looks as if it's in a snow globe, blanketed with silence, the air sweet, wet and crisp. No one is in the vast garden today, so it feels like I have Paris to myself. As I leave to catch the Metro, I view my trail of footprints behind me, a small ants' trail up to the arch, behind loom the Pei pyramids and buildings of the Louvre.

At school Chef Dufour has the ovens cranked. Our practical dish today will be *feuilleté de poireaux et oeufs pochés sauce Albuféra,* or puff pastry with leeks and poached eggs with Albuféra sauce.

Feuilletage is a rich and delicate pastry, made up of very thin layers, suspiciously similar in concept to phyllo dough. Some food reference books suggest that puff pastry can be found in medieval recipes and may even date back as far as ancient Greece. To get an idea of how tricky making puff pastry can be, consider that Julia Child spent twelve pages on it in *Mastering the Art of French Cooking, Volume II.*

Chef begins by making standard pastry dough. Then he adds in a thin, hard brick of what in France is known as *"beurre sec,"* or dry butter, a high-fat butter with a low water content. Chef pounds the butter into the dough, then rolls it out in an even rectangle. The rectangle is folded like a brochure. This gets a ninety-degree "turn" and is rolled out into a thick rectangle and folded again. After these two turns, the dough is chilled, often overnight. The next day, we give it four more turns. In theory, it now has 512 layers of dough and butter. If made properly, these layers cause the dough to puff and rise when baked to as much as five or six times its size—a light, flaky pastry. The smell escaping the oven reminds me of a bakery with fresh croissants.

"When it is golden brown and it feels almost weightless, it's done," Anne the translator says. The recipe seems straightforward enough. We will make a vol-au-vent, a fancy name for a pastry shell, line it with sautéed leeks, a poached egg, and Albuféra sauce, a basic cream sauce blended with stock.

The puff pastry proves a hurdle. The patient Chef Bertrand oversees our inaugural attempt. Both Anna-Clare and I add too much water to our dough and must start over. In demonstration, Chef made neat rectangles each time after rolling out his dough; mine have ragged edges. We do two turns, wrap the results in plastic, then put our names on them so they can be stowed overnight in the walk-in coolers downstairs. The class assistants retrieve it the next day, and we finish our turns.

I put together several little vols-au-vent. They look as if a kindergartener put them together with Play-Doh. I agonize over my leeks to cut them into a perfect julienne. Then, I work on my eggs. We must make them the classic way, by dropping them in simmering water with vinegar and, with a ladle, wrap the egg white around the yolk as it cooks. Poached eggs should look like shiny, smooth parcels. Mine look like gnarled creatures from a horror film. As I finish the last egg, a strong burning smell hits me, a mix of burned grass and onions. I forgot my leeks. They've burned to black. I feel a tap on my elbow.

"Attention! Regardez votre pâte," warns Chef Bertrand. He points to the convection oven at the end of the room.

I rush to pull the heavy, cast-iron baking sheet out of the oven. *Oh, no.* My pastry's surface has a dull brown cast. It's heavy and hard, not light and airy. My only hope is to cover this mess with my sauce. Just then, I turn to see my cream boil over. I race back to my stove, nearly knocking down Anna-Clare. To finish the sauce, I frantically whisk in chicken stock and butter. I taste. The sauce has no flavor except scalded cream. I look at the clock. It's too late. I must plate what I've got.

The vol-au-vent hits my warm plate with a thud. I put my least burned leeks in the bottom and tuck a grotesque poached egg on top. I drench the entire affair with my scalded sauce. I add a piece of parsley, for color.

Unsurprisingly, Chef Dufour is not impressed. He patiently explains everything I've done wrong. My hands were too hot for my pastry. I overworked it and didn't let it rest enough. A bit of water and attention would have saved my leeks. My poached egg looks bad, but it's cooked to the right degree. My sauce—well, I have to work on my sauces. It all needs more salt.

As I clean up, I overhear Chef comment on other plates. Only the meticulous L.P. passes the puff-pastry inspection, but even she had a little trouble with the eggs. Still, I'm disappointed with myself. I want to do so much better.

Outside, the snow has turned to freezing rain, a perfect match to my mood.

I call Mike with plans to detail my ruinous day. But he's got other news. He passed his flight exam, so now he's a pilot. He's got the house rented. He'll be here in exactly one week. We talk for an hour, about nothing and everything.

"I've been so excited about flying," Mike says, "I forgot to ask about your day. How did class go?"

"It was fine," I say. His voice made my disastrous afternoon fade away.

I open the fridge and eat the last wedge of quiche as I draw a hot bath. In the tub, I read Escoffier's instructions on puff pastry. One day, I'll get it right. I sink into the water and consider Chef Bertrand's comment that pastry is like people.

You can't hurry love, and you can't rush puff pastry, either. You can knead too much, and you can be too needy. Always, warmth is what brings pastry to rise. Chemistry creates something amazing; coupled with care and heat, it works some kind of magic to create this satisfying, welcoming, and nourishing thing that is the base of life.

It's cold in Paris. I long for Mike's warmth.

Quiche aux Oignons d'Or et aux Tomates Rôties

GOLDEN ONION AND ROASTED TOMATO QUICHE

Makes one quiche (six to eight slices)

Quiche is like pizza—it can be made with almost anything. This version uses the onions and tomatoes from the *pissaladière*, but try asparagus, ham, artichokes, or whatever. The onions will seem an insurmountable pile, but they reduce drastically in cooking. If good tomatoes aren't available or time is short, use soft sun-dried tomatoes. Prepared pie-crust dough may be used, or make your own *pâte brisée* from the "Extra Recipes" in the back of the book (see page 275). Quiche may be served hot, warm, or chilled, and it reheats well in a low oven. This pairs nicely with Chardonnay.

ROASTED TOMATO PETALS

6 to 8 roma tomatoes

3 tablespoons olive oil

1 clove garlic, roughly chopped

4 sprigs thyme

1 teaspoon coarse salt

CARAMELIZED ONIONS

2 tablespoons butter

1 tablespoon olive oil

3 large onions (about 2 pounds), sliced

1 bay leaf

1 tablespoon flour

Salt

Prepared pie dough or *pâte brisée*

1 egg, beaten

FILLING

3 large eggs

¾ cup (175 ml) heavy cream

3 ounces (90 g) Gruyère cheese, grated

1 teaspoon salt, ground pepper

½ teaspoon thyme

Preheat oven to a low heat, 250°F/120°C. Slice an "x" on the bottom of each tomato. Drop into boiling water for a few seconds, then plunge into a bowl of ice water. Tear the flaps on the "x" to remove skin. Cut out the core and then quarter each tomato and remove the seeds. Line slivers on parchment atop a baking sheet. Drizzle on the oil and add garlic, thyme, and salt. Gently bake for about 1½ hours, or until the slivers are tender.

Meanwhile, in a large sauté pan melt the butter with the olive oil. Add the onions and bay leaf. Cook and stir patiently over medium-low heat until they're brown and soft, about a half hour. Once browned, sprinkle with flour and a dash of salt and cook another two minutes. Set aside and let cool until completely cold.

Remove the tomato petals from the sheet, let cool.

Increase oven heat to 425°F/220°C. Roll out the dough, and press it into a metal quiche or pie pan. Pierce the bottom with a fork. Set parchment or aluminum foil in the center and fill with pie weights or dry beans. Bake for five minutes. Remove weights, brush the pastry with beaten egg, and return to oven for seven minutes. Cool slightly.

Whisk the eggs and cream in a bowl. Stir in about one third of the cheese, and the salt, several grinds of pepper, and thyme. Stir in the cooled onions and then pour into the pastry shell. Arrange the tomatoes in decorative pattern on top. Sprinkle on remaining Gruyère. Bake for twenty minutes, then reduce oven heat to 400°F/200°C and cook for another fifteen to twenty minutes until firm, browned, and a bit puffy.

CHAPTER 6

LA VIE EN ROSE

Lesson highlights: Roasted sirloin fillet, beef bourguignon, a tour of a Parisian market, and Mike's arrival

"Mmmmm," says LizKat groggily, as she fishes around inside her Louis Vuitton shoulder bag and pulls out a big pair of sunglasses. "I need some coffee." She looks like a movie star trying to hide from her fans.

We all could use some coffee. It's 8:00 a.m. and we're wandering through the Saxe-Breteuil market in the Seventh arrondissement, one of the city's largest outdoor markets. The Eiffel Tower looms at the end of the stalls, presiding over the market like a guardian.

This Marché de Paris, or market visit with a chef, is a staple of the Basic Cuisine curriculum. Our entire class, shivering in the brisk January air, is led by Chef Alexandre Colville, whom we've never met before. Younger than the other chefs, somewhere in his thirties, he's a handsome guy with mischievous blue eyes and slick black hair. He's the only chef at the school who has trained as both a chef de cuisine and a chef de pâtisserie, and therefore is the only one who teaches both disciplines. I know little about him, other than that he worked at one of Paris's most famous restaurants before joining Le Cordon Bleu. Also along for the tour is a new translator, Janine, an affable, down-to-earth Australian in her late thirties, with boy-short blond hair.

As at all French markets, the purveyors began assembling around 5:00 a.m. Within two hours, everything is in place, the fruits and vegetables arranged attractively, priced with handmade signs. Portable meat counters are hoisted down from trucks. The fishmongers, or *poissonniers,* build their displays as if by erector set to create tiered levels, topped with tarps and dozens of bags of ice, before the fish and seafood are brought in from chilled trucks.

Chef Colville wanders through the market, stopping among the stalls to give us insight, buying a bit here and there, distributing the plastic bags of his purchases among the students. Our lesson is to understand how to recognize good produce and to start learning how to select meat, fish, and cheese. As we walk, we're bombarded by the aromas: nose-searing stinky cheeses, sweet simmering pots of choucroute (sauerkraut, ham, and sausage), and pungent mounds of dried spices.

Our first stop is the butcher, where a woman skewers trussed chickens on a large swordlike device to put into an upright portable rotisserie. The main display case is standard brutal French fare: a rabbit with head and fur intact, a variety of chickens with their head feathers, a generous selection of small, tender birds. The fur and feathers are left on so buyers are assured of what they're purchasing, Chef explains. How do you know it's really a certain kind of chicken if you don't see its feathers? He gives us a lesson on quizzing stall managers. Vital questions to ask include: Where did it come from? What did it eat? What does the seller know about the people who raised it? How long has it been hung to dry or waiting to be purchased? A good chef is not shy about asking such questions, Janine says, translating it all.

We continue this way until we come to a charcuterie stand. Much of charcuterie centers on transforming every part of a pig—snout to hooves—into an edible something. The result is a vast spectrum of ham, sausages, pâtés, terrines, and pressed meats, some of which we're looking at right now. Chef points out various types, starting with a *saucisson à la cendre,* a tough white pork sausage rolled in ash so that as it air-dries it takes on a smoky flavor. Then, he points to a string of *andouillette.* There's a collective groan. Not to be confused with American andouille, the fat, spicy pork sausage from Louisiana cooking, French *andouille* and *andouillette* are made mostly out of tripe, the muscular linings of an animal's stomach. The whole process for making tripe sounds unpleasant. Let's just say there's a lot of soaking and washing involved to rid the stomach of the animal's last meal.

Amused by our chagrin, Chef Colville asks the butcher to prepare slices for us all.

"Chef says that you cannot be a chef without knowing how things taste, even if you don't like them, because often what you are asked to prepare is out of your control," says Janine. "And come on, guys, it's not really that bad."

L.P., LizKat, Anna-Clare, and I all gather together, eyeing the white, paper-thin piece of the sausage. The cut shows the cross-section of the sausage and the pinkish-white swirls of tripe. L.P. goes first. Her expression is unchanged. "It is not very good, but it is not that bad," she says.

LizKat pushes her sunglasses atop her head and nibbles thoughtfully. Her eyes widen. "I've never fancied tripe, and that hasn't changed."

Anna-Clare is the least inclined. She screws up her nose and shakes her head as L.P. hands her a piece. "I just know I won't like it."

"You are not serious about cooking," says L.P.

"Because I won't eat pig's stomach?" balks Anna-Clare. L.P. nods. Anna-Clare takes a bite, and her face contorts. It's my turn. The cold sausage has a chalky yet fatty feel on the tongue. The flavor is almost sour, with a metallic aftertaste. L.P. had it right. Tripe is an acquired taste. To the untrained palate, it's not very good, but it's not especially bad, either. It's just foreign.

We finish with fruits and vegetables. Chef picks out some tender endives, crisp radishes, white turnips, a head of fennel, and a pair of cabernet-colored beets—vegetables common in France but likely to be unfamiliar to many students. We head back to school, crammed on a city bus.

Chef and an assistant spread out our cache buffet-style on a table in the window-lined demonstration room on the second floor. There's a raft of cheeses, olives, fruits, and vegetables, and a variety of sausages and breads. We cradle plastic tumblers filled with Chablis. It feels elegant but a bit odd to be sipping wine at 11:00 a.m.

★　★　★

In Paris, music haunts the Métro. Some musicians are not content to sit still at a station and instead spend their days moving from train to train. A few even tote portable amplifiers and audio players strapped to luggage carts to provide accompaniment. On my train today, a saxophonist plays a soulful rendition of "La Vie en Rose." When you're in love, every love song gets your attention. I hum along, Louis Armstrong singing the words in my head.

> *Give your heart and soul to me*
> *and life will always be*
> *la vie en rose.*

The song finishes just as I alight at Saint-Placide, the Métro stop for the Alliance Française language school. While I can order in a café, hire a cab, navigate the Métro, and buy shoes, my French needs bolstering for the rigors of culinary school. An unsmiling woman hands me a placement test. Among the grammar questions, there's a writing test. It directs: "Write a letter to a friend about Paris." Huh. I have much to say, but how to write it in French? I agonize and chew my pen for nearly an hour. The unsmiling woman's face changes as she grades it. She starts to chuckle, but it's a laughing-at-you-not-with-you sort of chuckle. She draws an "X" across my paper with a red pen. "You are what we call a false beginner," she says dismissively. "You have to start all over."

Ugh. Well, I thought I knew how to cook, too. I take the school's brochures home without signing up.

I read that Julia and Paul Child tacked a large map of Paris on their wall and then crossed off each area as they visited it, to be sure not to miss a speck of the city. I vaguely recall a shop in the Gallerie Vivienne that sells posters and maps. There, sure enough, I find an inexpensive reproduction of a 1925 map of Paris. Holding it up to a new one, I see that it appears central Paris is largely unchanged. I want the map to feel like a blank canvas, not just to show how much of Paris Mike and I have to explore together, but how much of everything.

"C'est un cadeau?" asks the efficient proprietress.

I stare at her blankly. *"Cadeau"* . . . Is it a hat? No, that's a *chapeau,* you idiot. *Cadeau* . . . is a . . . *gift.* Of course! I nod yes. She reaches under the counter and pulls out a heavy piece of white paper and a long, shiny red ribbon. In seemingly one movement, the map is wrapped with an expert bow. She hands it to me with a cheery *"Bonne journée,"* the French version of "Have a nice day."

I walk to busy avenue de l'Opéra and step into a wine store to buy a bottle of Veuve Clicquot champagne. At home, I put it in the refrigerator but then catch myself before closing the door. I stare at it hard. When I open it tomorrow, Mike will be here. My heart pounds at the thought. I am nervous, excited, and about a dozen other emotions all at once. How can you miss someone so much, in only a matter of weeks? How can you fall in love so quickly with someone you've known for years? I pace the flat. I can't be here alone with all this nervous energy. I run down the six flights of stairs and out onto the street. I walk fast past the Louvre and don't stop until I reach the Seine. I pull my coat around me, the cold wind stinging my face, and stare at the city, the sky dim with twilight.

"Mike Klozar."

Three unrelated people—a friend in Oregon, a former colleague in Germany, and my downstairs neighbor in Seattle—all mentioned the same name when I asked if they knew anyone working in the London office. I emailed him, and our exchanges turned chatty. When we agreed to meet on his next business trip to Seattle, I was intrigued. Was this a job interview or a blind date?

It was around the fourth of July 1999. I watched him walk into the restaurant I selected, one of my favorites. Mike searched the room for a woman matching a description I had sent him. (He swears now that I had said I'd be wearing leather boots, a short black skirt, and a white top. Boots? Surely not in July. The miniskirt? Well . . .) His pale blue eyes locked on mine, and then he smiled a dimpled, impish grin. The attraction was intense, immediate, and mutual, something neither of us expected. I had been arranging a portfolio of my work on the table in front of me. This forced a split-second decision on his part: sit in the chair across from me as expected, or slide in beside me on the bench. As he slid beside me, with only incidental contact, the electricity felt powerful.

He asked why I wanted to go to London. "Adventure, to try something different," I replied. As we talked, Mike casually mentioned that he had booked a flight to Spain that left in just three hours and that he'd recently climbed Mount Kilimanjaro. He sailed, he hiked, and he loved to cook Thai food. So he was a funny, smart Renaissance man *and* he had an amazing sense of adventure. Exactly what I was looking for in my life—except that we both were in long-term relationships.

So when I moved to London we became friends. But as we got to know each other, something always lingered below the surface. One night years later, in my London flat, we began to kiss. For the first time, neither of us was in a relationship. After a moment, I pulled away and, from out of nowhere, I heard myself say: "If you stay . . . it will be forever." He didn't. We found reasons to avoid each other for weeks. "Forever," it seems, was a scary word for each of us.

A year later, Mike left the company. He took off traveling, enjoying his newfound freedom from corporate life. On his way through Europe, he and I arranged to meet in Milan, where I was going to be on a business trip. After dinner the first night, we strolled along the Piazza del Duomo, gently lit by a hazy moon. He asked softly, "Are you OK with forever now?" With a kiss in the middle of the shadowy piazza, we crossed the thin line between platonic and passionate. It took three years for us to get to that kiss.

I've got to hear his voice. I dial directly to Seattle on my cellphone, even though I know it will cost two dollars a minute. "Good morning, sexy," he says groggily, tugged from sleep.

"Good evening, handsome." I try to make my voice light. Across the Seine, I see the Eiffel Tower explode with strobes, as it does on the hour every evening.

"I was just dreaming about you," he says.

At school today, I can barely concentrate, even though we've moved on to red meat. We'll prepare the meat and marinade for *boeuf bourguignon*. We'll cut palm-sized pieces of meat from a jagged hunk of shoulder and steep them overnight in a crimson marinade of red wine, garlic, onions, and herbs. Tomorrow, we'll retrieve our marinade, add veal stock and a bit of sifted flour to the top of the meat, and let it braise leisurely as we prepare the dish's *garniture,* or signature vegetables, separately. Once cooked, the meat will be "decanted," removed piece by piece from the now hot stewing liquid. After straining the vegetables from the sauce, we'll reduce it, and then add the beef and separately prepared onions, mushrooms, and bacon, along with a dash of chopped parsley.

Chef moves on to the mashed potatoes that will accompany the grilled sirloin we'll prepare in the rest of our practical. "You should add roughly half as much butter as potatoes," Anne translates as the chef churns soft just-boiled potatoes through a food mill. *"Un petit peu de beurre,"* Chef says—"a little bit of butter"—tossing three sticks of butter in. He beats them in with a wide plastic spoon and pours in a generous dose of cream. Mike will love them, but my thighs will not.

Our practical class cannot end quickly enough. I prepare my *bourguignon* marinade in record time. I poke repeatedly at my sirloin on the grill, urging it to cook, and take it off at the first hint of doneness. "Bien," Chef says of my *jus*. My meat earns a *"très bien."* Cooked *bleu,* it's so rare that it's almost still mooing, the way many French people prefer it. I've worked so quickly, I finish with Amit. Anna-Clare waves me to leave. "I'll clean up your station, don't worry," she says. Everyone knows that Mike arrives today.

"Have a great time!" calls out LizKat. "Tell him we can't wait to meet him."

L.P. is typically pragmatic. "Don't forget, we have an early class tomorrow."

At home, huffing onto the sixth floor, I see Mike's bags dropped just inside the door. I put the food in the fridge and then creep over to the bedroom. He's wearing the deep blue sweater that I bought him for Christmas. Kissing his neck, I coax awake my jet-lagged boyfriend and murmur, "Welcome to Paris."

Later, I lead him on a tour of the apartment. He marvels at the view across the rooftops, delighted that we can see the flag flying above the Palais Royal. His interest in architecture is piqued by the clever uses of small space, by the whole wall that slides over to reveal the master bedroom.

Mike leans out far to see the Sacré Coeur as I sauté the sirloin until it's closer to medium-rare, reheat the potatoes, and make a salad. For the first of what will be many similar dinners, we feast on my day's work, talking and laughing. I tell him about the beef bourguignon that's marinating in the basement for tomorrow, and I show him the schedule of what's to come. He lifts up a glass of champagne in a toast.

"We're here," Mike says, and we clink glasses. "Isn't it odd we talked about this years ago? How do you feel about it now?"

I ponder the thoughts I had standing at my window in London. Sitting here, with my binder from school open, from the look on his face I know that my grandmother would agree: I've picked the right lane.

"Are you kidding? No regrets, none at all."

He takes my hand and kisses each fingertip, one by one. "Good," he says. "Because I feel the same way. I would give up anything to be with you."

By 9:00 p.m., he's wide awake, so we bundle up and go out with a vague plan to find somewhere to kiss in the cold, clear night air along the Seine, to mark off our first place on the map. We end up at the same spot I called him from just a day ago. A dinner boat passes by below, and a familiar song drifts up from it along the water:

Give your heart and soul to me
and life will always be
la vie en rose.

Boeuf à la Bourguignonne

BEEF BRAISED IN RED WINE

Serves eight to ten

Marinate the meat at least six hours, although overnight is better. Serve with hot buttered noodles or boiled potatoes. For entertaining, make a day ahead, reheat, and voilà. The ideal pairing here is to serve the same wine you used in the marinade.

MEAT AND MARINADE

2½ to 3 pounds (about 1.5 kg) lean beef stew meat, cubed

1 bottle (750 ml) red wine, preferably Syrah

2 medium carrots, chopped

1 medium yellow onion, chopped

4 cloves garlic, peeled, smashed

Parsley stems from one bunch, tied with string

½ teaspoon dried thyme

1 bay leaf

½ cup (125 ml) cognac or brandy

2 teaspoons coarsely ground black pepper

2 teaspoons coarse salt

3 tablespoons olive oil

8 ounces (230 g) pancetta or unsmoked bacon, cubed

1 teaspoon thyme

2 bay leaves

3 tablespoons flour

2 cups (500 ml) brown beef stock

3 cloves garlic

½ sweet onion, sliced

8 ounces (250 g) mushrooms, sliced

1 medium carrot, chopped

2½ cups (20-ounce can) tomatoes, chopped

2 medium white potatoes, peeled, cut into ½-inch chunks

2 tablespoons balsamic vinegar (optional)

3 tablespoons chopped parsley

Combine meat with marinade ingredients in a large, nonreactive bowl and stir to mix. Cover with plastic wrap and refrigerate overnight.

Preheat oven to 350°F/180°C. Separate the meat, vegetables, and red wine. Discard the parsley bundle and bay leaf. Bring the marinade liquid to a boil. Vigilantly skim foam off the top. Dry meat with paper towels and season with salt and pepper. Add oil to a large Dutch oven over high heat.

Brown the meat in batches and set aside. Lower heat, and add pancetta or bacon. Cook slowly until slightly browned. Remove half and set aside to add before serving.

Add the meat, the vegetables from the marinade, and the thyme and bay leaves to the pan with the pancetta. Sprinkle with flour and stir to coat. Add the boiled wine and stock (and water if needed) to cover meat. Bring to a simmer, cover, and bake in the oven for an hour.

Then add the garlic, sliced onions, mushrooms, carrots, tomatoes, and potatoes and cook until the meat and vegetables are tender, about forty-five minutes. Check seasonings, and add the reserved pancetta, balsamic vinegar (if using), and parsley.

CHAPTER 7

NO BONES ABOUT IT

Lesson highlights: Introduction to les farces, caul fat,
meat-stuffed meat, and dinner at Le Fouquet's

Two nights after Mike arrives, Basic students go to our "class dinner" at Le Fouquet's, an institution on the Champs-Élysées heavy with Old World decor and well-coiffed patrons who drip with diamonds.

Upstairs, in a private room, we're a tough crowd. Students pick apart everything, from the seasoning of the grilled lamb to a muted red-wine sauce deemed too thin to the turn of the carrots served on the side. Only a light lemon-artichoke mousse passes inspection. We're seated at round buffet tables of ten and at ours is a woman whom I've seen around school but not yet met. Lely hails from Jakarta, her face graced by large dark eyes, dark straight hair, a flat nose, and a beatific smile. I've never met someone from Indonesia; I could see her wide frame cascaded in leis.

At dinner, Mike meets everyone for the first time. Known for his quick wit and well-timed puns, he is an immediate hit when he starts a long string about the waiters, who seem to be on a mission to provide our table an endless supply of bread and butter.

"I don't know why they keep coming over here," muses Lely. I look at LizKat, tonight clad in a fetching low-cut black top, and then around the rest of the table loaded with beautiful women. Personally, I think it's obvious.

"Maybe they are trying to butter you up?" Mike says to Lely. (Groans, laughter from the crowd.)

"Hey, you're really on a roll," I say. (More groans and laughter.)

"You could say that I've risen to the occasion," Mike says.

Lely's first language is not English. She looks confused. "I don't get it," she says. Butter, roll, rising dough, I explain, thinking this will kill the humor. Instead, as if a light goes off, she begins a shriek of delayed laughter.

After dinner, we all walk in a bitter wind along the Champs-Élysées in search of a drink. We lose part of our large crowd to the lure of warm taxis, and others to clubs throbbing with Euro dance music. Oddly, we end up at an Australian pub.

Beers in hand, our crowd of global nomads raises its pints to make a toast: "Here's to caul fat!" says Lely. I clink my glass to it. After all, who knows what mysterious substance ties people together?

Caul fat soaked in a large bowl of water spectacularly resembles brain matter. Also known as *crépine,* caul fat is the spiderlike veil of white fat that surrounds the internal organs of animals. This week, Chef Bertrand has been demonstrating how to use it. The day after our dinner, for example, he unwinds a thin, lacelike layer of the membrane and then gently wraps it around small, stuffed veal parcels known as *paupiettes.*

We've moved onto *les farces,* the French term for absurd comedies and "stuffing." Although anything can be made into a *farce,* there's a whole repertoire of classic dishes (such as the *paupiettes*) that involve stuffing meat with more meat.

Paupiettes sound simple, but they're typical of the laborious recipes we undertake here. First, Chef bones a hefty piece of veal shoulder, then grinds it with a chunk of marbled pork and sheer white pork fat. He combines the ground bits with sautéed shallots and mushrooms, seasonings, and a *panade* (a blend of fresh bread crumbs and cream). This gets wrapped in a veal escalope—a slice of meat made flat by pounding the hell out of it with the bottom of a small saucepan until it's as "thin as cigarette paper," says Chef Bertrand. He wraps the *crépine* around the veal-stuffed-veal to form the parcels into little balls before they're braised in veal stock.

To use caul fat, we each rip off a large piece. It tears like thick crêpe paper, and in hand it feels like rubbery, delicate wet lace. Anna-Clare takes a photo. "You don't see a bowl of wet brains every day," she says, and who can argue—until we use it for almost a week.

The next day in class, we flatten chicken breasts into escalopes with sauté pans. These are stuffed by piping in a mixture of ground chicken and cream, then topped with a mushroom-cream sauce.

I carry the mushroom-stuffed chicken home in a Hefty OneZip plastic bag, a favorite of my sister, who calls them "zipbags." As a surprise, Mike brought me a cache of them in two sizes from Seattle, a thoughtful gift inspired by my daily complaints about the cake-sized Tupperware. I reheat the chicken. When Mike cuts into it, the filling oozes everywhere. He loves it.

"So when are they going to teach how to make chicken cordon bleu?" he asks. Huh. I have not seen that dish listed in my binder. I ask the next day. Turns out it's not in the curriculum. According to Madame Madeleine Bisset, the woman with the purple pashmina the first day, despite its name the dish has nothing to do with the school. "It is a very old recipe that might have come from Austria," she says. "Or it could be German. Either way, it's not ours."

My stepfather is worried. "Let me tell you something about men," he says one day after wrestling the phone away from my mother. "You don't want more than one hound in the henhouse; it messes up the whole system."

I have no idea what he's saying, but I know what he's getting at.

This week, our first houseguests arrive. One of them just happens to be a friend of mine. Well, maybe that isn't exactly the extent of it. Bill, an NPR host back home, is someone I dated a couple of times years ago.

His visit does not sit well with my mother. After observing my love life as a spectator sport for two decades, she believes that Mike is serious marriage material. She begins to counsel me on strategies to ensnare him. They sound suspiciously like tips from 1950s home-economics classes, ranging from "always make the bed every day" to "invest in some really nice lingerie—men love that."

She's so concerned that Bill's visit will offend Mike that she offers to pay for a hotel for Bill. They don't accept my protests or assurances that we're just friends.

Mike arrived only last Wednesday, but by the following Monday he has already enrolled himself in a grueling thirty-six-hour-per-week intensive French class at Langue Onze, a school in the République area. Slowly, details of his classmates drift out that are a bit worrying.

Jacqueline or "Jackie" is the worldly nineteen-year-old daughter of an Australian embassy official. A.J. is a young, scarlet-haired Danish woman who speaks four languages. Tia sounds stunning—a South African who also happens to be a professional hula hoop dancer. (I didn't know that this was a profession. It turns out that she gets paid to wear skimpy clothes and hula-hoop in nightclubs.)

But this Wednesday night, we wait for Bill. And we wait. I verify the time of his train from London. Two hours later than we expect, we hear the buzzer. Again, the wait is long. "It *is* six flights," I remind Mike.

"Maybe he needs help with his bags," Mike says. He goes downstairs to investigate. There's a muffled conversation on the steps. Suddenly, Bill hurtles into the flat. His six-foot-two frame is hunched, his face a stark, ghastly white.

"Hi Kat, uhm, where's your bathroom?" he asks, and then flings himself in its direction, slamming the door behind him.

Mike appears in the doorway, arms loaded with Bill's coat and cases. "Food poisoning in London," he says, nodding toward the bathroom. So, for his first twenty-four hours in Paris, the man that worried my mother remains wrapped, miserable, in the fetal position on a foldout couch in the postage-stamp-sized den.

The next night, Bill is feeling better. We end up waiting on my good friend Marietta, who is a couple hours late arriving from London, too. "I hope she didn't eat what I ate," adds Bill. We had planned to meet Mike and "the girls" from his class at a bar/restaurant in République called the Chat Noir. As soon as Marietta arrives, she, Bill, and I bundle into a cab, but by now we are hours late.

The real Chat Noir was a celebrated cabaret. This bar is a popular brasserie, with solid tables and Stella Artois signs scattered around to perk up the decor. The group started drinking red wine at 4:00 p.m. while waiting for us to arrive. Apparently, some of them never stopped.

Rail-thin Jackie is the first to greet me, wearing a black T-shirt that says:

Sorry I Missed Church
I Was Busy Practicing Witchcraft
And Becoming a Lesbian

She moves over to shake my hand and promptly loses her footing, taking a couple of chairs with her. For some reason, I had imagined her as very proper and embassylike, sort of an Anne Hathaway after she's cleaned up in *The Princess Diaries*. Instead, here she is, splayed on the floor, the result of having consumed no food and half her body weight in *vin rouge*.

"I'm all right!" she slurs mightily, as Mike and A.J. raise her up. "It's so nice to meet you. Mike talks about you all the time. He loves you sooooo much." Then her lids droop, and her body follows.

Mike says, "Okay, let's get you home." He puts her in a cab back to the embassy. "I told her to go, but she wanted to stay and meet you," he says to me.

The other two aren't what I expected either. Tia is very pretty, to be sure, but a bit goofy, dressed in a sort of wanna-be-a-gypsy getup. She keeps wandering off to flirt with men at the bar.

I'd pictured A.J. as a severe Nordic Bond Girl, but she turns out to be a soft-figured beauty with an engaging smile. With her four languages, she's taken a job at a currency exchange to pay the rent, allowing her to attend language classes full-time. She thought it would be undemanding, but it sounds horrific.

"People yell at me constantly. They say horrible, mean things. Today, some guy from Alabama called me a whoring bitch," she says, her blue eyes starting to water. This genuinely pains her. "We post how much commission we take and all the exchange rates, but people can't do math anymore. All they know is that they get back less than they expected, so they yell at me. It's awful."

Mike tactfully interrupts. "Hey, there's a DJ downstairs. *Allons-y!*" Indeed, a jumble of decks are set up in an underground chamber with ancient brick arches, the space just large enough for us and a handful of Parisians. We dance until midnight. Mike chats with a friend of the DJ, and it turns out they both play jazz trombone. His new friend insists on taking us to another club, so we're off en masse through the backstreets of République to an unmarked dance club. Then, his friend produces a whole round of drinks, this time gin and tonics and bottles of Stella Artois.

The rest of the night is a blur. French techno music blares on the speakers, melding into what I'm convinced must be one endless song. We dance *ensemble,* sometimes infiltrated by men hitting on the girls. By 4:00 a.m., I'm wiped out. I look for Bill, who, undeterred by his food poisoning, has escaped to get a kebab from a street vendor outside the club.

Sometimes it is tough to know what's good for you.

The next afternoon, Bill, Marietta, Mike, and I walk over the bridges to the Île de la Cité and Notre Dame. We stop in our tracks at the sight.

Scaffolding with snaking hoses, cranes, and massive fans accompany a full cadre of cameras and lights and a film crew in front of the church. We wait. An American voice yells "Action!" and suddenly it rains. It's puzzling, though: it's been raining here on and off for weeks. Leave it to Hollywood to wait for the first beautiful sunny day to create fake rain in Paris. With nearby British tourists, we amiably debate if we're watching a scene for *The Da Vinci Code,* rumored to be shooting early scenes here. After watching a couple of takes, we walk on toward our planned destination, the Marais.

This neighborhood in central Paris near the Hôtel de Ville is not what you think of when you hear the word "swamp," which is what *marais* means in French. Nor do you look and think, "That's what I imagine a Jewish ghetto would look like." It was once that, too.

The Marais was never demolished to make way for the grand boulevards under Baron Haussmann in the 1800s, and so it's one of the few places in Paris that feels almost ancient, not just old. One of the oldest houses in the city is found here—a half-timbered number built in 1407 by a French writer and alchemist. The rest of the area is rife with sagging, gray, eclectic architecture laid out amid twisty, narrow streets, a few still made of cobblestone. Its old infrastructure is a major contrast to the updated storefronts that are part of the area's rebirth in the past couple decades as a trendy shopping and eating area and the epicenter of the city's gay community.

As we walk, I learn that my mother had nothing to worry about with Bill. He's madly in love with a woman in Seattle named Sara, and they plan to get married. Not that anything could distract me from Mike.

My mother always says, "Eighty percent of what you worry about never happens anyway." She worried about Bill; I fretted about the "girls." But it turns out neither of us had anything to be concerned about. So much of life is a farce, in both meanings of the word. Much of our life is made up of situations one might find in a traditional comedy—misunderstandings, wrong expectations, and odd situations that, in retrospect, seem quite amusing. How much of what happens is just *stuff?*

Of course, there is always that other 20 percent.

Poulet Cordon Bleu

CHICKEN CORDON BLEU

Serves four

Let's set the record straight: The Paris-based cooking school has nothing to do with this dish. The specific origins remain a bit of a mystery, but the original (with veal) is likely a cousin in Germany's schnitzel family and may have originated in Austria. Taste the ham and cheese before you start; overly salty or smoky versions of either can overwhelm this dish. Secure the chicken parcels by threading a trussing needle with string and sewing up the sides, or wrap them in caul fat; in a pinch, toothpicks work. My sister adds shredded cheese to her sauce as it finishes. Serve with a crisp white, such as a Sauvignon Blanc or Fumé Blanc.

4 chicken breasts, about 6 ounces (170 g) each
Coarse salt, ground black pepper
4 teaspoons Dijon mustard
4 slices (2–3 ounces) Swiss cheese, preferably Gruyère

4 slices (about 2 ounces) very thinly sliced prosciutto or ham

1 cup (about 100 g) flour

2 eggs, beaten slightly

1 cup (about 100 g) seasoned bread crumbs

½ cup (125 ml) dry white wine

1 cup (250 ml) chicken stock

1 tablespoon butter

1 tablespoon flour

1 cup (250 ml) cold milk or cream

Salt, pepper to taste

1 tablespoon grated Gruyère cheese *(optional)*

Preheat oven to 350°F/175°C. Butterfly each chicken breast, using a sharp knife to carefully cut into one side until it opens like a book. Season the interior with salt and pepper and coat with 1 teaspoon mustard. Top with a slice of cheese, then a slice of prosciutto or ham. Close and secure with string or toothpicks, or wrap them in caul fat. Dredge this chicken preparation in flour, then dip it in the beaten egg, and then roll it in bread crumbs. Repeat for the other breasts. Bake in a dish lined with parchment paper or foil for thirty-five to forty-five minutes, or until the parcels are firm to the touch and juices running from the chicken are clear and no longer pink, and a meat thermometer reaches 180°F/80°C.

Heat the wine in a saucepan over high heat and reduce by half. Add the stock, bring to a boil, and reduce to a simmer. Keep warm until ready to add to the sauce below. (Don't skip this step; your sauce will break.)

In another saucepan, make a roux by melting the butter over medium heat until bubbly. Whisk in the flour and continue to whisk for eight to ten minutes, until it smells like popcorn. Add the cold milk and whisk in completely. Whisk in the wine-stock mixture, and season with salt and pepper. Adjust consistency by adding more stock if sauce is too thick. If desired, add in the grated cheese. Remove the string from the chicken. Top with the sauce.

Chapter 8

SPLITTING HARES

LESSON HIGHLIGHTS: RABBIT WITH MUSTARD SAUCE, HAKE STEAKS
WITH HOLLANDAISE SAUCE, AND THE IMPORTANCE OF DISHWASHERS

In France, butchers leave the heads on whole rabbits to assure their customers that they are not buying cats.

Or at least, that's the rumor among students as we watch Chef Dufour cleave the rabbit's neck with a loud *thwack*. As when anything gruesome happens in a demonstration, half of the class recoils in horror; the other half leans forward in fascination.

After the guillotining, I head to the basement. It's one of my weeks to act as assistant, working with Ramona. As I open the door to the walk-in cooler, I find her standing frozen, staring into the large plastic basket. She tears her gaze away to look at me, her face heavy with anguish, as if she just stumbled onto a horrific car accident. Walking over to the box, I see why. The dead eyes of ten rabbits stare straight back at us.

I see the confusion with a skinned cat. Long and lean with pink muscle, the extended legs and short torso certainly resemble how I'd picture my late Tessie to look without her fur. The head's similarity to that of an alien cannot be dismissed. The wide skull narrows into a pointed nose and shallow mouth. Most disturbing are the eyes; they seem almost perfectly intact.

Maybe I don't want to learn French cuisine after all.

The rabbits are heavy. It's a struggle to move the box into the dumb-waiter. We lug a huge stainless-steel pot filled with chicken stock onto the shelf next to them and finish off with two plastic crates loaded with vegetables. We hit the button to send the lot upstairs and run up two flights to greet it. When we arrive, L.P. has already set out everyone's cutting boards.

The worktable is set up the same way each day for a practical. Assistants dole out the ingredients in equal measure among five bowls to be shared by two students on each side of the worktable. Next to the ingredient bowls sit *les poubelles,* or little waste bowls for trimmings, used paper towels, et cetera. Nothing is ever to be left on our cutting boards. Cut vegetables or prepped meats or fish go into other stainless-steel bowls or pans. We are to cut, then wipe off our board and all around it after prepping each ingredient.

Amit thumps a naked rabbit on my cutting board. "It's better to just get it over with," he says, outlining the best route to cut. The scene reminds me of surgeons giving one another tips. Will he suggest how to cleanly remove the appendix next? Looking across the table, I see the model-beautiful LizKat sawing off her rabbit head with a bread knife, blood splattered onto her forehead. I have no stomach for that. I grab my heavy cleaver. *Thwack!* It's done. I drop it into the *poubelle* and contemplate the rest of the lean body.

I hear Anna-Clare's voice, polite and even. "Um, ah, Kat?" I look up. The rabbit's head landed in an unfortunate position. It's staring straight at her. "Do you, uh, mind, removing that DEAD RABBIT HEAD from our bowl?"

"Oh, sorry, Anna-Clare," I say, meaning it. "Give me yours." She picks up her rabbit head between her index finger and thumb and with great distaste adds it to the bowl. I bang it hard against the edge of the trash can, and the heads are out of sight.

She smiles. "Thanks for that." I wave her off.

"No problem," I tell her and lean back over my rabbit. After ritually removing the organs, I trim the body into pieces and craft a square known as its "saddle" from its tummy. I "French" the delicate rib structure with a small paring knife, scraping the meat to expose the tiny end bones. It's like making a rack of lamb for a dollhouse.

Always working well ahead of the class, Amit has already browned his rabbit, coated it with mustard, and shoved it into the oven. I start multitasking at a quick pace. For the next hour, I simultaneously prepare my rabbit, sauté potatoes, clean my station, and measure everything for the mustard-cream sauce.

Today's sauce calls for roughly three tablespoons of butter and about a cup of cream. At 55 calories per tablespoon of cream and 90 for the same amount of butter, I calculate that these ingredients alone contain more than 1,500 calories. Perhaps this explains why I've gained seven pounds in five weeks.

Before Le Cordon Bleu, I had 119 pounds on my five-foot-four frame. I've never weighed more than 125—until now. I barely buttoned my houndstooth trousers before class.

I assemble my plate for my day's grade. Opening the grade book, the kind-faced Chef Bertrand peers through the bottom of his glasses to examine my day's work. He cuts into my potato. "Bien." He tries the rabbit. "C'est bon," he says but then adds a quick comment about the sauce. "Plus" and "moutarde" are all I understand. Hmmm, did I use too much mustard? Or do I need to add more sauce to the plate? He flashes me a quick smile and then moves on.

At home, I climb the six flights of stairs to the apartment. Mike has just arrived home from his French class. His arms envelop me in a soothing hug as he kisses all over my face, then proudly announces that he walked the two miles from République for some exercise.

"Good thing. I've got another cream sauce," I tell him.

I dump the rabbit unceremoniously into a saucepan and then pull out some greens for a salad. As Mike opens some wine and cuts up a baguette he bought on his walk home, I put the plates on the table. We sit down. Suddenly, an image flashes in my mind. I see the rabbit's head rolling away from its shoulders.

"What's wrong?" Mike asks, seeing the odd look on my face. So I tell him about the day's beheadings.

"You did what?" We both stare down at our plates.

We put the food back into the zipbags and then head out for fondue in Saint Michel in the Fifth. It's the second Le Cordon Bleu meal we haven't eaten. Mike teases me that nothing at Costco comes with its head on; it is usually bagged and boneless. As at most supermarkets, they remove every bit of evidence that the meat came from anything that was ever alive.

Dishwashers, or *plongeurs* in French, play an important role at Le Cordon Bleu. They're the only ones who can get you a *passoire* when urgently needed. So far, I've encountered three *plongeurs* who rotate through our kitchen on the first floor.

My favorite is a tiny, pleasant Algerian who comes up as high as my shoulders. He has a shy smile and a gentle manner, yet he can wash through a stack of pans in record time. I make a point to be nice to him and give him food from time to time. He washes whatever I need promptly and makes sure my station stays stocked.

Then there's a tall Moroccan who fancies himself a lady-killer. In the first month, he's given every woman in Basic Cuisine his phone number, with little success. He punishes the women who don't call, including me, by not refreshing their stations with pans when they run out during class.

Then there's one that I've nicknamed Jules as he reminds me, in both physical appearance and attitude, of the Samuel L. Jackson character in *Pulp Fiction*. He arrives more than an hour into our class, just after the kitchen is entirely out of pots and pans. He walks slowly, sometimes offering high fives to the male students.

Once, I stood behind him in the dishwashing area waiting for a pan. He stopped, turned around, leaned against the sink, and crossed his arms, his hands in industrial blue rubber gloves. Then, he casually asked, "Qu'est-ce que vous regardez?" *What are you looking at?*

But the worst is when Jules wanders around the kitchen helping himself to tastes of students' food. One day, he dips into Kim's carrots, cooking on the stove.

"WHAT ARE YOU DOING?!" she cries. "It took me half an hour to *turn* those!"

He shrugs and walks away unfazed, chewing on the carrot. Later, he filches a simmering potato from Anna-Clare, who fumes.

Then, it's my turn for a run-in, thanks to someone else's fish.

I do not have high hopes for the poached hake with hollandaise sauce when Chef Dufour begins the day's demonstration.

"Take care to remove all the scales," Anne translates. "This is a particularly scaly seawater fish." Chef saws each thick black fish into one-inch steaks and then ties each piece with a string around the middle to keep its shape. He deposits the steaks into a vinegary vegetable-stock bath known as a court bouillon, meaning simply a "short boil." The fish is added to boiling stock, covered, and then taken off the burner to allow it to gently soak up heat and flavor. A court bouillon is often used to cook delicate fish and shellfish. "The acid from the vinegar will keep the flesh firm and white," Anne says.

As assistants, Ramona and I struggle with a box of fat, lazy-looking hake, or *colin* in French. "These *colin,* I hate them," she says, her Mexican accent thick with disgust. Like many Americans, I've never heard of hake. Best described as a big, ugly fish with gray flesh and a slack mouth, it's often used as an inexpensive substitute for cod. The *tronçons de colin pochés* is not a difficult recipe, though it takes fifteen minutes just to remove the fishes' scales. The bouillon gives the kitchen a harsh, acidic smell.

While the hake bathes in the bouillon, I turn over my cutting board. We are assigned just one cutting board each per practical, and we are to flip it over whenever we conclude prepping meat or fish to avoid contamination. I'm dubious that this truly prevents cross-contamination, but I do it anyway. I mop up the scales and flop the bloodied side down, planning to prep vegetables.

Just then, Ramona comes up to Chef Dufour with her hake.

"Ch-eff, j'ai un problème." Without a word, he takes her hake, picks up my clean fillet knife, and proceeds to scale it and cut it on my clean cutting board. Afterward, Chef hands me my knife with a polite *"Merci,"* and walks away. My board is again littered with gray, wet scales and blood.

With a sigh, I lug it into the dishwashing station. But Jules the dishwasher attacks me like a pit bull at a junkyard. "NON!" he screams, so loud that I literally jump back two feet.

"Mais, le chef à coupé un poisson—"

"APRÈS LA CLASSE! Seulement après la classe!" he yells, *only after class,* pointing back toward the kitchen. Meekly, I walk back to my place at the worktable. What to do? I try to wash it as best I can in the kitchen's small sink, meant for washing vegetables, knives, and our hands. But there's no soap.

Sometimes, I'm just not sure about the hygiene here. In theory, we're graded on sanitation, although specifics aren't discussed. If you watch carefully in demonstrations, the chefs use good sanitation habits. The sous-sol assistants change their cutting boards as often as six or seven times during a class. So why can't I have *my* cutting board washed midclass?

I shake it off and move on to the hollandaise. "The more gently and the slower you cook something, the less chance that it will run away from you," Chef Bertrand told us in demonstration when explaining how to slowly bring egg yolks to the right temperature for the sauce. "It's like courting a difficult woman."

I divide my eggs, sliding the yolks into a metal bowl and dropping the whites in a communal Tupperware dish; those will be used in pastry classes later. Then I snuggle the yolk bowl into a saucepan of simmering water and start to whisk.

And I whisk.

My yolks aren't cooperating. I have no upper body strength. Lurking in our practical kitchen is the mustached Chef Dufour. He frowns, mildly exasperated. He roughly grabs my whisk from my hand and then places my palm against the lukewarm bowl.

"Ça n'est pas chaud." Cranking up the electric burner, he waits until the yolks are warmer. He hands me back my whisk with a bored gesture.

Once they are frothy, I transfer the bowl with the yolks to the worktable. I hold a pan with clarified butter overhead and pour it in a steady stream into the yolks, then whisk madly again as my bicep burns.

For presentation, I make a crisscross pattern with the hollandaise, with the grayish *colin* steak in the center, circled by delicate lemon slices and parsley. I almost forget to take off the string, an inexcusable faux pas.

Chef has little to say. The hollandaise is all right. On the *colin,* he is less generous. "Le colin a besoin de goût." My fish lacked flavor. In English, he asks if I forgot to add salt to my bouillon. *"Merci,"* he inspects my name tag, "Miss Flinn." He writes down my grade. Without enthusiasm, I zipbag the fish.

Nothing in the world is as unappetizing as this fish, I think as I walk from school. Then, I see the smartest homeless man in the world.

Once or twice a week, an older French gentleman dressed in a fraying blue sports jacket sits on a doorstep with his dog at the end of rue Léon Delhomme. It's a discreet spot yet directly in the path to the Métro from Le Cordon Bleu. He never asks for food—he doesn't have to. I know now that some students routinely give their food away to the dishwashers, to their roommates, to friends, or to beggars on the street.

As I approach this man, his dog gives a welcoming sniff. "Excusez-moi, monsieur," I begin, tugging the fish from my bag. "Est-ce que vous désirez du poisson?" I hope my pronunciation is correct. If not, I've just cheerfully asked him if he'd like some poison.

"OK, yes," he says in English. I don't know why I'm surprised; everywhere in Paris, if you ask something in French, the response is invariably provided in English. He inspects the bag. "Ah, *le colin*. I am often getting this." I start to turn away, but he motions for me to wait. He reaches his fingers into the bag to pinch a bit of the fish to taste. "More salt, *peut-être?*" he says good-naturedly, grinning to expose an incomplete set of dark teeth.

"Er . . . *ah, oui. Merci, monsieur.*"

Even he agrees my dish needs more salt.

Lapin ou Poulet à la Moutarde

RABBIT OR CHICKEN WITH MUSTARD SAUCE

Serves six to eight

You can make this dish with either rabbit or bone-in chicken thighs. Rabbit is similar to the dark meat of chicken but with a gamier flavor. This dish pairs nicely with simple green beans. Traditionally, you'd drink white wine

with this, perhaps a Sauvignon Blanc or a Pouilly-Fumé. But if you're partial
to red wine, try a soft one, such as Pinot Noir. In cold weather, I add cream
for a richer dish.

2½ pounds (1 kg) rabbit pieces or chicken thighs
Coarse salt and freshly ground pepper
1 tablespoon dried thyme
All-purpose flour
3 tablespoons olive oil
4 tablespoons + 2 tablespoons Dijon mustard
1 tablespoon butter
3 shallots, finely chopped (about ¼ cup)
1 large onion, finely chopped (about 1¼ cups)
2 cloves garlic, chopped
⅓ cup (75 ml) brandy
⅔ cup (150 ml) chicken stock
Bouquet garni (parsley, bay leaf tied)
4 or 5 sprigs fresh rosemary or 1 teaspoon dried
⅔ cup (150 ml) heavy cream (optional)

Preheat the oven to 350°F/180°C. Sprinkle the meat with salt, pepper,
and dried thyme. Dredge lightly in flour, shaking off excess. In a Dutch
oven large enough to hold all the ingredients comfortably, heat the oil
over medium-high heat. Brown pieces on all sides, in batches if necessary.
Remove meat from the pan and drain the oil. Using a pastry brush or the
back of a spoon, apply a generous coat of mustard to each piece; set
aside.

Over medium heat in the same pan, melt the butter. Add the shallots
and onions and cook until translucent. Stir in garlic. Add the brandy and
chicken stock, and simmer until slightly reduced. Add the bouquet garni
and rosemary. Return the chicken or rabbit pieces to the pan. Cover and
cook in the oven for about forty-five minutes, or until an instant-read meat
thermometer reads 160°F/75°C degrees. Remove the meat and cover
loosely with foil to keep warm.

Put the pan on medium heat and bring the pan juices to a simmer for about five minutes, until slightly reduced, skimming off any fat from the surface. (Rabbit is oilier than chicken and will require significant skimming.) Add the remaining two tablespoons of mustard and the cream (if using) and let simmer for seven to ten minutes, until the sauce thickens enough to coat the back of a spoon.

Once it has thickened, pour sauce through a fine-mesh sieve, pressing it through with a spatula. Check seasonings and adjust, adding salt and pepper to taste. Spoon the sauce over the chicken or rabbit pieces.

CHAPTER 9

THE SOUFFLÉ ALSO RISES

Audrey Hepburn failed the soufflé class at Le Cordon Bleu.

At least her character did in *Sabrina*. Inspecting her uncooked soufflé, the chef sniffs "far too low." A suave, elderly baron in her class quickly grasps the situation—it isn't her soufflé that's a problem but her heart.

"A woman happy in love, she burns the soufflé," the baron tells her. "A woman unhappy in love forgets to turn on her oven."

I turn mine on the minute I get to the kitchen.

Chef Jacques Bouveret oversees the soufflé class. A substantial man with a celebrated appetite, Chef Bouveret looks like the quintessential French chef, sort of like Santa Claus without the beard. Specializing in sauces and fish preparation, he's been a chef longer than I've been alive. He earned international acclaim as chef of a famous three-star Michelin restaurant in Paris and won numerous culinary awards before joining Le Cordon Bleu in 1990. Despite his impressive résumé, Chef Bouveret may be the least temperamental of the lot. He whistles and hums his way around the kitchens. Sometimes, he even sings.

"Oh, Champs-Élysées. . . . Oh, Champs-Élysées. . . ." His off-key voice precedes him to the kitchen. He gives us eight minutes to whisk our egg yolks and water over gentle heat to nudge them to a generous froth. Then, he gathers us around the worktable. In unison, we whisk the egg whites for a good fifteen minutes with huge balloon whisks, until the whites form stiff peaks. It's a song of its own, the clattering of all those metal whisks on stainless-steel bowls.

The key to a good soufflé, we learn in demonstration, is the careful folding of the stiff egg whites into whatever else is going into the soufflé. They must be blended but not *too* mixed. Chef Bouveret oversees our folding efforts and then instructs us to pour the mixtures into prepared, chilled soufflé dishes. We all put our soufflés into the convection oven at the same time. As the minutes tick down, I wring my hands. "Soufflé" translates roughly to "blow up." I'm certain that's what mine is doing in the oven.

Ding!

"Look, look," Chef says. (I think these are the only English words he knows.) We gather around the oven to claim our soufflés as he pulls each one out. It begins badly. The first one has fallen deeply and cracked.

"Le vôtre?" he says to Tai Xing. She nods forlornly. He shakes his head. The next two are lopsided, the third one has fallen, and the next two have risen too much.

"Ooh la la," he says, pulling out the seventh. "C'est parfait!"

I can't believe it. "C'est le mien!" I exclaim.

"Très bien, mademoiselle, très bien," the chef says, pushing it toward me. He gives me the thumbs-up, his ultimate endorsement. I float home on the Métro, as my soufflé suffers in my Tupperware.

Back at the apartment, I'm greeted by Mike's best friend from Seattle, James, and Amy, his girlfriend of eight months. A thoughtful, Oxford-educated American, James is a voracious reader who is into paragliding, an extreme sport that requires jumping off a mountain with a special parachute. Amy is a veterinarian who owns her own power tools and isn't afraid to use them.

Their romance started marvelously after they met at a book club. They cuddled in public. James developed "mention-itis," meaning he'd bring up Amy regardless of the topic being discussed. ("You know, Amy power-washed her house, too.") So when James called to say he was bringing Amy to Paris for Valentine's Day, we assumed he planned to propose.

I burst into the flat, still exhilarated by the soufflé class. I can't talk fast enough. "It was perfect, wait until you see it," I ramble on, taking the lid off the Tupperware. It's fallen and soggy. My heart sinks. We eat it anyway. Success can be so fleeting.

For dinner, we head down an alley and spot a tiny place called Restaurant Incroyable. As we walk in, the conversation trails off at the handful of tables. The patrons are all clearly regulars. "Bonsoir!" says the owner, getting up from one of the tables while holding a panting white puppy. It's common in Paris to see dogs and diners together, yet this is the first time I've seen an owner with a pet tucked under his arm.

"Une table pour quatre, s'il vous plait?" I ask.

"Ah, oui, madame," he says. He asks tentatively. "You are English?"

Mike, burnishing his new French, replies, "Non, nous sommes Américains."

"Oh, yes, good, Americans! Then you are welcome to dine here," he says in English, clearly relieved we're not British. A thousand years of war with your neighbor can have that effect. Over the next three hours, he smiles and showers us with his hospitality, even ferreting out a last prized bottle of his favorite wine, a Côte de Beaune, to go with our grilled salmon fillets and braised lamb shanks. We ask him to join us for a glass of port as we finish our apple tarts.

Amy asks the age of his puppy. "Oh, he's very young. He hasn't even had his first examination," he says, scrubbing behind the puppy's ears.

"I'm a veterinarian; can I have a look?" He thrusts the tiny fur ball toward her. Amy inspects his teeth, coat, and ears. Then, she slips her chair back a bit from the table, flips the surprised puppy on his back in her lap, spread-eagle, and nonchalantly conducts a thorough probe of his privates. "Everything's in great shape," she announces brightly. "Both of his testicles have dropped already!" She hands the furry ball back to his owner.

This has drawn the attention of the patrons at the two remaining tables, now quiet with disbelief. Not missing a beat, the owner sets the puppy on the floor, slides back in his chair, and assumes a spread-eagle position. "Perhaps I am next?"

The restaurant erupts in laughter. *Incroyable,* indeed.

I wake to an empty apartment the next morning. James and Amy are off to sightsee, and Mike left for French class at 7:00 a.m., as usual. I work on cleaning my uniforms.

Culinary school is a messy affair. Every day, new stains and smells assault my whites with vigor. I always wonder who came up with the idea of the standard kitchen uniform. Why *white*? Le Cordon Bleu uniforms have a deep-blue logo emblazoned on the center of the apron and on the left breast of the chef's jacket. Simply washing them in strong bleach and detergent seems to destroy the blue in the logo yet leave intact the blood, fish guts, veal stock, and other unpleasant residue of our practicals, not to mention a cast of repulsive smells.

Thus I've begun to haunt the cleanser section of the nearby Monoprix. Perusing labels and thumbing through my pocket dictionary, I add a curious mix of words and phrases to my vocabulary: *détachant* (stain remover), *eau de javel* (bleach), *solvent de sang* (removes bloodstains), *nettoie tout* (cleans everything), *décapant puissant* (powerful cleanser), and *odeur fraîche* (fresh smell). Like a stain-fighting apothecary, I concoct a potent, very likely lethal mixture to apply to the stains. Then, I cram the garments into the tiny washer embedded in our kitchen and set it at the highest possible temperature. As in many European apartments, there's no dryer. A painfully complicated drying rack must be assembled. Later, I iron the whole lot. With just two jackets and three aprons, it seems like an endless cycle. Treat stains, wash, struggle with the rack, then iron.

I've just hung the last apron on the rack when the apartment phone trills with its typically French "purr purr" ring, I hear a familiar Cockney accent. "Roight, hello then!"

"Albert! Where are you?"

"Roight, we're downstairs, and it's just stopped pissing rain out here."

Albert's the first person from my office I've talked to since I lost my job and was shunned from the herd. He'd phoned a week earlier to say that he and his fiancée, Vickie, were coming to see his relatives somewhere in the murky outskirts of Paris. We agreed to spend my Friday off from school sightseeing together.

Albert joined my former company when his career in biochemistry provided disturbing insight into what really goes into nonfat cheese, as well as into the true prevalence of airborne diseases. Half French and half English, he had previously worked for Mike in London, then later served on the management team with me. "Bunch of twits," he concluded and changed jobs.

I run downstairs to meet them. Vickie's fragile five-foot frame swims in a camouflage-patterned parka. A former cult member who is now a practicing witch, she gardens part-time for some minor British royals in Sussex. I'm utterly intrigued by her, though she rarely speaks.

"So Vick's never seen the Sacré Coeur, and I thought that it would be cool to go see it," says Albert, finishing the last of a *pain au chocolat*. We take a cab to avoid the mountainous climb that would be required if we took the Métro to Abbesses.

We emerge in front of steps leading up to the Basilica. As we get out, I back up and bump into Amy.

"What are you guys doing here?"

She looks glum. "Well, only I'm here."

"Where's James?"

"I have no idea," she says, shrugging. "We had a fight at breakfast."

Oh. Insert uncomfortable conversation pause here. Albert saves the moment by clearing his throat, forcing introductions.

We wander around the Catholic cathedral with Vickie, the practicing witch, and then agree to climb to the top of the dome. At the bottom, we see a temporary sign in English: "Caution: Precarious steps. Steep climb. Proceed at your own risk." As we navigate the steps, it occurs to me that the sign isn't in any other language. Amy and I speculate that it is probably there for Americans. As a result of our overzealously litigious society, it seems like much of the world is undergoing childproofing on our behalf. I'd once visited the Cliffs of Moher in Ireland, where an unprotected overlook juts above a sheer drop of more than seven hundred feet straight down into the icy waves of the Atlantic. A couple people walk off the edge each year. "They're always Americans," the Irish caretaker told me.

"I think they assume that if there aren't buckets of warning signs and guardrails, it just isn't that dangerous."

Here at the Sacré Coeur, we scramble over broken steps and dislodged bricks and balance along a thin precipice wall before reaching the safer confines of the dome, where we share the endless view with a handful of Italian tourists. Maybe it comes from living daily with history, but Europeans seem so much more accustomed to the fragility of places.

Later, we wander through the touristy shops near the cathedral. Vickie and Albert duck into a *tabac* for cigarettes. At one of the outdoor stalls, Amy picks up an apron with an image of a black cat that says in English, "My cat loves Paris."

"So are you OK?" I ask.

She avoids my gaze. "I don't know. I think we may have broken up."

"Oh." So much for that proposal, I think.

Albert and Vickie catch up. We weave through Montmartre to rue Lepic, a spirited market street. We take a seat under a heat lamp at the Café des Deux Moulins, the café from the film *Amélie*.

Albert updates me on the office. I'd been anxious to hear work gossip, but I'm surprised to find that the corporate intrigues now seem pointless and petty, the hypocrisy rampant. As our lunch arrives, I think of the "Delight the Customer" initiative started before I left the company. It occurs to me that unlike in the corporate world, customer satisfaction is a real and immediate matter in cuisine. Every plate, every meal is another test of a kitchen's ability to satisfy its customers. A chef is judged by whether plates come back empty to the kitchen, the food happily consumed—or not.

Albert shifts to a truly engaging topic: his and Vickie's upcoming nuptials.

"So, it's going to be a thoroughly traditional wedding," Albert starts. "Traditional pagan, that is," he says, laughing. "You know, in the country, out in a field, goats, that sort of thing." Amy and I laugh, until we realize he's not kidding.

"We decided to forgo getting naked to consummate the marriage right in front of the guests, though," he explains. "We're supposed to sacrifice something, but we think putting a pig on a spit should do."

My mobile phone bleats. "So, uhm, James is here, and I guess that he and Amy had a big fight." It's Mike. I get up and walk around the corner.

"Oh, yeah, I know. Amy is here with us, I'll explain later," I tell him.

Cautiously, we plot. He'll take James to the florist downstairs now and urge him to make up. "Tomorrow's Valentine's Day, after all," he says.

We hop a cab back to our apartment on rue de Richelieu. As we arrive, James approaches Amy at the door with a single white rose and gently enfolds her in a hug. They whisper to each other and exchange a couple tender kisses.

Although James and Amy reach a truce that night, the residue from the fight lingers. The next night, the four of us end Valentine's Day over a late candlelit dinner in a stone-covered basement restaurant not far from the Comédie Française. We laugh and talk, but underneath the cheerfulness there's an undercurrent of uncertainty.

There comes a time when every couple knows they're a couple. In our case, it occurs when our visitors almost become uncoupled. As we stand in the February rain to watch James and Amy leave in a cab, I wonder if it will be the last time we see them together.

The week makes me appreciate that love is a fragile thing. It can be as precarious as those steps on the Sacré Coeur or as unpredictable as the eggs in a cheese soufflé. And in love, there are no handrails or any safe recipes to keep your heart from falling.

Soufflé au Chocolat

CHOCOLATE SOUFFLÉ

Serves six

Like love, soufflés can be tricky. This recipe is adapted with permission from the 1999 book *Le Cordon Bleu at Home.* I've added some orange liqueur in honor of André Cointreau, who owns Le Cordon Bleu. Soufflés go more quickly made with two people, especially if whisking the egg whites by hand. Mike and I sometimes make this recipe together.

CHOCOLATE PASTRY CREAM

4 ounces (100 g) semisweet chocolate, chopped

2 cups (500 ml) milk

1 teaspoon vanilla extract

4 egg yolks

½ cup (100 g) sugar

7 tablespoons all-purpose flour

6 egg whites

1½ tablespoons orange liqueur, such as Cointreau (optional)

Confectioners' sugar for dusting

Unsalted butter, softened, and sugar for soufflé mold

Preheat oven to 425°F/250°C. Brush a six-cup soufflé mold with softened butter and carefully coat with sugar; tap out the excess. Refrigerate until needed.

Prepare the chocolate pastry cream: Bring one to two inches of water to a simmer in a saucepan. Put the chocolate in a heatproof bowl and set it over the pan of hot water. Let stand, without stirring, until it melts. While the chocolate softens, heat the milk and vanilla in a heavy-bottomed saucepan and bring to a boil. Combine the egg yolks and sugar in a heatproof bowl and beat until thick and pale yellow. Whisk in the flour. Then whisk a couple tablespoons of the hot milk and a bit of the egg-yolk mixture into the pastry cream. This will "temper" both, bringing them closer to the same temperature. Whisk the rest of the milk into the bowl with the yolks. Pour the yolk-and-milk mixture back into the saucepan. Bring to a boil over medium heat and then simmer until thick. Stir constantly—the cream burns easily. Whisk the melted chocolate into the hot pastry cream. Remove from heat, but keep warm.

Beat the egg whites with a whisk or electric mixer until stiff peaks form. Stir one third of them into the warm chocolate cream to lighten it, and then gently fold in the remainder with a spatula. Remove the soufflé dish from the refrigerator. Pour batter into the prepared soufflé mold and bake for fifteen minutes. Reduce the heat to 375°F/190°C and bake until the soufflé is puffed and firm to the touch, about ten to fifteen minutes longer. The soufflé is ready when it has risen yet still jiggles when moved from side to side.

Punch a hole in the center and pour in the Cointreau. Sift confectioners' sugar over the top and serve at once.

CHAPTER 10

AS THE VEGETABLES TURN

"We could call it our underground lair," Mike says. "Wouldn't it be great for parties?" That's his optimistic take on a warren of rooms in a basement apartment in République. The place could be a set for a Stanley Kubrick film: red and black inflatable furniture set against stark white walls and floor. A hole in the floor offers a sharp descent via a staircase to the bedroom below. In the end we agree this is a place of broken necks and bad dreams.

Finding a good yet affordable apartment in a major city is never an easy task; Paris is no different. We've been renting our place on rue de Richelieu from Nigel, an affable Brit who came to Paris about fourteen years ago and just never left. He helps run an online rental agency along with his friend Theo, a good-looking blond Frenchman with deep dimples. Mike's been lending them some free technical consulting on their website and helping to repair a couple of wildly infected laptops. Nigel apologizes regularly about making us move out, but months earlier he'd agreed to rent our apartment to a wealthy Jordanian woman who can pay one thousand euros more per month for it.

"Really, if I could keep renting it at this rate, I would," he tells us more than once. We don't debate. We like the apartment, but it's so modern, it could be anywhere. Mike and I agree that our next place should feel like we're truly in Paris.

So in our search, we crisscross the city, looking at a dozen places. We inspect an intriguing apartment with exposed, decaying beams and a view of the Panthéon just outside. Everything feels ancient, including the rudimentary bathroom surely built by the Romans. Access to a mattress in what's euphemistically referred to as "the bedroom" is limited to a rickety wooden ladder. The agent proudly discloses the price. A bargain, she assures us. The rent is three times the price of the Richelieu apartment, *plus* there's a monthly commission equal to our current rent—and that apartment has modern plumbing. We pass.

A well-dressed French woman from a different agency leads us up six flights to a loft in a building on rue du Faubourg St.-Antoine in the Bastille neighborhood. It's great, even if it does have a bizarre, blood-red tile shower. We look out a window and realize it's across from Barrio Latino, a notorious late-night four-story dance mecca.

"Oh, no, it's not noisy at all," she assures us. We thank her and head downstairs to meet Nigel for a drink at the Barrio. Nigel laughs at her response.

"This whole street rocks with bass until about six a.m.," he says.

The next day, we meet Chef Henri Gaillard, who will introduce the classic method of clarifying a stock to make consommé.

A stout, handsome man, Chef Gaillard's reputation precedes him.

"He's the one who made a girl cry last term," says L.P. as we watch him prepare for the demonstration. Born in Cognac, he began his restaurant training at the age of thirteen. He arose each morning at 5:00 a.m. to receive the deliveries of vegetables, meat, and seafood. Then, he broke down the crates to start the fires in the ovens. The rest of his early days were spent doing whatever the chefs requested. At the end of the dinner service, he cleaned up the kitchens, only to get up a few hours later to do it all again. His tenacity over the years was rewarded. He moved up the

ranks to hold prestigious positions in kitchens throughout France, eventually heading up one of the most prominent kitchens in Paris, in a restaurant
made famous by Hemingway.

"Est-ce que vous désirez une petite histoire?" he asks. Do we want a
little story?

"Oui, Chef," we reply.

Chef sets a massive stockpot on one burner, heats up a cloudy veal
stock, and adds ground beef, egg white, and tomatoes. For the next hour,
he lovingly tends to the consommé, pulling the ingredients as they cook
into a floating ring known as a "raft." The stock gurgles at a languid pace.
The beef adds flavor, while the egg whites and tomatoes draw out the impurities in the stock, he explains. The result should be a bright-flavored,
clear bouillon. As he does all this, he occasionally takes a small taste with
a fresh spoon and tells us his theory that soups similar to consommé led to
the creation of restaurants.

"Everyone says that the Revolution brought about restaurants," he
says via Anne the translator. "What really happened was that the monarchy made people tired and sick." So, street vendors began to peddle inexpensive thick bouillons or thin soups—said to *restaurer,* or "restore," one's
vigor—to hungry peasants, weary travelers, or tired city workers. More
places offering this "restorative" nourishment began to appear in the sixteenth century, until the first establishment known as a "restaurant"
opened in France in 1765. Even then, it was operated by a French soup
seller, the chef says.

Shortly afterward, elite heads rolled throughout France, and chefs for
the upper classes had to find some new customers. That's when the idea
of a "restaurant" expanded well beyond soups, Chef says.

Chef carefully removes the clarifying ingredients and pours the consommé through a *passoire.* He tastes again with his spoon. Satisfied, he adds
perfectly diced vegetables.

"Goutez, goutez, goutez," Chef begins. "C'est très important . . ."

Anne translates. "Always taste, taste, taste, as you cook. Chef Gaillard
believes this is very important. If you wait until a dish is done, then it is
too late to fix the seasonings. You must taste everything as you go along,
every ingredient."

As I taste his consommé after class, the clean flavor does indeed feel as if it could *restaurer* my body, now growing weary of looking at substandard apartments.

That afternoon, I nurse my consommé and finish yet another round of disappointing puff pastry. As I do, I consider how wonderful it would be to toss some hamburger, egg whites, and tomatoes into the soup of life. Suddenly, everything would be clear and the purpose of it all would be revealed.

Chef Dufour oversees the practical. My consommé is fine, but my puff pastry raises an eyebrow. Without a word, he picks it up off my plate and drops it to the marble work counter. It hits with a *clunk*.

"Maybe you should practice—at home," he says.

Some people believe that Julia Child dropped a whole chicken on the floor while filming *The French Chef*. In truth, she dropped only some potatoes she was trying to flip in a pan. But how I wish it were true. Then, I wouldn't feel so bad about the duck.

Everything is going well with *canette rôtie aux navets,* roast duckling with turnips. Aiming below the knee joint, with a whack I take the webbed feet off in one swift blow. Chef Bouveret whistles as he walks around the room and collects the feet in a large stainless-steel bowl; the sight looks as if a host of Daffy Ducks were bumped off and stored, feet-side up. I pick off the excess feathers, cut out the wishbone, and truss what remains into a neat package. Then, I follow Le Cordon Bleu's precise roasting instructions.

La canette goes on its side in a hot oven for ten minutes. Then, the duckling is turned to the other side for ten minutes. After I add mirepoix, it is turned on its back for fifteen minutes to finish. I'm dubious about the short cooking time until I see the duckling, brown and tender, its skin just ever so taut. I rest the pan on the open oven door as I insert my roasting fork into the cavity to turn it over for the last minutes of cooking.

Then, my wrist hits the edge of the hot pan.

My duck flies from the roasting fork into the air and drops onto the floor. It keeps rolling, like a succulent little football, to the edge of Anna-Clare's stove.

Now, there is one thing that's true about Julia Child. She said that you should never confess to mistakes that were not witnessed by others.

"Remember, you're alone in the kitchen," she would say. "You must stand by your convictions and just pretend that was the way it was supposed to turn out."

Of course, here I am not alone. There are nine other students, plus the nosy Algerian dishwasher in the kitchen, restocking pans. Mercifully, Chef Bouveret is out of the room. Anna-Clare eyes the duck with a look of horror—for a good reason. The *sous-sol* sent up only five ducks today. We're sharing this one.

I put a finger to my lips to Anna-Clare and the dishwasher. Without a word, I scoop up the hot duck with my side towel and toss it into the pan, shove it in the oven, and slam the door. I stand up and bump into L.P., standing in front of me. Her face says it all. She doesn't approve, and I sense a lecture coming. But then, Chef Bouveret returns to the room, whistling and triumphant, having found the turnips that had been missing from the class basket.

"Look, look," he says, holding up the bowl.

I proceed with my recipe and plate as usual.

By now, whispered word has spread in the kitchen of the dropped duck. The dishwasher peeks around the corner. Will I let the chef taste the contaminated duck?

Chef tries the sauce. Good consistency, he says, but it needs more salt. My vegetable cuts earn a *"bien."* He tastes a tender turnip. His hand, clutching a small plastic spoon, hovers above the duck-breast meat, sliced thin and fanned out on the plate. Instead of taking a bite, he directs my attention to the coloring of the meat.

"Look, look, *ici. Pas assez cuit,"* Chef says. It needed two more minutes of cooking on one side, he says. But otherwise, it's *"bon travail,"* nice work, "Meeze Fleen."

In the locker room, Anna-Clare and I debate the duck. Didn't some researcher find that the "five-second" rule wasn't a myth? That you could reclaim food as long as it had been dropped on a clean floor? Surely, our duck wasn't on the floor that long.

Still, when I take my half home, I tell Mike, "Just don't eat the skin."
He asks why. "I'll tell you later."

Such intrigue over a duck is nothing. We are learning that it's best to keep
the chefs happy, even if it requires the occasional bit of clandestine work.
The following day, we are to sauté three pieces of beef to specific doneness. We are instructed to make one bleu (bloody), one rare (a little less
bloody), and one what the French call à point (sort of medium-rare). The
chefs have taught us a trick to determining the doneness of meat using our
hands. It goes like this: relaxing the hand, hold thumb to forefinger, as if
making the OK symbol, and touch the soft pad under the thumb with
your other forefinger. That's bleu. Touch the thumb to the middle finger,
the bump gets a bit taut. That's the way that rare meat feels. The thumb
to ring finger equals medium-rare.

The thumb to pinky? That's well-done, or "Américain," as one chef
says.

At the other end of the table, there's some shuffling when Chef Bertrand
leaves the room. Ramona has overcooked all her steaks and utterly destroyed
her béarnaise sauce. Students quickly converge to assemble an adequate plate,
chipping in a piece of meat, some sauce, and some warm potatoes Pont
Neuf, which are essentially large French fries. Chef returns, looks her plate
over, deems the sauce too salty,. and leaves. A minute later, he returns, tastes
the same sauce presented by L.P., and declares it perfect. C'est la vie.

Such teamwork is common, but we realize in a week's time that we
will not be able to help one another on the final exam. In Basic and Intermediate Cuisine, it's always the same. The chefs provide a list of ten of the
thirty or so recipes that we have prepared during practical. Of those, two
will be used in the exam. In B4, half of us will receive one recipe, and the
other five will complete something else. Typically, the dishes include one
fish and one meat dish.

Students also must perform a technique. This we learn in advance.
Our technique will be to fillet two whiting, or merlan.

In class, we present a single plate. In the exam, we must plate all our
work—every piece of food, every ounce of sauce. A trio of Parisian chefs

will be brought in to judge the work. We will have exactly two and a half hours to complete our dish, aided by only the ingredient list. The steps, the taste, the technique, and the procedures for everything must be from memory.

This list includes the dreaded hake with hollandaise, a fragrant chicken fricassée, and the veal paupiettes. There's immediate and heavy speculation about which dishes will be part of our test.

"The tarragon chicken is the most common test dish, so everyone should study it carefully," says L.P. seriously as the women from B4 gather after class in the Winter Garden. L.P. has questioned Superior students about what dishes typically turn up at the Basic Cuisine exam. She's been able to find out the test dishes for the past five semesters. She's charted them roughly on a piece of paper and developed a simple statistical model for what we're most likely to get. We all hunch around the list. "Now, the duck is also common, probably because it requires precise cooking. The hake has been used twice, so review the hollandaise sauce. . . ."

Chef Bertrand returns early from a trip to Costa Rica and spends a day just observing classes. He's not happy.

"You do not taste as you cook, so you ended up with bland or over-seasoned consommés. Your puff pastry was nothing special," he lambastes us via Anne the translator. We were not careful enough with the meat, and some of us did not follow instructions for cooking the duck. "Some of you are taking too much liberty. You are to reproduce what you see in the demonstrations, consistently and faithfully."

Later that day, chefs conduct our first uniform checks. Diego makes up a complicated lie about why he hasn't yet purchased professional chef shoes. He's given forty-eight hours to comply. Kim's attire is usually spotless, but she's gotten lazy with houseguests and today wore a dirty apron. Chef Savard expels her from the kitchen. She clandestinely purchases a new one from the front desk so that she can continue class.

Everyone seems to struggle to "turn" vegetables. Starting out with large potatoes, I keep turning, trying to get the right shape, whittling it down to a half-inch clumsy cylinder. Chef Savard is unimpressed when I present mine along with some pork medallions soaked in a sauce.

"Everything is OK, but these vegetables are not acceptable, although I can see you know that, Meess Fleen."

So on my way home, I stop by Monoprix and buy four pounds of carrots and five pounds of potatoes. I buy flour, fresh yeast, and butter. Mike comes downstairs to help me lug them up the six flights. I start puff pastry, making two turns and letting it rest overnight. Then, I sit for four hours practicing turning until my hands are almost too sore to move. Mike practices a few, too. Irritatingly, his are almost perfect.

Everyone seems to be under fire from the chefs. We can do nothing to please them. They have been easy on us for weeks. But the mood has changed among them and among us. It's their time to find out who is serious.

When the going gets tough, the tough, well, throw a party. We decide to invite over all of B4 and the twenty-somethings from Mike's language class for one last *fête* at our apartment. The culinary students bring food; the language students bring alcohol. I spend two days concocting great vats of gumbo and jambalaya. Amit brings bags of artisan bread at the bakery where he's working. Anna-Clare offers to make a round confection known in New Orleans as a "King Cake." By tradition, a plastic baby representing Jesus gets tucked inside before it's glazed with yellow, gold, and green icing. Whoever gets the slice with the baby is "king" for the day.

"I got very strange looks when I asked store owners whether they had a plastic baby Jesus, and for once it's not my French," Anna-Clare reports. She settles, and uses a plastic coin instead.

There's too much of everything, and some feel compelled to stay and consume it all. Our final visitors stumble out at 5:00 a.m., so we claim the party a success.

The day after the party, we answer an ad in *FUSAC, France USA Contacts,* a biweekly magazine consisting mostly of classifieds and ads for British-style pubs and French-language schools. The apartment manager, a young o, shows us a place on rue Étienne Marcel, not far

, we know that it's different. Elegantly furnished, it
ome, not a rental. The built-in bookcases sag with
and French. Aged Persian rugs lie on the floor. The apartment is in the corner of a traditional old French building; the nearly cir-
cular living room is lined with windows. Then, we walk into the
kitchen.

Much as in New York City or London, many Paris apartments have
only cramped kitchens, some without even an oven. Yet this is a large
room with every appliance, even a dishwasher and a separate fridge and
freezer. The countertops and walls are covered in a warm, soothing rustic
tile. But it's the window that sells us. A modern remodeling changed the
wall into a light-flooded ten-by-twelve-foot bay window overlooking the
lively five-way intersection of rue de Turbigo, rue Étienne Marcel, and
rue Pierre Lescot, the last of which is a pedestrian street leading into
Les Halles. Classic French buildings sit on each corner. It truly feels like
Paris.

Thoroughly transfixed, without taking our eyes off the activity of the
street scene below, we say in unison: "We'll take it."

It is too good to be true.

Gombo de Paris avec Saucisse, les Crevettes et le Poulet

GUMBO FROM PARIS, WITH SAUSAGE, SHRIMP, AND CHICKEN

Serves eight

Gumbo is a post-Thanksgiving staple in my family, as it's a great way to
use up leftover meat for the turkey carcass for stock. True gumbo uses a
dark roux that smells of lightly roasted coffee. Roux can be made ahead and
refrigerated for up to a week, but take care with its preparation: if it has
many black specks, it's ruined, and you need to start over. Also, hot roux is
known as "Cajun napalm" for the nasty burns it can cause, so be careful.
Always use gloves when handling hot chilies; they can burn and irritate eyes
and skin. Gumbo requires good stock; see the recipe on pages 44–45.

ROUX

1 cup (250 ml) olive oil

1½ cups (375 ml) all-purpose flour

¾ pound (375 g) raw shrimp, shells reserved

3 quarts (3 l) brown chicken or turkey stock

2 tablespoons olive oil

2 medium onions, chopped

2 bay leaves

4 ribs celery, chopped

1 green bell pepper, seeds removed, chopped

1 pound (450 g) cooked chicken or turkey, cut into bite-sized pieces

1½ pounds (750 g) cooked andouille sausage, sliced

1 (28-ounce) can (about 800 g) peeled, seeded tomatoes

2 habanero peppers, minced

6 cloves garlic, minced

1 tablespoon chopped fresh thyme, or 1 teaspoon dried

¾ pound (375 g) okra, thawed if frozen

2 cups chopped fresh parsley

1 tablespoon filé powder *(optional)*

1 to 2 lemons, juiced

coarse salt, ground pepper

Cayenne pepper or hot sauce, to taste

Cooked white rice

Preheat oven to 315°F/160°C. For the roux, combine olive oil and flour in an ovenproof sauté pan over medium heat. Stir constantly until the roux is light brown, with a nutty smell. Put into the oven and let cook undisturbed for the first hour. Then *carefully* stir every half hour afterward until it's a dark, almost chocolate brown. This will take from three to five hours. Set aside and let cool.

To start the gumbo, combine the shrimp shells with the stock and simmer while you prep everything. Heat the olive oil in an eight- to twelve-quart pot. Cook the onions with the bay leaves over medium heat until translucent; then add the celery, carrots, and green bell pepper. When the vegetables soften, add the chicken, sausage, tomatoes, habanero peppers, garlic, and thyme. Strain the stock and add to pot with vegetables. Bring to a simmer and then stir in one third of the roux until it's absorbed in the liquid. Keep adding roux a tablespoon at a time until the gumbo reaches the desired consistency. Bring to a simmer and add the okra, parsley, shrimp, and filé powder, if using. Cook until the shrimp are bright pink and the gumbo thickens. Finally, stir in the lemon juice, add cayenne or hot sauce, and serve over hot rice.

CHAPTER 11

FINAL EXAM: BASIC

LESSON HIGHLIGHTS: STUFFED CHICKEN LEGS, BAD GNOCCHI,
DUCK À L'ORANGE, BASIC CUISINE FINAL EXAM

Chef Savard seems like he's going through the motions of the *jambonette de volaille*. As he scrapes the meat from the bones, he systematically peels back the skin as if he's turning a sweater inside out. He stuffs the legs with a mixture of ground chicken and sausage and then sews up the ends with a trussing needle and string. Once stuffed, the leg appears as if it is still intact.

Thus the final week of Basic Cuisine begins. The air feels like it does at the end of a school year. The smell of a fresh March day wafts through a window of the second-floor demonstration room. Students bored by yet another demonstration on how to bone a piece of chicken itch restlessly in their kitchen whites. Sitting next to me, Diego looks up long enough from a travel magazine to see Chef spooning meat into the empty leg cavities and goes back to photos of women in bikinis.

Then, Chef grabs at carrots on the stove. "Les carottes sont cuites," he says, dryly. The carrots are cooked. Some students laugh.

"What's funny?" I ask LizKat.

"It's a French idiom," she says dully, not moving her chin off her hand. "'The carrots are cooked' means it's about to end badly, or you've had it. Like you Americans would say, 'Your goose is cooked.'"

Kim gets up in the middle of class to phone her nanny. Of the students, only L.P. sits straight, as usual, taking detailed notes on her legal pad.

The afternoon's practical is uneventful, save that it has the same bittersweet end-of-an-era feeling that school years often bring. Of B4, I know that at least four of us will not return after Basic. I look around, watching Anna-Clare joshing with Kim and LizKat flirting with Chef Savard as she presents her plate. It's so calm and pleasant.

The next day, we study duck à l'orange in our last lesson before our exam the following day.

Then it all goes wrong.

Ramona and I are class assistants again this week. Prepping for exams and preparing to change crews, the usually efficient downstairs crew has set up incomplete baskets all week. We have enough duck breasts for just eight, only four oranges, and there's no veal stock in sight. We're making gnocchi today also, although it was demonstrated three weeks ago, yet there are no potatoes. We finally get the ingredients assembled, and it's an enormous lot of stuff; the dumbwaiter sags under the weight.

Everyone's set up when Ramona and I enter the room. An odd feeling permeates the kitchen.

"Who's the chef?" I ask.

Anna-Clare looks at me and shakes her head and just then in walks Chef Gaillard. He's in a palpably bad mood. No one talks, and everyone goes right to work.

I start with the *magret,* scoring the back to allow the fat to release when it's cooked. I slice the orange peel fine. Using a hand juicer, I make fresh orange juice. This I reduce by half and then combine it with the orange peel and veal stock. Starting late, I remain a half step behind the others in the class. Just then, I hear a growl behind me.

"Où est la liqueur pour la sauce?" Chef is standing fewer than four inches behind me. He's dripping out the words as a taunt.

"Ugh, je suis désolée, Chef. Je vais la chercher au sous-sol," I respond, wiping my hands on my side towel. *Damn, damn, damn,* I think, trotting quickly down the stairs to search for the orange liqueur. This will put me even further behind.

At first, I can't find Le Maestro. The assistants don't have the key to the liquor cabinets. They send me to the pastry kitchen. I run up three flights to find him leaning on the industrial mixer. Le Maestro waves away my breathless and ill-formed French request for Cointreau. Expensive alcohol goes only to the chefs, he says dismissively, and Chef Gaillard knows that. I run downstairs, practicing my response in French for Chef. On my arrival, he scowls at me, a bottle of the liqueur in his hands.

I return to my station. A few minutes later, I hear another growl.

"Où sont les oeufs et le fromage pour les gnocchis?" I turn around. He's sniffing with fury like a taunted bull.

Oh, shit. I apologize and run downstairs. After hauling three dozen eggs and a three-pound package of Gruyère into the dumbwaiter, I head back upstairs. I unload it and head directly to my station. I remove my cutting board, clear away all knives, and toss flour onto the marble. Then, I take a deep breath.

I've never made gnocchi, small dumplings whose name means "lumps" in Italian. Although I took notes, I don't remember the demonstration well. Sometimes, this happens at Le Cordon Bleu. The chefs sense some spare time in a demonstration and add in an extra lesson. I follow my notes, which I've taken to putting into plastic sleeves to protect them from the dirt and grime of the kitchen.

While the results seem gnocchi-like, meaning they look like lumps of potatoes and dough, I cook one by itself and taste. *Tasteless.* We aren't making a sauce for the gnocchi, and Chef suggests that we sauté them. I do it, hoping a brief hot-butter bath will add some flavor.

I nurse my orange sauce. It's sweet, but it has a good, almost velvety consistency. I've caught up to the rest of the class, although some students are presenting their plates.

It isn't pretty.

On every plate, Chef complains the sauce is too sweet. At Kim, he decries her duck as so overcooked it's criminal. He picks up a piece of Amit's gnocchi, tastes it, and throws it back onto his plate. Amit begins to protest, and Chef holds up his hand.

After four too-sweet sauces, he's agitated. Loudly, he advises the rest of us to finish the sauce with a bit of vinegar. I grab an almost-empty bottle on the table.

"Don't use it all, I need some," says Anna-Clare. "Mine is really sweet, too."

I add two drops and taste. Too sweet. Two more drops, no changes. Four drops. Better. Another couple drops . . . and I detect a hint of vinegar. Do I make it less sweet or risk having it taste like vinegar? Do I use the rest? No. I hand the bottle to Anna-Clare.

I slice my duck, fan it out, then drizzle a spoonful of the dark sauce in a crescent around the meat and arrange five of the still-warm gnocchi in a fan shape on the other side. They look like naked little rolls of flesh, but then so do everyone else's.

I'm the eighth person to present my plate. Perhaps it's just bad timing, perhaps it's me. But the moment he tastes my sauce, his face contorts into a grotesque gesture and turns visibly red.

"C'EST HORRIBLE!" he screams. The clattering noise of the training kitchen fades in the background.

Being yelled at by someone is unpleasant enough; it is worse when you're not sure what that person is saying.

"Vous ne pourriez pas servir ceci!"

My mind rushes to translate. *You . . . not . . . serve this.*

"Pourquoi vous me donnez cette assiette." *Why . . . you . . . give me this plate?*

"Vous n'avez pas honte?" *You . . .* shit, what is he saying?

I'm stunned by the tirade—so much that I can't speak. I stand in a daze. To punctuate a point, he slams his fist against the counter and accidentally touches the edge of my plate. It spins hard, skidding across the surface.

By now, nothing else is happening in the kitchen. Everyone stands frozen, watching. After what seems like a lifetime, he just stops, nearly breathless. Everyone stares at me. I can almost hear their hearts beat. What will I say to defend myself?

My mind is blank for a response. I open my mouth. Nothing.

Chef sighs and turns away. Disappointed, he asks LizKat to translate as he stares at me, shaking and breathless.

"He wants to know if you think what you presented was acceptable," she says stiffly. "He said if this were the exam, you would have failed." Then, more casually, she adds, "Evidently, he thinks that you ignored his request to put in vinegar, and that you didn't taste it."

"Of course I tasted my sauce. It was sweet, I used vinegar, and it seemed to tone it down. Anna-Clare watched me do it." Anna-Clare nods. "I tasted it about a half-dozen times." She chats to him some more in French, explaining my response.

"Tell him I'm sorry about my French," I add. "I couldn't . . . think of anything to say." She nods sympathetically.

I hear her offer my apology. "Elle est désolée pour son français, mais elle comprend. . . ." He waves LizKat away. People begin to move around in the kitchen, my humiliation seemingly complete. He gestures to a horrified Tai Xing to come forward with her plate. As I turn away, I hear one last assault.

"Vous perdez votre temps!"

I turn on my heel to look at him. My mind races to translate.

You're wasting your time.

I turn back to my oven. I slam my unwashed knives loosely into my canvas bag. I throw all of my food into the trash. I can't get out of the kitchen fast enough. I begin to cry, and I hate myself for it. Anna-Clare has been watching me.

She puts her arm around my waist. "Kat, I'll clean your station," she whispers soothingly. "You should just go."

I collect myself and walk out of the kitchen in obvious tears. I run down to the basement locker room. I lock myself into a bathroom and collapse onto the toilet in a heap. My body shakes as I gulp down my tears.

What a disaster. I've spent my adult life thinking that I was a good cook. What about all those ambitious dinner parties? I'm struggling through Basic Cuisine, and according to one chef I'm wasting my time. I feel as if I am failing at the one thing that I'd always loved.

After ten minutes, I get up to wash my face. As the cold water hits me, I remember: I am a class assistant. I pull myself together and go into the locker room, now filling with students returning from classes. Ramona finds me.

"Don't worry about the kitchen, I put everything away," she says in her heavy Mexican accent. She embraces me. "I have to go, but you call my mobile if you are sad, yes?"

I get my phone to dial Mike. Once I hear his voice, I start crying again. I huddle against my locker.

"Come right home," he says. I rush to dress, bumping into everyone around me in the cramped room. On the way out, I run into LizKat, her eyes heavy with sympathy.

"That was thoroughly appalling," she says in her crisp English accent. She tugs off her necktie. "I mean, everyone's sauce was too sweet. I told him that after you left. He kept saying he thought you hadn't tasted it."

"But I did," I protest, "I tasted it over and over as I added vinegar."

"I know, I know," she said, holding her hands up in the air in surrender. "That chef is so unpredictable. He is just a man of gray moods."

On the Métro, I can think of plenty of responses to the chef, now that it doesn't matter. It's a long way to the top of the sixth floor, what will be our home for another ten days. Mike hears me on the stairs and greets me with a long hug.

"It's better to make your mistakes before the exam," he says. He pulls me inside. He's drawn a bubble bath, lit candles, and poured me a glass of cold Chablis. He rubs my neck in the bath and tries to bolster my confidence. But the words keep coming back to me:

"You're wasting your time."

I can't sleep. All I can think about are percentages. I have no idea about my grades so far. The final test makes up nearly half of the overall grade for the course. Fail the final, and I will not pass Basic Cuisine, dropping me out of the diploma program.

At 6:00 a.m., I give up and leave Mike in the warm bed. I study the recipes for the exam in the living room until it's time to leave for school. We have a final demonstration at 12:30, followed by our exam at 3:30.

As Chef Bertrand goes through preparation of rack of lamb and ⸍ Alaska, I can't focus on any of it, consumed as I am with dread a⸍ exhaustion.

We assemble outside the kitchen door at 3:25. Chef Colville doesn't let us enter until nearly 3:45. He hands each of us a slip of paper with the name of a dish. Damn. I have drawn the horrid hake steaks with hollandaise sauce. The other five students have been assigned the chicken fricassée with tarragon, a straightforward stew.

Amit offers a hug. "Don't think about yesterday. You're going to do fine."

I collect the basket the assistants set up for me. I store the hake and a duo of hazy-eyed whitefish in my fridge. My hands are shaking.

I go through the routine of the court bouillon, clumsily cut up the hake, and then start on the sauce. My hollandaise breaks, and I have to start over. Both test recipes call for turning thirty-six vegetables as garnishes. L.P. asks Chef Colville if we need to present all the vegetables.

"*Bien sûr,*" he replies and waves a warning finger to all of us, "and no less."

Despite all my practice, it takes me a long time just to turn so many vegetables. I start to get anxious.

And then, a final blow.

"Une *demi heure,* a half hour," the chef warns, to a wave of protests. That's 6:00 p.m. But we started late, we argue. We should finish at 6:15 p.m. No discussion, he says.

I steady myself. I am forty minutes away from finishing.

At 5:50 p.m., I plate my hake and cover it with plastic wrap as instructed and pour my sauce into a *saucier.* But although I've practiced filleting about eight fish in the past week, I get only halfway through the duo of whitefish when Chef Colville roars, "Arrêtez!" Stop!

All of us are seemingly midtask. We put down our knives. It's over.

We clean out our lockers. Weighed down with their contents and the unpleasantness of the exam, we gather for drinks at a nearby *tabac.* We are downbeat and dejected. No one feels good about the test. We feel cheated on time. LizKat orders a *Martini blanc,* and half of us follow her lead. Amit couple of Stella Artoises. We toast the imminent demise nd Chef Gaillard, "the Gray Chef."

ther student appears, fresh from her own exam. In her trand told them they had to turn just twelve vegetables, and he gave the class fifteen minutes *extra* at the end. It strikes us as so unfair that we order another round of drinks.

Eventually, we say good-bye to Anna-Clare, LizKat, Kim, and Amit. Anna-Clare must return to her life as an ad exec, while LizKat has been offered a glamorous job with a PR agency working to bring Krispy Kreme doughnuts to Europe. Kim has signed up for cooking lessons with a French woman who teaches in her home; Le Cordon Bleu was too brutal. Amit is heading off to study French *boulangerie;* for him, the school was not challenging enough.

Just as the group disperses, Mike arrives. He offers to take me to dinner to celebrate. Picking up my bags, he asks me what I want to eat.

"Anything but French," I reply.

Canard à l'Orange aux Figues

DUCK WITH ORANGE SAUCE AND FIGS

Serves two to three

Fresh ducks can be found in Asian markets or ordered from a good butcher; allow ample time to thaw a frozen bird. Wild or organic ducks cook more quickly, so monitor closely. This recipe uses a roasting technique that we learned at school as described in *Le Cordon Bleu at Home,* used here with permission from the Paris school. I've updated the classic orange sauce by adding sliced figs, tempering the sweetness with balsamic vinegar. Pairs well with a Sauvignon Blanc, or Chablis, or a fruity red such as a Sangiovese or Beaujolais Nouveau. Make two ducks for four to six guests.

ROASTED DUCK

3 tablespoons butter, softened

1 teaspoon salt

1 teaspoon ground pepper

1 teaspoon + 1 teaspoon dried thyme

½ teaspoon ground cumin

1 4-to-5-pound (about 2 kg) duck

1 large onion, quartered

1 bay leaf

SAUCE

2 tablespoons water

¼ cup (50 g) sugar

1½ cups (350 ml) fresh orange juice

1 teaspoon grated orange zest

2 tablespoons minced shallots or onions

1½ tablespoons balsamic vinegar

1 cup (250 ml) brown chicken stock

¼ cup (about six) dried figs, sliced

1 tablespoon orange liqueur, such as Cointreau

1 to 2 tablespoons butter

⅛ teaspoon salt, cracked black pepper

Preheat the oven to 400°F/200°C. Mix the butter with the salt, pepper, 1 teaspoon dried thyme, and cumin. Rinse the duck inside and out; pat dry. Cut off the tips of the duck wings and cut off the tail completely, remove two yellow glands underneath. Season cavity with salt and pepper; put in the onion, bay leaf, and remaining thyme and truss tightly. Rub the skin with the seasoned butter, covering the skin completely.

Place the duck on its side in a roasting pan and roast for twenty minutes. Turn the duck to the other side and roast for another twenty minutes. Turn the duck breast-side down and roast the back for twenty minutes. Turn over, breast-side up, and roast until the juices run clear when the thigh is pierced with a knife, about twenty-five to thirty-five more minutes. When done, let the duck rest for fifteen minutes before carving.

After you turn the duck for the final time, start the sauce: Combine the water and sugar in a small saucepan over medium heat. Stir until darkened and browned like caramel. Take off heat and immediately add the orange juice, orange zest, shallots or onions, and a half tablespoon of the balsamic vinegar. Return to heat and reduce by half, scraping the bottom to loosen caramel. Add stock and figs. Reduce by one third, until it becomes a light syrup. Add the rest of the balsamic vinegar and the Cointreau. Just before serving, whisk in the butter and check seasonings, adding salt and pepper to taste. Carve duck into eight pieces, discarding the cavity seasonings.

PART II

INTERMEDIATE CUISINE

"If you are lucky enough to have lived in Paris as a young man, then wherever you go for the rest of your life it stays with you, for Paris is a moveable feast."

—Ernest Hemingway

CLASS BREAK: SPAIN

During the break between semesters, Mike's planned a trip to Barcelona, with a side trip to Valencia in southern Spain for Las Fallas. Meaning "the fires" in the local dialect, it's an unusual annual tribute to St. Joseph, the patron saint of carpenters. Locals erect more than three hundred massive paper-and-wood statues, most lampooning local politicians and celebrities, in key intersections. While the statues may appear comical, the residents of each neighborhood agonize over what to build, then spend months physically erecting their statue.

"Then in one night, they burn them all down," says Mike. He's taking me to Fallas for a reason, to see beyond the pyrotechnic fantasy to the core message of it all. "They build something beautiful, only to destroy it. And they celebrate, because the joy of the statues isn't in keeping them but in creating them."

We check into our hotel and set off to find a café on the Plaça de Cataluña. We're to meet Maria, a classmate of Mike's. I've never met her, but Mike says she's insisted on showing us around Barcelona, her hometown.

As I see her walk toward us, shouting to Mike and waving wildly, I mentally note that he forgot to mention that she's a beautiful green-eyed Catalan. Worse, Maria turns out to be interesting: she just left her career as a lawyer, with vague plans to travel in search of what she calls "her life's true passion."

She grabs his arm and says, "I can't wait to show you my city." As she guides him—er, *us*—around Barcelona's Old Town, just off La Rambla, she gazes at him fondly. Struggling at times to keep up, I feel like a third wheel.

A day later, the trip feels as if it might fall apart. We check out of our hotel and drag our luggage a half mile to the train station. But *damn,* we left our driver's licenses back in Paris, so we can't pick up our rental car. Trains to Valencia are sold out; the only seats available depart late the next day.

Ever-optimistic Mike says, "Well, this just means we get to spend another day in beautiful Barcelona." *With Maria,* I think, as we drag our luggage back to our hotel. It's fully booked, and so are most of the city's hotels, thanks to a major football match, the manager informs us.

Mike and I exchange exhausted looks. The manager catches this.

"Well, I might have *something,*" he says. A bit later, he motions to the door adjacent to the front desk. We assume he's set up cots in a broom closet. At this point, we'd be thrilled with such an option.

We could not be more surprised.

It turns out to be the hotel's premier suite, a split-level with two bedrooms, a sitting room with leather furniture, a fireplace, two wet bars, and a vast marble bathtub. The manager's pleased with our reaction. "We keep this set aside for . . ."—he searches for the word—". . . special guests."

Mike stretches out on one of the couches while I take a long bubble bath before dinner. Afterward, I put on my best lingerie (purchased on my mother's advice) and a splash of perfume. I slip on one of the hotel robes and pull it down alluringly around my shoulders. I descend the spiral staircase holding two glasses and a bottle of Cava, the Spanish version of champagne. Mike looks up to see me as I reach the base of the stairs. I feel like Jean Harlow making an entrance in a 1930s movie.

"You look gorgeous," he says. "Just what are you up to?"

We snuggle in front of the fire and toast each other with Cava. Mike kisses my neck and murmurs, "You know, I've been trying to find the right place to ask you something." My hearts pounds. "I almost asked you on a bridge one night in Paris and thought about asking in our lovely loft, too. But I want it be something special and someplace unforgettable, like you." He takes my hands and kisses my fingertips.

"I hope you forgive me for quoting a line from a movie," he says. "But when you realize you want to spend the rest of your life with somebody, you want the rest of your life to start right away . . . ." he stops. "No, wait, let me do this right."

He gets down on one knee and takes my hand. "Is it wrong to propose without a ring?

I cradle his face with my hands. "Are you kidding? I would marry you if you gave me a rubber band in the frozen-foods section of a Monoprix. Yes, yes, yes . . . ."

For the second time in a week, I begin to cry. This time, I welcome the tears.

CHAPTER 12

C'EST LA VIE, C'EST LA GUERRE

LESSON HIGHLIGHTS: GUINEA FOWL WITH CALVADOS SAUCE,
RABBIT LEGS SIMMERED IN WINE

Returning to Paris, my grades from Basic bring me back to reality. I scored high on my midterm and two other tests, above average on my daily work, and passed the final, but barely.

"You must let it go," L.P. advises, as we change in the locker room. "You have much work to do until you get your diploma. If you cannot let go of the past, then you cannot focus on the present." Somehow, everything she says sounds like Chinese philosophy or, as Mike says, a bit like the pronouncements of Yoda.

When the Gray Chef enters the demonstration room for our first lesson, he looks expressionlessly at me. L.P. whispers in my ear, "Remember, you are just as tough as him." *Young Jedi,* I mentally add.

Chef breaks his gaze and begins.

With just thirty-four students, Intermediate Cuisine is roughly half the size of Basic. Culinary Darwinism at work, Basic tends to weed out the recreational cooks and those who want something else in a culinary program. Intermediate's curriculum differs from the rest of the Le Cordon Bleu training in focusing on regional cuisines. We begin our culinary tour in Normandy.

"Quel dommage, les gens pensent seulement à la guerre," Chef begins. I agree: it's a shame that most people associate Normandy only with World War II. Its lush pastures provide grazing for *vaches d'or,* or "golden cows." Their milk churns into wonderful cream, remarkable butter, and prized soft cheeses such as Camembert. Nine million acres of orchards produce tons of crisp apples each year, some of them turned into cider or Calvados, a stiff apple brandy.

"Le Calvados est le champagne de la Normandie," Chef says, adding a bit to deglaze the pan in our principal recipe of the day, guinea fowl with apples in a Calvados cream sauce. As the pan simmers, the sharp, sweet aroma of the brandy drifts over the room. L.P. looks at me and frowns. To her sensitive palate, the taste of alcohol in cooking is too strong.

Afterward, we walk upstairs and bid each other good-bye as we head into different kitchens. I've been assigned to Intermediate Group 1, which lacks all my friends. My effort to change groups musters no sympathy from the administrators.

This first day, I take the only open space, a corner among four Koreans. I'm on time, but already the two communal ingredient baskets at this end have been ransacked, leaving me nothing except a withered apple. I gather onions, garlic, and all the ingredients from bowls on the other end of the table. I feel like a beggar going through trash cans. No one is speaking French or even English here—it's all Spanish and Korean. I feel utterly isolated. Just when I think it can't get any worse, the Gray Chef swaggers into the kitchen.

"Bonjour, mes petits amis!" he bellows to the room. He pats one guy on the back. He chats quickly with a woman with blond curls. He ignores me. I take out my frustration on the guinea fowl.

The large semiwild hens are known to partner for life. Newly engaged, I try not to think of this one's mate as I take the bent handle of a soup ladle, tuck it behind the bird's tendons above its ankles, and rip them out with one swift tug. With no one to talk to, I work efficiently, alone with my thoughts for two hours, turning my apples, tending my sauce. I carefully check all the flavors before I plate my dish for Chef.

Be confident, I think to myself. *This is a great plate.* Yet my hands shake as I take it to where he stands, arms crossed, at the end of the table.

Chef cuts into the guinea fowl, then tastes an apple and some sauce. He chews thoughtfully. "Ça marche," he says, and pushes my plate back to me. I'm disappointed. All that work, and I get the equivalent of "It's OK, it works."

Deflated, I bag my food and silently clean up. On the way out of the kitchen, I run into Lely in the hallway at the top of the stairs. She looks like a lot of us do after a practical: smiling, sweaty, her hat askew as if she'd run a quick half mile.

"What happened to you?" she asks.

"I had the Gray Chef for my practical today," I begin. "I don't know anyone in my group, and some Koreans raided my basket at the beginning of class. There's no one to talk to. I'm stuck in the corner. It's . . . just . . . very lonely." I begin, preparing for a cliff dive into self-pity. She puts up her hand like a traffic cop.

"No, no, missy, I don't want to hear any of that," she says. She gets behind me, puts her hands on my back, and directs me forward, down the stairs. "You go home, drink some wine with your man, and come back here with a better attitude."

As we continue down the stairs, she tells me to work by the woman with the blond curls in my class, Jovina.

"She's from Colombia, I think," Lely says. "She's nice." Lely has heard her fiancé is an American soldier in Iraq. "You'll have plenty to talk about." We pass by a photo of Julia Child on the stairwell wall. "And, hey, you think that Julia would let a chef get to her? I don't think so, no, ma'am, I don't."

You can't argue with Lely.

Mike and I eat the guinea fowl in one of our last dinners at the apartment on Richelieu. Mike chuckles at Lely's domineering advice. With shared intensity, we talk about wedding plans and the Allied invasion of Normandy. For the ceremony, we agree to invade the beach on Anna Maria Island in Florida, close to the "castle" where we broke the bed.

The next morning, I'm the first one in the practical kitchen. I stake out a spot next to where Jovina worked the previous day. By luck, she arrives next. With creamy blond hair in tight ringlets, stormy blue eyes, and skin like a porcelain doll's, she doesn't look Colombian.

"My parents are American," she says in a midwestern accent. I've never heard her speak English, only Spanish or French. We start to unpack our knives and set up. "Lely says you've just gotten engaged," she says. "Congratulations."

I start to say the same, but "congratulations" seems like the wrong word from someone with a fiancé at war. Just then, the Korean students file in. One of them insists, in Korean, that I move from the space he had the day before. I put my hand on the table. "C'est ma place." My place.

We stand staring at each other, in a game of kitchen chicken. A slight Korean woman starts talking to him, apparently taking my side. He takes the place at which I worked yesterday. She smiles at me. "Merci bien," I tell her.

Shifting three feet down the worktable changes everything. Across from me now is Benita, a round Spanish woman who wore thick bandages through most of Basic Cuisine. She sliced her palm open the first week of school. Just as it healed, she burned both hands by grabbing the lid of a hot braising pan just out of the oven.

On the other side of Jovina is twenty-two-year-old Brian, who used to work as a line cook at a California yoga retreat. He saved for two years to afford the tuition here. Across from him is Elena, a shy beauty from Madrid. The banter changes from Spanish to English.

We're making *lapin mijoté aux carottes fondantes,* a stew made with rabbit legs braised in wine with carrots. Halfway through class, I look at Jovina. She is going on like everyone else, boning rabbit legs, preparing sauce, turning vegetables. I cannot think how I would cope, knowing Mike was far away, walking daily in body armor in one of the most dangerous places in the world.

The Iraq war has never felt personal to me, partly because I never understood it. Living abroad, I was not in the United States when the arguments for war unfolded. I was in London, where a million people—including many people I knew—took to the streets to protest it. News in the UK routinely covered the French military's efforts in Afghanistan. So I never grasped the antagonism so many Americans developed for the French, epitomized by the likes of "Freedom Fries." (Another misunderstanding: "French fries" are Belgian.) One American acquaintance was horrified that Mike and I were going to live in France. "Those frog bastards," he said. "We should bomb them along with Saddam."

Now in France, I'm working next to someone deeply affected by the war.

"How long has your fiancé been in Iraq?"

"Forever," she says, looking down, chopping onions. "It's been eleven days since we talked." He was on his way to Karbala. "In the beginning, my parents thought it was a good thing when he went into the army because they worried we were too young to get married. But then the war in Afghanistan happened, and now there's Iraq. I thought he'd be home by now. I thought—" she stops abruptly and looks over at me. Her eyes are wet. "It's just the onions," she says, wiping the tears away with the back of her hand.

Just then, the Gray Chef walks into the room. If Jovina can survive having her fiancé at war, I can achieve détente with the Gray Chef. I make a point to say loudly, "Bonjour Chef, est-ce que vous êtes notre chef aujourd'hui?" *Are you our chef today?* It's a dumb question, with an obvious answer.

Chef stops, looks at me. He smirks a little. Chef means "chief" in French. He knows his place. "Oui, je suis votre chef," he says to me directly, and adds in French, "today—and tomorrow."

At the end of class, I present my plate. His critique is tough: my rabbit's overcooked, my vegetables don't look good enough, and my potato flan lacks salt. Overall, my plate is *"sans rien de spécial,"* nothing special.

I am undeterred. "Merci, Chef," I say.

On the way home, a musician on the Métro plays "Imagine" by John Lennon on his violin. The words drift through my head:

Imagine there's no countries . . .
Nothing to kill or die for, and no religion, too.

I read somewhere that any war remains an abstract concept until it has a face associated with it. For me, it's Jovina, stifling tears over her onions.

Her knife is sharp, but her heart is elsewhere.

★ ★ ★

Things have gone wrong with the apartment on rue Étienne Marcel. The Italian manager, Arturo, speaks little English and marginal French. He interprets an innocent email the wrong way. We are baffled how "we are looking forward to moving into the flat" and "you should receive our wire transfer on Thursday" could incite such hostility.

"You are a bad man," he begins an email to Mike in response. The email tosses a slew of insults against us and Americans in general, ending with "I could keep your money, and not let you move in."

That's when we freak out.

We've wired several thousand dollars to cover the three-month security deposit and the first month's rent. We develop startling scenarios. What would be our recourse if he took off with our cash? Perhaps he's an Italian shyster who has signed up several hapless couples as "tenants"? Or, now convinced that we are "bad" people, could he find a legal loophole to keep our money?

Mike crafts a careful response, in French and English. This prompts more emails in return, each increasingly venomous—all directed toward Mike.

For those who believe in such things, Mike has what astrologers consider a typical Cancer male personality. He's loyal, trusting, and honest to a fault. The worst thing anyone can do is to question his integrity. Arturo's messages do just that. So by Thursday night at 7:00 p.m., when we are to move in, the typically sanguine Mike is ready for fisticuffs. An irate Arturo answers the door.

"Do you want a Nescafé?" he asks us through gritted teeth as he leads us to the kitchen. We shake our heads. He paces. He makes himself some instant coffee. A friend of his shows up, in case we untrustworthy people try anything. His friend sits limp in the chair, saying little, a long, mauve-colored scarf wrapped closely around his throat. Arturo offers him Nescafé. He doesn't want any either.

Finally, Arturo sits down. "In the kitchen here, you seem all right. But I am upset," he begins. "I don't know how I feel about you living here. But if you do, I will be like a French landlord: I will not help you with anything."

Mike, who has been sitting in his chair like a coiled snake, springs to life. "Well, I am upset, too!" I've never seen him angry. "You said TERRIBLE things to me in email! Why would you want to rent to someone who is as bad as you say that I am? Why would we want to live here?" They stare at each other, the anger palpable. Across the table, Arturo's friend raises his eyebrows.

Arturo is a college student in his late twenties. He had been living in this amazing apartment, a place he could never afford, until his uncle told him to rent it. Maybe we are not the ones with whom he's angry.

"Arturo, why did you agree to rent to us in the first place?" I ask.

He shrugs. "You seemed like a nice couple."

"Do you think that your uncle would approve of us as tenants?" He nods. "So why do you now think that we are bad?" He shakes his head. "We have done everything you requested. We got insurance. We sent our money as fast as we could. We have shown faith."

Arturo gets up and paces the kitchen again like a caged panther. "Are you sure you don't want a Nescafé?" he asks. He opens cupboards, looks in them, and closes them. He sits back down. "Maybe my English not so good," he begins. "But you also made me mad," he says, nodding toward Mike.

"That's OK. We are sorry about that," I say quickly before Mike can respond. "Let's agree that it was a misunderstanding, and no one's at fault."

He grabs at this. "Yes, I misunderstand you, but that wasn't my fault. You see that?" He gets up again and puts the kettle on. "You do not want Nescafé?" he asks me. Mike doesn't drink coffee; I loathe instant.

"I'd love one," we say in unison. Twenty minutes later, we've signed the rest of the rental papers. Arturo has calmed. His friend still hasn't uttered a word. We think we're done, but then there's the *état à louer,* the "state of the rental."

For this, the landlords have supplied Arturo with an exhaustive inventory of everything in the apartment, complete with hand drawings: every fork, each dish, the hand towels, every one of 414 books, some 87 figurines, 22 framed photos, 11 decorative bowls, 7 plants, and a one-eyed gargoyle inlaid in plaster over the door. A missing teaspoon prompts a panicked call to Rome. Even with Arturo's friend helping, it takes more thaₙ hours.

When we shut the door behind them, we breathe a sigh of relieₑ. Then, we both blurt out that we could use a drink.

We head to the closest bar, a safe, quiet, elegant one with an American name: Joe Allen. As we sit down, we meet two shoe salesmen from Brittany.

"Is no one in Paris French?" one of them asks, smiling, when they hear our American accents. They insist on buying us drinks and then lead us to Le Tambour, an all-night hangout nearby.

Le Tambour is the opposite of Joe Allen. It's a smoke-filled dive packed with locals, decorated with old Métro paraphernalia. Pierced guys with Mohawks sit shoulder to shoulder with men in business suits. The shoe salesmen squeeze us in at a crowded table and introduce us as their new friends. Mike heads to the bar to get a couple bottles of wine for the table. He does not return.

Mike thinks he's done a good job ordering the Côtes du Rhône. But his request is greeted with a stern *"Non"* as the bartender crosses his arms in defiance. The scene attracts the interest of patrons around the bar.

The bartender reaches high atop a stack of wine crates. He brings down a dusty old munitions box covered in drab olive burlap. On the side are stenciled the words "No Service for English or Americans."

"Well, then, what are *you* having?" Mike says.

After a short pause, and with the crowd quiet and attentive, the bartender produces a shot glass and a bottle of clear liquid that curiously contains a full-sized pear. Without a word, he pours a shot for himself.

He looks Mike in the eye and produces another glass, pours, and slides it Old West–style across the bar to Mike. *"C'est très fort,"* he says, following in English, "It's from Normandy, do you like it?"

Mike, feeling he is defending the fortitude of all Americans, drinks it down.

"C'est bon . . . . it's great," he says. The crowd applauds.

The bartender reaches for another bottle, this time Calvados. As he pours another round, the bartender explains that the sign is from World

Allied forces liberated Paris, the French women flocked
...ldiers.

... the few bars where Frenchmen had a chance to meet
...an," he says. They then talk and drink for hours. The
...der refuses to let Mike pay for anything.

La Poêlé de Normandie

PAN-ROASTED HENS IN CALVADOS SAUCE

Serves two to four

This recipe employs extra chicken wings to extend the sauce's flavor, a
common practice at Le Cordon Bleu. Use a heavy ovenproof pan large
enough to hold both birds. Each hen can be a single serving for a healthy
appetite, or you can use half if serving it as part of a larger meal. The
Calvados butter may be made a day ahead. Craft it with simple brandy
if you don't have Calvados.

2 tablespoons butter, room temperature
1 tablespoon Calvados or brandy
½ teaspoon + 1 teaspoon dried thyme
2 Rock Cornish hens
Coarse salt, ground black pepper
1 teaspoon granted lemon zest

2 tablespoons olive oil
4 or 5 chicken wings, chopped into pieces
1 medium carrot, chopped (about ¼ cup)
1 medium onion, chopped (about ½ cup)
1 rib celery, chopped (about ¼ cup)
4 shallots, chopped
3 sprigs thyme
1 bay leaf
½ cup (125 ml) white wine
1 tablespoon Calvados

1 Golden Delicious apple, cored, chopped

⅓ cup (75 ml) chicken stock

1 tablespoon butter

4 ounces (125 g) mushrooms, sliced

½ cup (125 ml) cream, heated *(optional)*

Preheat the oven to 350°F/200°C. Make the Calvados butter by blending the warmish butter with the alcohol and ½ teaspoon thyme. Refrigerate the Calvados butter for at least a half hour after mixing; if warm, it will be slippery and difficult to work with. Rinse hens with cold water and pat dry with a paper towel. Carefully work your fingers under the skin and rub the cold Calvados butter directly on the meat. Season the interior of each bird with salt, pepper, lemon zest, and the rest of the thyme. Truss or tie with string to keep their shape. Season the outside with salt and pepper. Set aside.

In a large Dutch oven, heat the olive oil over high heat. Add the wings and sear until well browned. Reduce heat to medium, add the carrots, onions, celery, half the shallots, thyme, and bay leaf, and sauté until the vegetables are softened. Add the white wine and Calvados and reduce by half. Add *half* the chopped apple and place hens on top. Add the chicken stock, cover, and cook in the oven for about one hour, basting every twenty minutes. The hens are cooked when their internal heat registers 170°F/76°C.

Meanwhile, melt butter in a sauté pan. Add the rest of the shallots and stir until softened. Add the mushrooms and cook until lightly browned. Add the rest of the apple and cook until softened. Remove from pan and set aside.

Untruss cooked birds and cover with foil to keep warm. Strain the cooking liquid from the pan through a mesh sieve into a saucepan. Simmer over medium heat to thicken, skimming if needed. Add the sautéed apples and mushrooms and, if desired, whisk in the warmed cream.

CHAPTER 13

A WEEK IN PROVENCE

LESSON HIGHLIGHTS: CALAMARI SALAD, BOUILLABAISSE, MAKING
SAUSAGE, EATING BONE MARROW, AND POT-AU-FEU

A chef gutting a squid is the last thing anyone with a banging hangover wants to see first thing in the morning.

Chef Savard holds the slimy creature over his cutting board and pulls its gray insides out. The calamari will be the basis for a salad, the first course in our lessons on the foods of Provence. Provençal food is distinctive in its reliance on Mediterranean flavors and ingredients such as olives, olive oil, tomatoes, fennel, oranges, and saffron.

"But it makes sense," says Anne the translator, "when you know the history."

Fertile soil, pleasant weather, and good fishing have made the southern edge of France hot real estate since prehistoric times. After being inhabited by the Greeks, the Celts, and a host of other invaders, the land was claimed by the Romans in the second century B.C.E. as one of their initial provinces outside of Italy. They called it Nostra Provincia, "Our Province." The name stuck, even after the Roman empire fell. Provence didn't become an official part of France until the fifteenth century, when Louis XV inherited its land from a noble cousin. Its flavors still reflect the region's invaded past.

Chef moves on from the calamari to present a variety of fish for bouillabaisse, the famed French fish soup. True bouillabaisse includes a *rascasse*, or scorpion fish, a brightly colored *poisson* studded with poisonous spines. They're getting harder to find off the coast of France, Chef says.

"Bouillabaisse is not simmered, it's always boiled," Anne translates for Chef. "The name itself comes from the French words '*bouillon abaisser*,' with *bouillir* meaning 'to boil' and *abaisser* meaning 'to reduce.'"

In class, Jovina and I divide the many tasks required to produce a proper bouillabaisse, from making julienne vegetables to filleting four types of fish. Despite my hangover, our bouillabaisse is smashing.

Mike and I invite Nigel and Theo from the rental website to dinner to thank them for their kindness to us. Theo took Mike all around Paris a few days earlier on the back of his moped to *faire les courses*, running errands. Nigel continues to help us navigate the complications of French life. We serve small cups of the bouillabaisse as an appetizer, followed by grilled lamb. On the side, there's potatoes Bercy, Mike's favorite dish from Basic Cuisine—essentially a cup of egg-fortified potatoes filled with cream sauce and topped with gratinéed cheese. We finish with chocolate macaroons scored from a pastry student.

As we sip Calvados after dinner, we watch the nightlife out of our kitchen window. Our window directly overlooks the Étienne Marcel Métro stop, and it's a busy one; people stream in and out constantly. An elderly man in a wheelchair pulls up to the edge of the steps and waits. With few exceptions, the Métros in Paris are not equipped with ramps. Without comment, two younger men grab each side and carry the man down the steps. Mike and I have seen this before, down on the platforms, when strangers will pick up the wheelchair by the arm handles and pull someone into a Métro car. Different strangers help them get off the train. They all go on about their business. No fuss. No pity. We ask our guests about it.

"That is just part of the French culture," Theo says. The national motto for France is *liberté, égalité, fraternité* (brotherhood). As part of *fraternité*, one must be a Good Samaritan. "From the time we are young children, it's taught that such things are expected."

I tell him about the man who helped me up the stairs with my groceries. "Of course. This surprised you?"

The next day, we make pot-au-feu, a name that literally translates into "pot on fire" and refers to meats and vegetables cooked slowly in water. Traditionally, the broth is served as a first course; the meat is reserved for the main course with the vegetables. It's a staple of French comfort food. In Paris supermarkets, the herbs and vegetables for pot-au-feu—potatoes, turnips, carrots, celery, thyme, and bay leaves—can be bought in one plastic-wrapped package. Traditionally, it's made with beef. For ours, we'll use duck legs, hand-made sausages, and poached marrow bones.

"Vous désirez une petite histoire?" asks the Gray Chef as he begins. *Do you want a little story?*

The class answers, "Oui, Chef." Today, he tells us about how his mother made pot-au-feu when he was a child, nurturing it over a hot stove for hours, extending it with various leftovers. I think of my mother's minestrone.

It's a busy class. He makes sausage first, showing off plain pork fat. It looks just like you think it would: great blobs of thick white stuff. "Your best fat comes from pigs which grew up in the Brittany area," observes John, the stand-up translator, adding his own aside, "I don't know why, they're not known to eat a lot of pizzas."

Chef puts cubes of the fat, veal, and pork through a meat grinder. He pulls out a natural sausage casing; it looks like a long white worm. This soaks in water as he stirs in a *panade,* eggs, seasonings, some orange zest, potato starch, and crushed peppercorns.

"Regardez," he says. *Watch.* Handmade sausage is prepared using a special nozzle tip at the end of a pastry bag. Using evenly applied force, he pushes the meat through the nozzle and into the casing, the sausage growing increasingly phallic. He holds it up. As he does when finishing most techniques, he asks, "Oui? D'accord?" *Yes? OK?*

Next, he moves on to the marrow bones. Sawed-off femurs are the most typical bones served for marrow. Via John, Chef explains that bone marrow is dense with nutrition as well as calories from fat, and for this reason was historically fed to the sick. "Chef says that England's Queen

Victoria ate bone marrow on toast every day for tea," John translates. He adds, "Which may explain why she was not a small woman."

"Where do you find these kinds of bones?" a student asks.

John translates. Chef has an easy answer: "Make friends with your butcher."

Chef turns various vegetables, many of which will be cooked separately in stock and brought together. He poaches the duck meat on its own and runs it under cold water. Finally, everything is brought together in one pot.

"This will be a very busy practical," observes L.P. during the tasting.

Chef Savard oversees our kitchen. All of us go right to work with little talk. Half of the class botches the sausage, either splitting the casings while filling them or bursting the sausage while cooking. Mine turn out all right and even brown nicely when tossed in the hot duck fat.

After I pull all the ingredients together, I taste my pot-au-feu. It has a clean flavor of broth, mildly seasoned with the meats and vegetables. Chef Savard thinks my plate is good, except for one point: I haven't put enough salt on my bone marrow.

"You have to use plenty of salt, and make sure the bones are very hot," says the handsome chef, "or it's disgusting."

On the way home, I stop at rue Montorgueil, about three streets from our flat. It's a historic pedestrian market street with various stores and stalls. Rue Montorgueil is thick with people, as it always is this time of day. I've read that in France at least one member of every household shops daily. Seemingly they're all buying bread.

Chef Bertrand told us that the government regulates bakers' vacations. In some remote towns, the local authorities subsidize bakeries. "You can't have all the bakers go on holiday at once, and you can't let the only bakery shut down," he said. "People need their bread." I pass the snaking line at the first bakery. Down the street, a *boulangerie* sets up a veritable baguette express station in the late afternoon that's worked by a competent, affable blond woman. I've been coming here four times a week.

"Vous désirez, mademoiselle?" she asks.

I've done this so often, I can respond perfectly. "Deux baguettes, s'il vous plaît."

She wraps two baguettes in a length of parchment. I put them into the heavy black canvas bag I carry around for such purchases.

"Vous êtes Américaine?" she asks. I nod. "Et vous habitez ici ou vous êtes en vacances?" I tell her I live on rue Étienne Marcel and add that I'm a journalist. She smiles. "Une journaliste? C'est intéressant. À demain, mademoiselle." *See you tomorrow.*

Customers pack the merchants along the street: a pâtisserie, a chocolatier, two butchers, a cheese shop, a horse-meat butcher,★ a charcuterie, four vegetable stands, a small supermarket, and a handful of other shops, or *magasins*. The air's thick with the intoxicating fragrance of roasted chickens, kept invitingly hot in upright rotisseries pushed outside the butcher shops each day.

Near our flat, there's a wine shop we keep passing, meaning to stop in. I walk in, and it's a pleasant shop, orderly and airy. A man with waist-long gray hair approaches me. He looks like an aging rock star, dressed entirely in black, silver rings on his fingers. "Bonjour, mademoiselle," he says. I sputter out that I'm looking for some wine.

"Ah, you're American." His English is perfect. "What do you like?"

"Well, I'm a culinary student, and today we made pot-au-feu with duck. What do you recommend?"

He puts his hand to his mouth. I see the skull ring on his third finger. "Perhaps a Côte de Nuits?" He talks me through his selections. In the end, I buy two bottles. He wraps each in white tissue paper and slides them into a sack. "Do you live around here?" I tell him we're on the corner. "So you speak some French?"

"I'm trying to learn," I say. "I need more practice."

"Well, I'll tell you what. When you come in here, speak only French, and I'll speak English and help you." He comes around the counter and gives me a kiss on each cheek. "*À bientôt, ma chérie.* Enjoy."

At home, we heat up the pot-au-feu and at our kitchen window talk over our day. We try the bone marrow, spread on toast. I feel rewarded

---

★ Horse meat is lower in fat than beef yet higher in protein and iron. Horses are not susceptible to BSE (mad-cow disease). For all these reasons, horse meat is still found on French tables.

and restored. It's the most satisfyingly buttery pâté
should make friends with a butcher.

Diffusion de Tomate Provençal

PROVENÇAL TOMATO SPREAD

Makes about 2½ cups

This spread uses quintessential ingredients from the south of France. This
is great served with crackers or bread. I also use it to accompany seared or
grilled fish. This spread is also used in two other recipes in this book,
Galette feuilletée à la ceviche de thon (pages 175–176) and *Rouget farcie
aux olives et aux tomates* (pages 218–219). "*Concassé*" refers to peeled,
seeded, and finely chopped fresh tomatoes. Use good tomatoes and do
not substitute canned tomatoes; the texture will be mushy and the flavor
flat. If you can't find Niçoise olives, substitute another rich, black olive.

4 tablespoons olive oil
1 medium red bell pepper, peeled, finely chopped
1 large onion, finely chopped (1½ cups)
3 to 4 cloves garlic, finely chopped
2 medium tomatoes, *concassé* (1 cup)
6 to 8 sun-dried tomatoes, chopped (¾ cup)
12 Niçoise olives, chopped
¾ tablespoon capers, chopped
2 cups chopped fresh basil
Coarse sea salt, black pepper

In a small sauté pan, warm the oil over medium heat. Add bell pepper,
onions, and garlic and cook until soft. Add the chopped tomatoes, sun-
dried tomatoes, olives, and capers and cook gently. Remove from heat.
When cool, add the basil. Add salt and pepper to taste.

CHAPTER 14

RITES OF PASSAGE

LESSON HIGHLIGHTS: COMPLICATED TROUT, JULIA CHILD,
AND THE HISTORY OF LE CORDON BLEU

Laying out a measuring tape on the marble work table, Tai Xing warns everyone in her kitchen: "Fifty-five centimeters. I am entitled to five-five centimeters." She will not be denied her fair share of space.

In Lely's group, students hoard equipment rather than share. For some reason, the Koreans at my table get in the habit of pilfering ingredients at the start of class. All this signals a subtle but important shift: classes are becoming more competitive.

One day in week three, as we study the Alsace region, the competition comes to a head.

Alsace's expanse of fertile land in northeastern France sits on the other shore of the Rhine River from Germany. Over a history of possessive squabbling, the land has shifted between French and German rule.

Chef takes a trout for *truite farcie aux morilles* and clips the fins. But this time, he doesn't go after its innards through the fish's tender belly as usual. Instead, Chef rips the red-and-gray guts out through its gills.

"Les alsaciens parlent avec un accent allemand," says the Gray Chef, explaining that the French in Alsace speak with a German accent.

Removing the main skeletal structure by cutting along the spine, he tugs out the bones. He stuffs the fish with finely chopped morel mushrooms sautéed with shallots, then settles it on top of parchment paper in a roasting pan, sprinkling a bit of coarse sea salt over the fish. He ladles in some fish stock and finishes by splashing Riesling wine on top. The fish braises in the oven, and the smell of the sweet wine drifts through the room.

"Chef says that in France fish are served with their heads to the left," translates John. "It's tradition, and customers here expect that."

Jovina and I arrive in the kitchen that afternoon, there are no more trout. Brian, the class assistant, is baffled. "The basement parceled out two fish per student," he says. "I don't know where they all went."

Someone discovers that two students have taken extra fish in case they make a mistake. Trout are fragile, and it's difficult to pull the guts through the gills without damaging the head. The chefs, like diners, expect a trout with an attractive head. The students want a good grade, and the recipe is among the most technically challenging in the curriculum.

The students refuse to give them up. It escalates. We argue, wasting precious time. Chef Savard arrives.

"Quel problème?" he asks. Brian explains the situation. Chef orders all fish on the cutting boards. The two students with extras hang their heads. Chef Savard takes the extra trout and evenly redistributes them, shaking his head. It feels like elementary school, when the teacher has to make children share their toys.

No one does well. It's like a surgical technique to extract the bones while leaving the fish intact. Chef Savard finds bones in everyone's fish. He extracts a huge one from mine. How did I miss *that*? As for my sauce, for the first time I've made something *too salty*.

"Just pray we don't get *that* for an exam," Jovina says, peeling off her uniform in the locker room. "That was awful." On the way home, I give my hard-won bagged trout to the world's smartest homeless man, perched at the end of the street. I don't wait for his critique.

Instead, I rush up to Montmartre to join Mike's language class on one of its regular walking tours. This one is led by a French historian with a long, gray silk scarf tossed around his neck. He delights in showing off the more unusual and odd elements of Paris.

He leads us south toward the Palais Royal via a series of passages built in the 1800s. Designed to allow Parisians to shortcut dense blocks, protected from the elements and away from streets dirty from horse manure, these passages, our guide theorizes, are the precursors to modern shopping malls. Passionately, he spins tales of love, murder, deceit, and the development of department stores as the sounds of our heels echo off the worn marble floors. A soft filtered light pours through the old skylights as we pass eclectic shops teeming with eccentricities. One store sells nothing but canes.

I'm thinking of the passages when I go to school the next day. There's a sort of passage here, too.

On my way up to the kitchens each day, I pass a huge original poster of the film *Sabrina*. On another wall, a yellowed press clipping from a London newspaper heralds the international acclaim of Le Cordon Bleu as "a diploma that raises the standard of cooking." It's dated 1927. Across from it, a smiling Julia Child in her mid-eighties looks resplendent in a magenta blazer with matching lipstick.

Every time I see the photo of Julia, I think of the two times I met her. The first was in the mid-1990s during a food writers' workshop at a swanky West Virginia resort. On the second day of the workshop, I arrived late. Just as I sat down, I heard a familiar warble ask, "Is this seat taken?"

Julia squeezed her giant frame into the seat next to me. It was as if God Almighty had saddled up on my left.

"That salmon at breakfast was so good, I had to finish it," she whispered in a conspiratorial tone. She took copious notes of the morning's session. As we broke for lunch, she closed her notebook with a satisfied smile. "I always love to come to this workshop. You learn so much," she said.

This amazed me. After all, she was Julia *freakin'* Child. I assumed she knew everything there was to know about food and cooking. I politely told her so.

She laughed. "Oh, no, you can never know everything about anything, especially something you love," she said, patting me on the knee. "Besides, I started late."

At an evening reception, I told her the story about the short obituary and the ad for Le Cordon Bleu at my desk and my plan one day to attend her alma mater. She listened with enthusiasm.

Our paths crossed again a couple years later, while I was working for the software company.

"When are you going to Le Cordon Bleu?" she asked. Shocked that my idol remembered me, I didn't have an answer. Instead, I changed the subject, and we talked about why her Internet connection was so slow.

Now, as I pass her photo on the stairs, I think, *I'm finally here, Julia, see? I told you I'd go.* I have *Mastering the Art of French Cooking, Volume 1* with me in Paris.

I always thought I'd send her a photo with a thank-you note when I graduated. She died before I could.

"To understand the history of Le Cordon Bleu," says Madeleine Bisset, "you have to go all the way back to the sixteenth century."

Madame Madeleine Bisset joined the school shortly after it was purchased by André Cointreau. She met the school's former owner, Madame Brassart, and attended her funeral. Madame Bisset is known for her exceptional knowledge of the school's history. One day, I ask her about the 1927 newspaper article.

In 1578, King Henry III crafted l'Ordre des Chevaliers du Saint Esprit, or the Order of the Holy Spirit. The group of knights reigned as the most exclusive inner circle of the privileged and royal class in France, until the Revolution in 1789 put an end to that sort of thing. To its esteemed members the king awarded special medallions made of silver. King Henry had the same medal encrusted with diamonds. Each hung from a thick blue ribbon—in French, a *cordon bleu.*

"The king did this for a reason," Madame Bisset says. "It seemed like an honor, and it was, but it also required these nobles to be a part of the court and encouraged their loyalty to the king." Membership had its privileges, and among them were legendary Cordon Bleu banquets. These sumptuous long-table feasts required dozens of cooks and assistants and grew increasingly extravagant and frequent. If nobles were expected to lavish cash on parties, clothes for court, and material displays of wealth, it lessened the likelihood they'd do something bothersome, like set up their own army or invade a neighboring noble's land.

From the feasts, the term was first applied in the realm of cuisine. By the eighteenth century, the term *"cordon bleu"* had evolved into shorthand for a craftsman who hit the pinnacle of his or her profession or developed impeccable skill.

When a journalist named Marthe Distel started a publication on cooking and entertaining, she naturally called it *La cuisinière Cordon-bleu,* "The Cordon Bleu Cook." To prompt readership, Distel offered subscribers cooking classes taught by professional chefs. The first class met on January 14, 1895, in kitchens of the Palais Royal.

Distel's aim was to have top professional chefs teach the classes. One chef in particular, Henri-Paul Pellaprat, had a lasting impact on the school. Chef Pellaprat joined the staff after World War I and stayed for thirty-two years. A disciple and friend of Auguste Escoffier's, Pellaprat took on the task of codifying the school's classic French curriculum.

On her death in the late 1930s, Distel willed the school to an orphanage. By all accounts, this turned out to be generous but misguided. The school shut down temporarily during World War II, when matters more pressing than cooking lessons loomed large in German-occupied Paris. Madame Elisabeth Brassart gave the school a fresh start by buying it in 1945, and she used her significant contacts to attract top French chefs such as Chef Max Bugnard, who taught Julia Child.

Child attended in the late 1940s, when the school was located on rue du Faubourg St.-Honoré. Julia adored Chef Bugnard but loathed Brassart, whom she called a "nasty, mean woman" and a poor administrator. Brassart didn't care much for Julia, either, saying that although she worked hard, Julia had "no natural talent" for cooking.

Years later, enter André Cointreau. He and the aging Brassart both belonged to the Club des Cent, an exclusive, celebrated dining club. He persuaded her to sell him the school in 1984. Four years later, he relocated Le Cordon Bleu to its present site on rue Léon Delhomme. An astute businessman, Cointreau injected both significant funding and marketing savvy into the operation. He purchased Le Petit Cordon Bleu in London, a school started by a former student in 1933 that had no official affiliation.

He simultaneously launched Le Cordon Bleu schools in Ottawa and Tokyo.

Expanding the number of schools is Cointreau's core focus. In 2006, Le Cordon Bleu had some twenty-seven schools in fifteen different countries, with more opening all the time. Most are set up through partnership deals, the largest being with the Career Education Corporation in the United States. Each year, some twenty-two thousand students graduate with a Le Cordon Bleu diploma. Only five hundred of them earn it in the kitchens at the flagship school in Paris. That's because it's now possible to become a "Le Cordon Bleu–trained chef" in Las Vegas, Pittsburgh, and Dover, N.H. Other deals have brought about schools in Korea, Mexico, Brazil, and Australia.

Madame Bisset says, "For [Cointreau], this is a spiritual mission. Food brings people together around one table. It's a business, certainly, but it's also very personal."

All of this started with a twenty-page magazine in 1895. I wonder what journalist Distel would make of it all.

I find myself alone with Lely, chatting, drinking Chablis sitting on the sidewalk during lunch. It's remarkably warm for an early April day. We sharpen our knives as we chat, and people cast worried glances in our direction. The combination of alcohol and knives makes people nervous.

"Did you ever see *Sabrina*?" I ask.

She just looks at me. "Are you kidding? I saw it as a little girl. That's part of why I always wanted to come here." But, like me, she took a complicated route.

Ironically, she started her career in the McDonald's corporate offices. After a decade, she got bored and started her own business and then worked for another international company that sent her to Chantilly. That was the trigger.

"I turned forty in 2003, and I wanted to give myself a BIG present," she says, sipping her wine. "So, I quit my job and flew to Paris a month later and started at Le Cordon Bleu the day after I arrived. It was cold and dark." She planned to stay only for Basic but was having so much fun in Paris she couldn't leave. For the first time in her life, she feels thoroughly free.

"In Paris, nobody knows Lely," she says. "So there is no certain image that I need to maintain. Back in Jakarta, my friends and I, we go to the same restaurants, the children go to the same schools, shop at the same malls. Wherever I go, there is a certain set of behaviors that I feel I must maintain.

"For example, in Jakarta I will not walk alone to enjoy the view," she says. "One, because there is no view, and second, it's unseemly and probably is not safe."

But in Paris, it's different. Everywhere in Paris is beautiful, and she has walked alone over much of the city. It's as if she wants to memorize not just what she sees but how she feels being open and free.

I tell her there's an Ernest Hemingway quote that says if you're lucky enough to live in Paris when you're young, then wherever you go for the rest of your life it stays with you, for "Paris is a moveable feast."

She smiles and raises her plastic tumbler. "Are we still young? Oh, forget it. Of course we are. Here's to feasting on Paris wherever we go."

That weekend, Anna-Clare and LizKat return for a visit. We head over to Lely's for dinner in her cramped Seventh-arrondissement apartment. Two dozen students crowd the flat, and seemingly all of them have brought food. The table is heavy with a crazy buffet ranging from sushi to fondue to the roasted-pepper bruschetta that Mike and I contribute. The highlight, though, is a slow-cooked bolognaise by an Israeli student named Sharon. Mike eats two helpings of it.

"You have to give Kat this recipe," he tells Sharon.

Anna-Clare is back at her corporate job. "When I got back, they moved me over to a big jeweler's account," she says. "A year ago, I would have been thrilled, and I like it. But now, I'm starting to think one day I'll shift my career and do something with food."

"Just quit," Sharon says. "Why not? I did."

It turns out that Sharon is a corporate refugee, too. "I wanted to cook for as long as I can remember, even as a small child," she says. She got a degree in hotel management that she never used. She somehow landed in high tech, starting as a production manager and later shifting to overseeing Internet projects.

"I liked it, but I always felt like something was missing," she says. "I would get bored really fast and change jobs all the time. Then I turned thirty. I found myself with no job, no real motivation to look for another one in high-tech." Her fiancé, Amir, asked why she didn't consider cooking as a career. "The idea had honestly never occurred to me," Sharon says. She persuaded the owner of a well-known French restaurant in Tel Aviv to apprentice her in his kitchen for three months. That chef had graduated from Le Cordon Bleu in London, so after the apprenticeship she decided to follow his path. She speaks French, so she opted for Paris. "It was almost a spur-of-the-moment decision," she says. "Suddenly, I was here."

Sharon and Lely's stories remind me of the passages. All of us have made the decision to enter into this experience with abandon, unsure of where we'll come out on the other side. Sometimes, the places that life takes us can be so unexpected.

Spaghetti Bolognaise de Sharon

SHARON'S BOLOGNESE SAUCE FOR SPAGHETTI

Serves six to eight

My classmate Sharon learned this in an Italian class she took in Israel. Very lean hamburger works best for this. You can use cheap Chianti or other red table wine. This results in a mostly meat sauce that's common in Europe yet may be unfamiliar to Americans used to a more tomato-heavy style. If so inclined, add in the tomato sauce from the grilled pizza on pages 156–157 near the end of cooking, in place of adding the cream, for a more traditional flavor.

2 large onions, chopped (about 2½ cups)

2 tablespoons olive oil

4 cloves garlic, minced

2 pounds (about 1 kg) lean ground beef

1 bottle (750 ml) dry red wine

4 tablespoons tomato paste

1 teaspoon Italian herbs

1 cup (250 ml) heavy cream
Salt and pepper to taste, at least ¼ teaspoon of each
3 tablespoons chopped fresh parsley or basil *(optional)*
1 pound (500 g) spaghetti, cooked and drained
Parmesan, grated

In a heavy-bottomed Dutch oven or sauté pan, cook the onions in olive oil over medium heat until softened. Stir in the garlic, add the beef, and stir until the meat cooks through and separates into crumbly pieces. Add the wine and turn the heat up so that the wine bubbles continuously. Reduce by about half. Skim off any gray foam. Add the tomato paste and stir. Cover and turn the heat down to very low, and cook for a minimum of two hours and up to four hours. Stir from time to time, scraping the bottom to ensure nothing sticks to it or burns. Shortly before serving, stir in the cream and Italian herbs. Taste, and then add salt and pepper. Let simmer uncovered another ten minutes. Taste again, adjusting seasonings as necessary, and stir in the parsley. Serve with pasta, sprinkled with Parmesan.

CHAPTER 15

THE SILENCE OF THE LAMB

LESSON HIGHLIGHTS: DEMONSTRATION OF MEAT CUTS,
KILLING LOBSTERS, AND THE LINK BETWEEN DEATH AND DINNER

I'm grateful the lamb arrives without its head. It appears naked, shorn, as if prepared for surgery. The tools of *le boucher* look cruel and primitive: a hacksaw, a host of rugged boning knives, and an enormous, well-worn cleaver.

The Gray Chef introduces Monsieur Robert, who scans the room, massaging the handle of his cleaver like a worry bead. Performing for the crowd, the butcher's thin voice trembles. For his first cut, he lifts his knife high and cleaves deeply into the animal's midsection. His hands shake as he wipes blood off the blade. Thus begins our lesson on meat cuts.

As he saws and hacks the lamb into chunks, he explains the idea behind each cut and how it's traditionally cooked. Anne observes, patiently converting his words to English.

Monsieur Robert does not look like a butcher. Thin, even a little gaunt, he has begun to comb his brown-turning-gray hair over to hide his bare head. Under his immaculate white butcher's jacket he wears a pressed lime-green shirt with a black tie. He appears more like a mild-mannered professor, the sort of man who spends his days with books, not engaged in manual labor in a bloodied Paris back room.

Monsieur Robert moves through the cuts at an impressive pace, setting each one on a plate as Anne writes its name in French on a piece of paper. There are *les gigots,* the legs, of course, plus pieces you see infrequently, such as *les poitrines,* or breasts, and *le collier,* the collarbone. He breaks the shoulder, or *l'épaule,* down into small pieces for stew.

"The shoulder," Anne translates, "should be roasted. The collar can be sautéed and then slow-roasted in dishes such as a cassoulet."

He cuts a vertical line down the back and then peels the fat off gently to reveal the skin on the other side. This results in a double chop. "Ceci peut-être désossé et bourré," he offers.

"This could be boned and stuffed," translates Anne. Sitting next to me are Lely and Sharon. They exchange eye rolls.

"Doesn't he realize that all we do is bone meat and stuff it with more meat?" Sharon whispers to us both.

At the end, the shy butcher spreads his hands over the lamb, now portioned into labeled cuts. It's a final, proud gesture. The room erupts in applause. Then someone asks how old the lamb was at the time of slaughter. "Four months, maybe five," Anne responds matter-of-factly. An "awwwwwe" sweeps the room.

So I've watched a lamb get hacked into bits, another first for me.

I conduct a quick mental inventory. As of today, I have gutted a couple dozen fish, boned a beef shoulder as big as my head, and ripped the tendons out of a guinea fowl with a soup ladle. Earlier this week, chefs taught us to cut a live lobster in half as part of the preparation for *homard à l'Américaine.* In the practical, the more compassionate Chef Bouveret offered us a second choice of torture to kill our lobsters: the time-tested boil-them-alive method. I did neither, opting to kill the lobster instantly with a sharpened trussing needle, pushed directly into the heart. I felt bad but not too bad.

I am going through the same thing that a friend is now experiencing in medical school: desensitization. At this point, our training kitchens often seem to double as anatomy labs. The ability to objectify something such as a lamb must be as vital to a chef as it is to a surgeon. That's especially true here in France, where the eating public consumes every part of a cow or pig with delight—and often with a cream sauce. At Le Cordon Bleu, we must come to terms with the simple math of meat, or as Peter Mayle once wrote, that "direct link between death and dinner."

All of this makes me think of my mother.

For about fifteen years, my family lived on a ten-acre farm in Davison, Michigan, that was inhabited by dozens of nervous chickens, some mean geese, and a languid dairy cow. Mom used to keep a stained ax hanging in a special spot in the hay barn. Every so often, she'd break the necks of a few chickens and give them a *thwack* with the ax. "Sometimes they'd literally run around with their heads cut off," she says, pleased at the memory. Born about a decade before me, my brothers and my sister were introduced at age eight or nine to plucking feathers off the limp, headless chickens.

Briefly, we kept rabbits. Two quickly grew to two dozen, each assigned a name by us children. "You can't kill something with a name," Mom says. So she gave all the rabbits away, destined to be someone else's dinner. She felt no qualms about killing all the geese, though. One attacked my brother on his way to kindergarten. My dad came home to find the headless birds lying on the kitchen table.

"I see the geese got after the kids again," was all he said.

By the time I was five, we'd uprooted from the farm into "town," a sleepy hamlet with a population of around two thousand. Retiring the ax, my mother started working full-time, and my siblings went off to college. Mom now prefers the lazy vagueness of boneless chicken breasts. Those years on the farm never left her, though. I must remember that, as my mother's daughter, I should be cut out for this.

Chef then moves on to one of the prized lessons of Intermediate Cuisine, the ballottine: *Ballottine de volaille à la mousse de foie gras aux pistaches,* or chicken stuffed with foie-gras mousse and pistachios. Sure, we've boned lots of meats, including chicken. But this time, we'll bone the entire chicken without removing its skin.

In our practical, it takes about forty-five minutes to ease and scrape the flesh away from the joints of the wings and hips. It's meticulous work, gently tugging and cutting while not puncturing the skin. The sound of ten students working, scraping metal to bone, sends shivers down my spine.

We stuff the chicken with a *farce* of ground pork, cognac, canned *mousse de foie gras,* crushed pistachios, and ham. It's then wrapped into a tight plastic package and poached in broth, where it is left to sit overnight.

Ballottine, day two: we clarify the chicken poaching stock like consommé. This is strained twice through two cone-shaped sieves with a paper towel placed in between. To this we add gelatin to make aspic, a jellylike substance. We stamp out shapes from blanched dark leek leaves, carrots, or even tomato skins and arrange them attractively on a large metal serving tray. We then pour the aspic over it until it coats the whole tray evenly. It chills and sets so the design cannot move.

Frankly, it's a lot of work, all to decorate a tray. But this is French cuisine at its most classic, dating back to grand royal meals of *les Cordon Bleus.*

Chef Bouveret loves my tray. "Oooh la la," he says. He calls over other students. "Look, look!" he instructs. The tray is the backdrop for the sliced ballottine.

The Gray Chef wanders into the kitchen. Chef Bouveret calls to him. The Gray Chef looks at my tray carefully, sniffs a hint of approval, and walks out.

I take the ballottine home to our visiting guests from Seattle, Amado and Nellie. Let's just say that cold poached chicken with foie gras isn't for everyone.

Exploring Paris with our guests, we head to the catacombs, a vast maze of subterranean tunnels holding the remains of five to six million dead residents. The result of mass church-graveyard consolidations in the late eighteenth and nineteenth centuries, the underground cemetery covers nearly seven miles of old mine corridors built beneath the city by the Romans. The official entrance to the catacombs is an unassuming stone building near Métro Denfert Rochereau. As we begin to descend the spiral staircase into the depths, Mike suddenly stops.

"What's wrong?" I ask.

He shakes his head. "I don't feel right. Maybe I need something to drink." The guard waves us through the exit turnstile, and we head across the street to a crêpe and hot-dog vendor. Sipping a Coke and chewing on a hot dog, he offers, "That was odd. Maybe the thought of going underground with six million dead people got to me a bit. Or I just needed some caffeine. I'm OK now."

We head down the stairs again, then walk for what feels like a mile in a nearly black, damp tunnel. It smells of wet soil.

We come to a crypt. I'm not sure what I was expecting. The corridor walls throughout much of the catacombs are made of actual, aging human bones: skulls, femurs, and arm bones, generally stacked in tidy, often artistic symbolic displays. Other bones are thrown or stored behind these ghastly, decorous fronts.

At this point, all of us feel something deeply. The macabre mood under the city is broken by the many pithy French comments etched in the walls by the grave makers. One etching, Mike's favorite, says: "Do not feel sad for me, for I am here with five million of my friends for eternity."

This one becomes my favorite:

Crazy that you are
why do you promise yourself to live a long time,
you who cannot count on a single day?

The visit haunts me. I'm thankful that the next few lessons shift to fish so I don't have to face any more bones.

Life seems so linear, a constant march toward the end. But in reality, the general flow is more cyclical. The brutal truth of nature is that it often takes the death of one thing to feed another. A chef never mourns an empty plate.

Agneau Grillé Mariné aux Olives, Haricots aux Artichauts, et Tomates

OLIVE-MARINATED GRILLED LAMB, WHITE BEANS WITH
ARTICHOKES, AND TOMATOES

Serves twelve

High-quality olives make all the difference in this dish, so don't skimp.
Get a glistening Mediterranean mix. Ask the butcher to butterfly the lamb;
it will cook more evenly. The lamb should marinate overnight in the

refrigerator and be brought back to room temperature before grilling. White northern and cannellini beans work well. I use rosemary, thyme, and parsley for the marinade herbs. The lamb is inspired by a recipe from *Bon Appetit*'s July 1999 issue; I was reading it as I waited to meet Mike for the first time. The lamb pairs nicely with a blended red table wine or a Syrah.

LAMB AND MARINADE

¾ cup (80 g) high-quality olives, pitted

1 tablespoon coarse salt

2 teaspoons ground black pepper

1 cup mixed fresh herbs, chopped

6 tablespoons olive oil

6 cloves garlic, peeled, smashed

Juice of 2 lemons

4½ to 5 pounds (2 to 2.5 kg) boneless leg of lamb, butterflied

BEANS

4 ounces (125 g) salt pork or unsmoked bacon, cubed

1 medium onion, chopped (about 1 cup)

2 medium carrots, chopped (about 1 cup)

1 pound (500 g) dry beans, soaked overnight, drained

2 bay leaves

3 tablespoons chopped fresh thyme, or 1 tablespoon dry

2 cloves garlic, chopped

2 quarts (2 l) chicken stock

1 (14-ounce) can chopped, seeded tomatoes

2 (16-ounce) cans artichoke hearts, drained

2 tablespoons butter

Salt and pepper

Hot sauce, such as Tabasco

2 tablespoons fresh parsley, chopped

Marinade: Combine the ingredients in a small food processor. Blend until the olives and garlic are minced and the mixture emulsifies. Slather this on the lamb, set it into a nonreactive bowl, and cover with plastic wrap. Marinate as noted above.

Start the beans in a large Dutch oven by cooking the salt pork or bacon slowly over low heat until browned. Add the onions and carrots and cook until softened. Add the beans, bay leaves, thyme, garlic, and enough chicken stock to cover the beans by about three inches. Bring to a boil, then reduce to a simmer and cook uncovered for 1½ hours. Do not add salt; it will toughen the beans. Add water or stock to keep beans moist. Add the tomatoes and artichoke hearts, then simmer for another half hour.

To start the lamb: Discard marinade; pat the meat dry with paper towels. When the grill is hot, start cooking the lamb with the fat side down, about fifteen to twenty minutes per side or until a meat thermometer reaches 125°F/51°C for medium-rare. Let lamb rest for ten minutes before slicing. Finish beans with butter, salt, pepper, and hot sauce to taste. Remove bay leaves; stir in chopped parsley. Serve with sliced lamb.

CHAPTER 16

"I AM A PIZZA FOR KATHLEEN"

LESSON HIGHLIGHTS: THE DIFFICULTIES OF ORDERING A PIZZA IN
PARIS, AND A BAD GROUP BLIND DATE

From the day the first outpost opened on avenue de l'Opéra, hip young
Parisians thronged to the comfy couches and €4 cappuccinos. Many
predicted the French would scoff when Starbucks finally came to Paris.
Hardly. By contrast, uncomfortable American tourists unsure how to ask
for a double-shot soy latte in French instead line up to buy Paris Starbucks
mugs and flee.

For fun, Mike and the twenty-somethings from his class head there
not long after it opens to study their early French lessons. One of his classmates is a young, blond missionary from Texas who's studying French as
part of her endeavor to "convert" the French to Christianity. She's obvious to that bloody part of French history in which the devout Christians
battled over whether they were Protestants or Catholics.

"Hey, did y'all get POO for DOO?" she asks in her thick Texas
drawl, meaning the *peux* (puh) for question number *deux* (duh). Then A.J.
sits up excitedly.

"Wow, I get it!" A.J. says. "I get the Creole Lady Marmalade song!
You know," she sings, *"Voulez-Vous Coucher Avec Moi."* The whole group
murmurs to one another.

"I see, *'VOULEZ-VOUS'* means 'would you' . . ." says Tia.

"Oh yeah, *coucher,* the root verb 'to sleep,'" picks up Mike.

"*AVEC MOI CE SOIR,* 'with me, this night!' I get it, I do!" Jackie exclaims.

They go around the table repeating the phrase. It's like when Helen Keller suddenly understood W-A-T-E-R. They say it over and over, animatedly shifting the emphasis on different words, toying with the nature of the question. *"Voulez-vous coucher avec MOI ce soir?"* *"Voulez-VOUS coucher avec MOI ce soir?"* *"Voulez vous coucher avec moi CE SOIR!"* Even the missionary chimes in, drawling. *"Non, VOO-LAY voom coochie ah-vect moi sir sour?"*

Mike notices a hush has fallen over the Starbucks. The French patrons are fixated on the group, though pretending not to be, as that would be rude. He realizes that to their ears and eyes, it must appear that he is surrounded by a group of young women so desperate to sleep with him that they're nearly begging, nay, vying to be chosen. "Would you go to bed with ME tonight?" "Would you go to bed with me TONIGHT?" "Would YOU go to BED with me TONIGHT?"

A young Frenchman in a business suit lifts his mug and offers a salute in the air to Mike, and goes back to his newspaper with a smile.

Although I studied French for one year in college and Mike studied Spanish in high school, we're not exactly soaking up the French language. The primary problem appears to be that we're older than twelve. That's the age some researchers believe that people's ability to learn language begins to decline. Research suggests that it's almost impossible for an individual past their midteens to learn a language and speak it without an accent.

I quickly tire of relearning *"bonjour"* and learning to conjugate *"être"* in the beginning class that I eventually signed up for as a "false beginner." So I start to sit in on Mike's classes, and sometimes I study with a private tutor. We listen to French music, watch French TV, and attempt to read French newspapers. I start listening to the chef's instruction, trying to figure it out before the translator gets to it.

But the real problem we have with French isn't French itself. It's English.

At Le Cordon Bleu, cliques form not by nationality but by language. For instance, the Spanish speakers from Mexico, South and Central America, and Spain hang out together. The Japanese students form a tight-knit, almost impenetrable circle. Students from the United Kingdom, the United States, and most of Europe, however, typically speak in English. At home, Mike and I speak to each other only in English. In Paris, if you ask someone something in bad French, they often answer you in English.

So it's fine, I suppose, that we're stunted learners. Until we really need to speak French to, say, report a problem with the electricity to the power company. When we moved in, Arturo called the power company to shut off the power in his uncle's name, but he did not have it reinstated in ours. So one day, the power just went out.

Utility companies are universally unhelpful anyway. For forty minutes, Mike sits with the phone cradled to his ear, a pile of phrase books and French dictionaries on the table. The operator continually batters him to repeat everything. When he hangs up, shaken and exhausted, he prays she's understood. The electricity comes back on a few hours later.

Mike moves past me in comprehension. His brain works differently than mine. As a technical person, he's used to taking in masses of data and then shifting them into comprehensible information for decision-making purposes. But his problem is that he's having real trouble speaking.

One day, an old man sidles up next to him at Mike's favorite escape, the massive hardware area in the basement of the BHV department store. The man is apparently keen to chat about handsaws and wrenches in French. Mike tells him that he doesn't speak French very well. The old man tries relentlessly to be helpful and speaks louder and slower.

"But I'm sure your French is fine," he says to Mike in French. "Tourists don't visit hardware stores in Paris."

Like me with the chef and the orange sauce, Mike can't think of a word to say. He feels a sense of panic and makes an awkward excuse to leave. He comes home out of sorts and paces the flat.

"I guess I'm just a perfectionist. The more I learn, the more I realize just how much I don't know," he tells me.

I've had days like that, so to cheer him up I make a call in my semi-confident faux-beginner French and place an order with Speed Rabbit

Pizza. Although Mike will try everything I bring home from Le Cordon Bleu, pizza remains his favorite food. It turns out to be harder than I think. For ten minutes, I struggle on the phone to place an order for a large pepperoni with mushrooms. I hang up, frustrated yet proud of my French.

"Did you tell them the name on the buzzer?" Mike asks.

Um, no, I'd forgotten that vital piece of information. Seeing that I'm reluctant to call back, Mike runs downs four flights of stairs and the six blocks to their store to intervene. As he bursts in, four guys behind the counter in the small storefront look at him expectantly. He exclaims, "Je suis une pizza pour Kathleen!" The puzzled workers exchange glances, then smile. He whacks his head, realizing he's said "I am a pizza for Kathleen."

"Kathleen? *Ah, la folle!*" they say, making circles next to their head with their fingers. They start to explain something about "another pizza" to Mike, but he doesn't completely understand. A teenager returns from one of the mopeds they use for delivery. Like a lot of teens in Paris, he speaks English perfectly.

"Since you live with a crazy woman, they want to give you a second pizza for free," the teen says. I thought the order had gone all right; they hung up thinking I was crazy. So much for my French.

Undeterred, I sign us up online for a promising monthly event. "Practice French language skills and meet new friends in a non-threatening environment," the description reads. Photos on the site had nothing but smiling, happy people holding up glasses of wine or waving at the camera.

It turns out to be a horrible blind date with ten people.

We meet in the dank basement of Le Petit Châtelet, a hotel near Les Halles. Everyone sits with folded arms. Mike suggests we make a round of introductions.

"I am from Sweden," says a square-jawed chap at one end of the table who wore an unrelenting scowl. He is dressed entirely in black. "I work here in Paris, but I have no friends and no one at work likes me, so I thought I would try this."

Mike gets enthused. "Where are you from in Sweden? One of my best friends is from there."

His scowl intensified. "You've probably only been to Stockholm."

"Yes, a couple times for work, but his wedding was in Linköping in the south, and then a group of us traveled to Åre, up north."

The Swedish guy jeers at him. Silence.

Mike fills in the gap. "Actually, it's funny, he's this really nice guy named Hakan, who—"

The Swedish guy interrupts, "Oh, I bet you think I know him."

Suddenly, a chubby American at the other end of the table pipes up. "I hate that, when people assume that you know someone just because you're from the same country. 'Oh, you must know Joe' since you're from America. No, I don't fucking know Joe! Why the fuck would I know Joe? So stupid."

Silence.

"Does anyone want another drink?" I ask. The drinks arrive at a glacial pace.

By then, we've excruciatingly met the rest of the crew. Highlights include Louisette at one end of the table, a pretty, slight woman who was born to a French mother but raised in the American Midwest. As part of her introduction, she goes into rapturous detail about the beef-tongue sandwiches her mother made her as a child. Inexplicably, she's with Ralph, the sweaty American chubster who doesn't know Joe. There's Jalor from Malta who refuses to provide any personal details.

Shaz from Tunisia is the only normal one in the bunch. He engages in friendly banter to practice his English. He's reading *Jennifer Government,* a novel set in the near future, when corporations rule the world. Peoples' identities eventually unite so closely with their careers that they adopt their employer's moniker as their own last name.

"What happens to the people who are unemployed?" I ask.

"They don't have last names, because without a job, they have no identity," he says. "It is a very scary book."

As if that were a cue, they ask about us.

Mike dreads two questions: "So where are you from?" and "What do you do?" or its foreign variation, "What are you doing here in France?"

An Air Force brat, he was born in Texas but then lived in five other states, including Alaska. He's between careers, living off income from wise investments. But this complicates his answers and for some reason often prompts interrogation.

"So you're just here to be with your girlfriend?" asks the Swedish guy.

"Well, yes," he says.

Ralph asks, "Yeah, but what do you *do*? I mean, for a living?"

"I'm just taking some time off," he says, not wanting to explain further.

"So you're not *from* anywhere and you don't *do* anything," Ralph says.

We leave before one of us strangles the sweaty American.

Two nights later, we have our first real clash when Mike wonders aloud that maybe he should return to the United States and get a real job. I react like the crazy woman the Speed Rabbit Pizza people expected. I storm around the flat, upset. Doesn't he know how lucky he is to be in Paris? That he can just be free to have time to enjoy it? Do you know how many would kill for just such an opportunity? And he wants to go home to rainy *Seattle*? The scene deteriorates into me sobbing.

"Is it me? Am I not making you happy?" I ask, always a dumb question from a woman in the midst of a tantrum.

He takes my hands and sits me down on the couch. "I love you and love being with you. But this isn't about you," he says calmly. "It's not about Paris, either. I love Paris, but I feel like I'm on the verge of becoming a perpetual tourist here. I feel like I am just spinning but in no direction and not going anywhere. I'm not used to this. You of all people should understand that."

I do understand. This calms me. If we are to survive a life together, I have to start seeing the world from his point of view. We talk about *Jennifer Government*. I realize that when I discuss my former company, I still say "we," as if I remain a part of it. Life is so much easier when you can wrap yourself within the veil of a big company's identity. People assume that so much of what you do is who you are, and it's easy to believe that yourself. There's a stamp of worth that you get automatically by association.

Without jobs, neither of us has that anymore. On top of it, we're in a foreign place without even the safety net of a familiar language. We went to the meet-up looking for a "non-threatening environment," but in the end even that wasn't safe.

I suppose it's like some tourists who go into a Starbucks in Paris. Do they really let themselves experience what it truly means to be foreign?

Pizza Grillée, Sauce Tomate aux Herbes et à l'Ail

GRILLED PIZZA CRUST, GARLICKY HERB TOMATO SAUCE

Makes two pizzas; serves four

This recipe was inspired by a pizza Mike and I ate in a small hamlet in southern France. Grilling the dough results in puffy, lopsided pies; such imperfections signal true artisanal pizza. Don't start the coals before you start prepping the dough, as it takes an hour to rise.

DOUGH

1 package (¼ ounce) active dry yeast

1 cup (250 ml) warm water (about 100°F/38°C)

2 cups (220 g) all-purpose flour

1 tablespoon olive oil

1 teaspoon Italian herbs

2 teaspoons sugar

½ teaspoon salt

¼ teaspoon garlic powder

Extra flour, for kneading

SAUCE

¾ cup finely chopped onion

1½ teaspoons mixed Italian herbs

4 tablespoons olive oil

5 cloves garlic, finely chopped

1 (16-ounce) can tomato sauce (about 2 cups)

½ cup water

1 tablespoon balsamic vinegar

1 bay leaf

TOPPINGS

Any selection of pepperoni, artichokes, mushrooms, tomatoes, onions, and so on.

2 teaspoons mixed Italian herbs

4 ounces fresh buffalo mozzarella, sliced thin

Put yeast in warm water and let rest for fifteen minutes. Mix the flour, oil, seasonings, sugar, salt, and garlic powder in a bowl. Make a well in the center and add the yeast and water, then stir to mix in. Gently knead for a few minutes on a floured surface. The dough should feel elastic; if it doesn't, add a few drops of water. Shape into a ball, put into an oiled bowl, and cover with plastic wrap. Let rise until nearly doubled in size, about an hour.

For the sauce: In a saucepan over medium heat, cook and stir the onions and herbs in olive oil until tender. Add garlic; cook and stir for one minute. Add the rest of the ingredients, bring to a boil, then simmer uncovered on low heat for twenty minutes. Taste, and adjust seasonings. Set aside.

Prepare the grill to a medium-hot fire. Organize all toppings. Set aside.

Divide the dough in two. Roll each piece on a floured surface to a disk about the size of a dinner plate. (Thicker crusts are easier to handle.) Spray grill with cooking spray. Grill dough two to three minutes per side. Remove to a baking sheet. Smear with sauce as desired, add the toppings, sprinkle with Italian herbs, and put the cheese on last. Place under a broiler until cheese melts.

CHAPTER 17

A SAUCE THICKER THAN BLOOD

One day, I find a young Asian woman hunched against the back wall of the locker room. Sobbing, she methodically rips up a recipe as if working a rosary, as quiet tears roll down her face. Whispers say a chef yelled at her for botching three separate attempts at a cream sauce.

A complex balance of heat, ingredients, and seasoning, even a simple sauce can go wrong. Chef Gaillard noticed nothing else on my plate when he screamed about my duck à l'orange. Yet last week, an overcooked fillet of veal slipped by, masked under a river of velvety mushroom velouté. It's easy to appreciate why sauces developed into one of the distinguishing elements of French cuisine: a great sauce can hide a host of deficiencies. A bad sauce hides nothing, especially not itself.

In the days before refrigeration, sauces were sometimes used to disguise meats or seafood that might be pushing their sell-by date. The great chefs each developed long libraries of sauces. Take for instance Escoffier's list of master sauces, which includes béchamel (white, based in cream), velouté (blond, a mixture of cream and stock), espagnole (brown, usually starting with veal stock), hollandaise/mayonnaise (butter and egg emulsions), and tomato (red, for obvious reasons). There's also *jus,* not usually considered a sauce in classic French cuisine but used in the place of one in modern cooking.

But the more sauces we make, the more it becomes clear that in French cuisine sauces are like jazz riffs: variations off a few basic themes. By my own estimation, we've been through about fifty sauces so far. We've made them with red wine, white wine, Calvados, beer, Muscadet, Madeira, and port. We've thickened our arteries with a legion of cream and butter sauces: béchamel, beurre blanc, *suprême,* béarnaise, Albuféra, hollandaise, mornay, tartar, and a nut-brown butter version known as *meunière.* We've learned to make sauces from crawfish, tomatoes, mushrooms, mustard, herbs, and coffee. For desserts, we've learned honey, vanilla, passion-fruit, chocolate, pistachio, cognac, and raspberry sauces. Add to this a slew of *jus* and a list of vinaigrettes.

Today, our sauce will be thickened with blood.

Traditionally made with a rooster (a *coq* in French), *coq au vin* is one of the most classic of all French dishes. Several regions of France claim it originated there; some dubious reports say it was created by Caesar's chef. But regardless of where it came from, the original dish was finished by adding rooster blood, which coagulates and thickens when exposed to oxygen, lending the flavor a certain *je ne sais quoi.*

"I am not sure why that would be appealing to anyone," Lely whispers to me as Chef Gaillard dives deep into a story about peasants keeping chickens and holding the *coq* for special occasions. "Why eat the blood?"

"Maybe it tastes good to them?" I whisper back. "Lots of countries make blood sausage, and some people really like that."

She sits back and looks at me. "*You* like that?"

I just shake my head. The record should note that I tried black pudding during an adventurous breakfast once in the wilds of Ipswich, England. It was not, as the English would say, my cup of tea.

Overseeing our practical, Chef Savard offers that we can leave out the blood if we want. But I'm game. I pour some nonbloodied sauce into a zipbag to reserve it for dinner at home with Mike. I take the rest of my sauce and add in the blood. As I stir, it thickens slightly, taking on a darker hue by the minute. As always, I taste. The blood sauce isn't bad. Rich, almost a bit like chocolate, the texture a bit gritty. Count Chocula would be happy.

I'm one of only three students who took the extra step to make the blood sauce. Chef seems pleased. I don't even need any more salt—the blood lends enough for his palate. "It's good with the blood, yes?" he asks. I shrug.

Afterward, I meet up with L.P. and Lely to walk down to the lockers. "What did you think of the blood?" L.P. asks.

Like so many things, it's not that it's bad—it's just unfamiliar. "Well, let's put it this way. I don't think that I'll become a vampire anytime soon."

My sister lived on the family farm for more than a decade; I lived there only until I was six. She spent most of her life there eating the same ten dishes. So while I have fond memories of my mother's minestrone, she rolls her eyes at the memory. "You forget she would top it with Velveeta cheese," she chides.

With little variation, it went like this: On Mondays and Thursdays, Mom made bread and an "oven dinner," either meatloaf or chicken casserole. Tuesday meant spaghetti, Wednesday minestrone soup. Friday, we had fried fish even though we weren't Catholic. "It can't hurt, might help," Mom would say. Saturdays, she made vats of chili or a macaroni-beef dish we euphemistically referred to as "goulash." Sundays meant fried chicken or pot roast.

In the 1960s in semirural Michigan, Sandy had no exposure to ethnic cuisine. All she knew was that some lady named Julia on public TV made food that was different than our mother's—sans Velveeta—and different was good. Sandy began to cook the likes of *coq au vin* when she was in junior high. Presumably, her fixation on France grew from there.

Now the editor of a travel magazine, my sister has been all over the world. But there's one place that she's spent little time: Paris. I don't think it's an accident.

Today, she arrives with her daughter, twelve-year-old Sarah. It's always hard to describe my relationship with Sarah. "Niece" feels like an inadequate descriptor. She's my younger sister and my surrogate daughter all wrapped into one. Sarah has met a few of my boyfriends, but she's never been keen on any of them. Then she met Mike at the "castle" in Florida. She called him "Uncle Mike" right away and insisted I marry him.

We want to show them everything. We feel like we're showing them our city, the nooks and crannies, the special places we've discovered along with all the usual tourist spots. Sandy and I haunt the markets and the restaurant-supply stores near Les Halles. We take them through the passages. One day, I take them to the first place I ever had a meal in Paris: Les Fontaines on rue Soufflot in the Latin Quarter. Over a lunch of roasted quail, veal stew, and salad with hot chèvre, my sister seems distracted and unusually quiet. I notice she keeps stirring her espresso, staring out the window.

"What is it?" I ask her.

She stirs her coffee. "I want to go see it."

"See what?"

"The Sorbonne."

Of course, I should have known. In suggesting Les Fontaines for lunch, I'd forgotten that the main campus for the core Université de Paris–Sorbonne would be literally around the corner.

We walk down rue Soufflot and take a right on boulevard St.-Michel until we come to place de la Sorbonne, a square anchored by the ornate domed church built in the thirteenth century and loud with the sound of fountains. To one side, there's a line of cafés; on the other, bookstores selling philosophy textbooks and a Gap.

Sandy takes in the details. We sit at the edge of one fountain next to a female student with long brown hair. She's wearing jeans and talking on her mobile phone. She's got an obvious American accent: "No, no, I'll meet you at the bridge first, and then we'll go get some coffee . . . . *Oui, c'est bien. Au revoir.*" She flips her phone shut.

This was the life that could have been Sandy's. But if it had been, would she be a different person? Would she have her daughter, or her happy twenty-five-year marriage? Where would she be now?

"Mama, what are you thinking?" asks Sarah.

Sandy thinks for a moment.

"Maybe you can go here one day" is all she says.

With that, we turn and leave the university behind.

★　★　★

It's intriguing to look at Paris through the eyes of a child. Sarah is not interested in haute cuisine or impressive architecture. She's bored after an hour at the Louvre.

To her, the highlights of Paris come in simple delights: watching a sleek woman feed her puppy terrier at an outdoor café, a sweet crêpe, and a ride on the carousel at Les Halles. She's intrigued by the mechanics of the standard street hot dog: a long rod gets pushed into the center of a foot-long half baguette to make a hole in the soft bread before the hot dog is surgically inserted.

Their last day in Paris arrives, and they plan a final visit to the Louvre. But it is Tuesday, so they find it closed and wander into the Tuileries gardens instead. Sarah spots a boy and girl her age at the playground and runs to meet them. She finds one speaks only French, the other Spanish. Somehow, the three manage to communicate, and they play together for hours, sharing swings and monkey bars, teaching one another words.

There's much to learn from their visit. Still a child, Sarah lacks the fear of things foreign that we all seem to foster as we grow up. She is less likely to see others who speak another language as "them" because once you play with other children, they are no longer foreign; they are just people. Her sheer curiosity and desire to play transcend any inhibition.

If Sandy had never dreamed of the Sorbonne, would I have been as drawn to the Le Cordon Bleu? If she *had* gone to Paris, who would we be now?

Coq au Vin et Thym

CHICKEN IN WINE AND THYME

Serves eight to ten

This is my sister's recipe. She grows fresh thyme in her garden—hence the bounty of it used here. She usually serves the chicken with wide noodles or mashed potatoes. This is great for entertaining, as you can prepare it a day ahead and reheat. Serve with the same type of red wine you use in the sauce.

3½ pounds (1.5 kg) boneless chicken thighs, skin removed
Coarse salt, freshly ground pepper

3 tablespoons olive oil

8 ounces (250 g) pancetta or unsmoked bacon, diced

2 medium yellow onions, chopped (about 2½ cups)

ribs of celery, chopped (about 1½ cups)

2 medium carrots, chopped

2 tablespoons brandy or cognac

2 tablespoons flour

1 bottle (750 ml) dry red wine, such as Syrah or Pinot Noir

4 cloves garlic, chopped

10 sprigs thyme, tied together

2 bay leaves

3 cups (750 ml) chicken stock

½ sweet onion, sliced

8 ounces (250 g) brown mushrooms, sliced

2 tablespoons butter

3 tablespoons chopped parsley

Mashed potatoes or cooked wide noodles

Preheat oven to 350°F/180°C. Season the chicken pieces with salt and pepper. In a heavy Dutch oven, brown in batches in hot oil over high heat. Set aside. Turn the heat to medium-low and add the pancetta or bacon and cook slowly until slightly browned. Add the onions, celery, and carrots and stir until tender. Add the brandy, then reduce slightly. Sprinkle with flour and stir until coated. Return the chicken to the pan. Add the wine, garlic, herbs, and chicken stock. The liquid should mostly cover the chicken pieces. Bring the liquid to a boil, skimming off any foam or fat. Reduce heat to a bare simmer. Cover tightly and cook in oven for about two hours or until meat is very tender.

Meanwhile, cook the sweet onions and mushrooms in the butter in a medium skillet.

Before serving, add the mushrooms, onions, and chopped parsley to the chicken. Remove bay leaves and thyme branches. Check seasonings, adding salt and pepper to taste.

Serve atop mashed potatoes or noodles.

CHAPTER 18

LA CATASTROPHE AMÉRICAINE

LESSON HIGHLIGHTS: THE INTERNATIONAL BUFFET, WHY YOU CAN'T
MAKE SUBSTITUTIONS WITH CHEESECAKE

I s there any food that's really American?

Chef Gaillard has revived an old Le Cordon Bleu tradition: the international buffet. He's tasked the Intermediate students to come up with dishes that represent their countries. Brian in my group leads Team USA. In the kitchen, as we braise some beef, the handsome Chef Savard hangs out, taking part in the debate.

"Apple pie?" Brian suggests. No, that's mostly French, based on apple tarts.

"Hot dogs?" suggests Jovina. No, they're sausages and probably German. We run through a longer list, but everything seems to have originally derived from someplace else.

Meatloaf? It's strikes us as a kind of meaty terrine. Maybe hamburgers? I offer that the origin of the hamburger is unclear, but the idea of grinding up meat and putting it between bread probably started with immigrants on ships coming to America. The ground meat, sometimes spiked with onions and lightly smoked, was called "Hamburg style" beef, named for a popular meat patty sold there, itself derived from Russian cuisine.

The Russians got the idea from Kublai Khan when he invaded them in the thirteenth century.

"How the hell do you know that?" Brian asks. Turns out I wrote a story about hamburgers a few years ago. I can never remember anything important, but I can remember shit like how Mongolian warmongers fed their armies patties made from ground-up meat.

I suggest some Cajun—say, my gumbo.

"Shrimp creole or gumbo, that's very American," Chef Savard says, nodding. But it's too French for Brian, the purist. After school, he searches online and finds information about Native American cuisine, looking for a dish based on indigenous foods and unspoiled by any European influence. He develops an intriguing recipe: quails stuffed with red berries. We need a dessert, so I suggest chocolate-chip cookies. But LeAnne, an American pâtisserie student on the team, thinks the chips will be too hard to come by and suggests butterscotch.

Without consultation, I somehow get assigned cheesecake. I don't like cheesecake, and I've never made it. Dutifully I go online to research recipes, and I find a pumpkin-cheesecake recipe from an American site. This bad decision starts a series of unfortunate events. Cheesecake is baking, and that's a science. Let this be a lesson that too many substitutions can ruin what's otherwise a fairly simple recipe.

American cheesecake is made with cream cheese. I can't find cream cheese in Paris. I settle on a kind of soft cheese I find at Monoprix that resembles it. I look all over, even trying the Bon Marché, but I can't find pumpkin puree as we know it in America. I settle on a can of roasted squash and mash it down. No graham crackers either in the City of Light. I settle on some ground gingerlike cookies meant to be served with coffee. My ingredients look like what's called for in the recipe. Looks can be deceiving.

Chef Gaillard directs John to explain that four students should not cook but set up the tables in the Winter Garden instead. I'm one of them.

"Mais, j'ai besoin faire une recette . . . pour cheesecake," I stammer.

He doesn't care. "Ici, dix heures, lundi matin." Chef turns and walks away.

I am to be there at 10:00 a.m. Monday to set up. L.P. and Lely have watched the scene.

"Maybe he believes you will do a good job setting up the tables. You're very creative," says Lely.

"Or maybe he just wants to keep me out of the kitchen," I snap back. To be singled out of cooking while at culinary school—it couldn't be any more humiliating. But I won't be defeated. I'll make that damn cheesecake *and* set up the tables. I'll show him.

The buffet will be *fête du premier mai,* a national holiday in France to celebrate the worker, sort of like what Labor Day should be, except a lot of people work on that day in America. Officially, the school isn't open, but by 8:30 a.m. it's a hive of activity, with students spread through all four kitchens. The chefs start to wander in, intrigued by this experiment of Chef Gaillard's. It's a switch; the students are in charge now, and the chefs only watch. The air has a sense of friendly camaraderie, rather than the tense atmosphere of the deadline-focused practicals. Chef Savard even brings a tray of orange juice into the kitchen where Brian is busy boning a dozen quail. His workspace is covered in blood. It's too early for such carnage. I head up to the pastry kitchen on the third floor. LeAnne is busy prepping her cookies. I pour the cheesecake batter into two springform pans, put them into the oven, and leave them in her care.

Downstairs, Monique, a cleaner for the school, directs me to a stack of eight long, collapsible banquet tables left in the Winter Garden. Her accent is a strong one from somewhere on the outskirts of Paris. "Vous blah blah blah blah," she says. *What?*

"Répétez?" I ask.

She does, and it sounds exactly the same.

"Vous parlez Français?" she asks, growing a bit irritated. I make a pinch with my thumb and forefinger to indicate "just a little." She rolls her eyes and pronounces very slowly and deliberately.

"VOUS-déplacez-les-TABLES. Je vais chercher les nappes." Oh, all right. I'll move the tables; she'll get the linens. I smile and give her the thumbs-up. She nods and goes away.

I stack and carry the eighty chairs from the Winter Garden into the demonstration room. I make a diagram for the tables. By 10:40 a.m., it's clear no one else is coming up to help me. Somehow, I slide each of the fifty-pound tables into position and leverage them enough to set them up. Monique returns and helps me lay out the blue-and-white tablecloths.

Chef Gaillard checks on the setup. He's pleased. "C'est bien, Meeeze Fleeen," he says, smiling. Then he notices that I'm alone. "Où sont les autres?" Where are the others?

I shrug. "Je ne sais pas." I don't know. Eyeing the large tables, he says nothing and heads back to the kitchens.

Suddenly, LeAnne appears with a tray of small tarts. "Um, I don't know how to tell you this, but there was a disaster with the cheesecake." It didn't bake, rise slightly, and set—it just blew up, spilling over the top of the pans and all over the interior of the oven. It didn't get firm but stayed a sort of gooey liquid. LeAnne engineered a clever solution. She lined small pastry cups with short crust, added a little gelatin to the goo, and called them tartlets.

"We'll pull a Julia Child and pretend we meant it to come out this way, OK?" We slide them off the trays and onto our table.

With that, the Winter Garden comes alive. Amazing food emerges. The Koreans craft an acridly perfumed batch of kimchi and piles of hand-cut noodles. The Japanese offerings look too pretty to eat, resembling art, not appetizers. Students scrounged up flags, knickknacks, and other tokens of their countries. Lely goes all out at the Indonesian table, where they've assembled a veritable Tiki hut with palm leaves, dolls, authentic hand fans, and the like. Where she found some of this stuff in Paris is beyond us.

Over at the table for États-Unis, we've neglected to bring in a single flag. Worse, unknown to Brian, a rogue American student made her own national dishes. Just as the buffet starts, she arrives with chicken pot pie and broccoli with cheese, both served in two enormous industrial food warmers, which tower over Brian's platter of delicate, beautiful quails.

Students and faculty swarm en masse into the Winter Garden, eating everything in sight and draining a vat of Chef Gaillard's marvelous sangria. Overall, the buffet is a huge success. No food is left on any table—except ours.

With seeming cafeteria fare on offer, people avoid our table in droves. We put the cookies and pumpkin tarts onto trays that Mike and LeAnne walk through the crowd, serving them hors d'oeuvre style. The reengineered tarts are the greatest success, earning raves for LeAnne from Chef Gaillard.

Cleaning up after the buffet, I hand a gigantic warming pan of untouched broccoli to the baffled Algerian dishwasher. I take home most of the lovely quail.

Sometimes, life doesn't follow the recipe, either.

"We bought our tickets! We're all coming to your wedding!" exclaims Shannan, one of Mike's closest friends. But he's confused; we haven't set our final date yet.

"That's great," he says. "When are you arriving exactly?"

He discovers they've bought them for the Fourth of July. Their tickets—for eleven people from Seattle to Florida—are nonchangeable, nonrefundable.

Somehow, there's been a break in our transatlantic communication.

It's hard enough to plan a wedding when you're in the country. Planning one from another continent adds a whole range of complexities.

Previously, we agreed on a beach wedding near the "castle house." Location solved, we started the date debate. August? Too hot. September? Height of hurricane season. We had talked for a few days about the Fourth of July. It's my mom's birthday, and this year it's a landmark one; my whole family is planning to be in Florida. But that's too soon, and I won't finish Superior Cusine until mid-August. We'd just started to target October 27.

He hangs up with Shannan, and I begin pacing in earnest.

"Well, on the bright side, most of your family will be there on the fourth, so that's about a third of the guest list already," he says. Mike is forever the optimist.

My heart beats wildly. "There's no way we can plan a wedding—from France—in two months. It's almost May! And I'll have to leave school. I won't be able to graduate with my friends," I say, my voice inching up to a shriek.

Mike grabs me and holds me close. "I'll support whatever you say," he says soothingly. "If you want to stay, we'll figure out how to pay them back for the tickets. It will all be OK."

I learned from Julia Child that if something goes awry in the kitchen, just pretend that was how it was meant to turn out in the first place. The pumpkin cheesecakes seemed like a disaster, but with a bit of inspiration they were transformed into successful tarts.

I have learned something that's not about cooking. I felt, for a time, I had it all when I was working at my corporate job in London. But I lacked something critical—I had told myself I was too busy for a relationship. Now I have the one who loves me as powerfully and passionately as I love him.

My life, it turns out, was missing its essential ingredient.

Even now, he's not worried about the money or the planning or anything other than how I will feel if we disrupt my training, damaging my dream. I look into the eyes that I first saw in the Seattle restaurant in 1999. That was around the Fourth of July, too. I kiss him softly. I've made my decision.

The chefs will have to wait. My heart has waited too long already.

Nasi Tumpeng Kuning, Beef Rendang

JAVANESE-STYLE YELLOW RICE WITH SLOW-COOKED BEEF

Serves six to eight

This recipe is adapted from a dish Lely served at the international buffet. Nasi Kuning is a rice dish, reserved for special occasions such as weddings or birthdays, that's formed into a decorative cone. You can use basmati, jasmine, or long-grain white rice. Sriracha is a red chili sauce found in the Asian section of many supermarkets. Round beef-roast cuts, particularly the tips, work well for the rendang. Before serving the beef, remove the tough outer skins of the lemongrass. Kaffir lime leaves, native to Indonesia, are often sold under the name makrut limes in Asian food stores. You can substitute lemon or lime zest, but add a good pinch of grated peel before serving to extend flavor.

RICE

2 stalks lemongrass, cut into 3-inch pieces

2 cups (360 g) uncooked rice

2 (13.5-ounce) cans coconut milk

1 teaspoon turmeric or a few saffron threads (for color)

1 tablespoon lemon juice

2 bay leaves

SPICE PASTE

3 tablespoons grated galangal root

½ tablespoon turmeric

½ tablespoon chopped ginger

2 to 3 tablespoons Sriracha chili sauce, to taste

4 cloves garlic, minced

Salt and pepper, at least ½ teaspoon of each

1 tablespoon fresh lemon juice

SLOW-COOKED BEEF CURRY

5 kaffir lime leaves or 1 tablespoon lemon or lime zest

1 stalk lemongrass, cut into 3-inch pieces

3 (13.5-ounce) cans coconut milk

10 shallots, thinly sliced (about 2 cups)

1 cup chopped Thai basil or cilantro *(optional)*

2 pounds (900 g) beef round tip roast, cut into 1-inch cubes

Smash the lemongrass with a knife and remove the delicate inner pieces. Discard the rest. Wash and drain the rice, then cook according to package directions, using coconut milk instead of water and adding in the other ingredients.

Make the spice paste by processing all the ingredients together or grinding with a mortar and pestle. Put the spice paste and everything for the curry except the basil and the beef into a saucepan and heat just to boiling. Add the beef. Lower the heat and simmer uncovered for about two hours, stirring frequently. Cook until most of the liquid evaporates and the beef is tender enough to start falling apart. Remove the lemongrass. Serve with the rice, topped with basil or cilantro.

CHAPTER 19

BON TRAVAIL

LESSON HIGHLIGHTS: PIGS' TROTTERS, PUFF-PASTRY WITH TUNA,
AND SHOPPING FOR WEDDING RINGS IN PARIS

Like many women, I started thinking about my wedding when I was a little girl playing with my friend's Beautiful Bride Barbies. As a thirty-six-year-old bride-to-be, I've had a *lot* of time to think about it.

On an impulse while walking in place Vendôme, Mike and I go into Cartier to try on rings. Inside, we immediately know we're out of our depth. My hands are ragged from cuts and burns, my nails heavy with the residue of chipped pink polish.

"I'm in cooking school . . . ." I start to explain to the well-coiffed, perfumed saleswoman. Just then, my elbow tips my purse, splaying the contents onto the Persian rug. Pens, tampons, receipts, a vegetable peeler, and a fortune in coins fly out. I drop to my hands and knees. "Oh, I'm so sorry, really . . . ." As I sit back on the silk-covered wing-backed chair, I say, "I can't believe I've done this in Cartier."

The coiffed woman looks like she's just been hit with a bucket of icewater. "This *isn't* Cartier," she sniffs in reply. "They're next door."

We're feeling the time crunch. We don't have rings, and with only two months to our wedding I have no time to order a dress. I see a sign for a Wedding Dress Expo in the Twentieth arrondissement, so I spend forty-five minutes on the Métro getting there. The "Expo" is a run-down wedding-dress shop. But what the hell, maybe they sell off the rack.

"Vous pouvez en essayer quatre à la fois seulement," a severe-looking woman says, standing protectively in front of a rack of dresses.

I'm too flustered to know how to respond.

"Pourquoi?" Why can I try on only four dresses? Does she think I'm a crazy American tourist who flits around unfashionable Paris neighborhoods trying on wedding dresses for fun?

She simply crosses her arms. "Quatre." It's four or nothing. My French isn't good enough to argue. I select four, while madame fusses over another customer—a French woman on whom she has imposed no limit. But I overhear their conversation and realize it's all pointless. She tells her *belle cliente* that none of the dresses is available for purchase; each must be made to order.

These are far from the worst issues.

The Fourth of July has become a big holiday on Anna Maria Island. Locals swarm to the beach in droves to shoot off illegal fireworks and to watch offshore boat races. When we try to find a hotel to put up our fifty or so expected guests, we find that *everything* is booked. Mike spends hours on the phone scrounging up a few rooms here, a couple of rooms there. We're lucky, though, to secure the castle house for two weeks. Mike comes up with an idea. He'll invite his best friend's family to stay with us there. After all, they are the reason we chose this date.

We have our first big fight.

"There's only ONE real bathroom in that house!" I yell at him. "Can't you understand, I don't want to share a bathroom with seven people on my wedding day?!"

"You're overreacting, Kat. There are two bathrooms," Mike says.

"The whole point of renting the castle house was to spend our wedding night there! So you're fine having three kids in the room next to ours watching late-night TV while we consummate our marriage?"

It escalates. I complain about everything to him, not the least that I feel rushed to the altar, resulting in chaos. I turn into Bridezilla.

"We have NO PLACE to have the reception! We have NO PLACE to have a rehearsal dinner. I have NO DRESS! We have NO RINGS! We're sending out invitations that neither of us have EVEN SEEN!"

I run into the bedroom, slamming the door behind me. I hear something break.

I sheepishly walk out into the living room. We search for what's broken, both of us thinking of Arturo and our small fortune in security deposit. The argument is forgotten.

I am blaming the kindest man I know for trying to be thoughtful of his best friend. I am blaming him, too, for things that are not his fault.

"I'm sorry," I say, and I mean it. We see what's broken: a souvenir ashtray my sister forgot to pack to take home. We breathe a sigh of relief.

The Saturday after the buffet, I review the remaining ten lessons for Intermediate Cuisine. Among them is another featuring puff pastry. I head down to rue Montorgueil and pack my collapsible shopping cart with two heavy bags of flour, dry butter, and fresh yeast. Mike lugs them up the stairs to our flat. For the next three days, I make no less than six batches of puff pastry. By the fourth batch, it's light, airy, and flaky. I work slowly and methodically, remembering that you cannot rush puff pastry. You must show it respect, like a person you admire. Showing remarkable restraint, I eat none of it, so that I can fit into a wedding dress, if I ever find one.

Back in school, I hear that the Gray Chef scolded the students who didn't help set up for the buffet. Like me, they felt slighted that they weren't asked to cook. So they skipped it altogether. But L.P. saw the whole thing differently.

"It was a test," she says, and one that only I passed. "Wait and see."

Today, we're studying Auvergne, the coldest region in France, says the Gray Chef, with the oldest mountains in Europe. Those mountains were once active volcanoes, and as a result this is an area of high yet especially fertile plateaus loaded with volcanic soil. The hearty people of the Auvergne eat a whole lot of pork and stick-to-the-ribs food.

Chef demonstrates pigs' trotters glazed with foie gras on toast. Pigs' trotters are exactly what they sound like. They aren't bad if you can get over the idea, and find the flavor of ham hocks studded with meaty gelatin appealing. In our practical, we make cabbage stuffed with veal, pork, and bread-crumb *panade* that's then braised in veal stock studded with slab bacon. We also start a batch of puff pastry.

The next day, we study Côte d'Azur, the southern, beachy edge of Provence, one of the warmest places in France and famous for its intense Mediterranean influences. Chef demonstrates *galette feuilletée au thon mariné,* a puff pastry topped with marinated tuna. Although not an especially complicated dish, the recipe calls for precision cuts. The tuna must be sliced to a specific thickness, then marinated and broiled to an exact degree. The whole thing is assembled like a pizza—glistening green, black, and red vegetables are slathered on the pastry, the tuna set gently on top. A garlic-basil dressing is drizzled across to finish.

The Gray Chef prowls the kitchen during the practical. He used to ignore me. This day, he offers a friendly "Ça va, ma petite amie?" midway through class.

"Bien, Chef, et vous?" I say.

He nods and inspects my vegetable cuts. "Bon travail."

Wait, the Gray Chef said I was doing "good work"? Huh.

I finish my pastry. Before I begin, I pay attention to my hands. They feel warm. I wash them in cold water to cool them down and then dry them carefully. I've learned to make this pastry by touch. Is it getting too warm? Is it sticking to the counter? Has the butter been absorbed enough? After the final turn, it should feel velvety. This time, it does. I roll it out to an almost perfect rectangle and place it on a piece of parchment atop a heavy baking plaque. To keep it from rising too much, I top it with a cooling rack for the first fifteen minutes. In the end, the pastry's light, airy, and golden.

I slice a square and work quickly to top it with the vegetables, the still-warm tuna slices, and the dressing. My plate is warm. I put an olive and a cross of tomatoes on the four sides with the tiniest drizzle of sauce. I take it to the Gray Chef.

Without comment, he cuts off a small bite of the pastry with a spoon. He tastes the vegetables and the tuna and the dressing, examining each carefully.

"Meeze Fleen," he says, putting down his small spoon with a flourish, "excellent, non, c'est parfait." It's perfect. He smiles at me and first shakes my hand, then on second thought throws his arm around my shoulders. He calls over Chef Savard, who is preparing for a demonstration next door. "Regardez cette assiette."

Chef Savard looks at my plate and smiles. "Chef Gaillard kept saying he knew you had it in you," he says. "He just wanted you to find it yourself."

Is there anything more satisfying than pleasing your hardest critic? I can't think of it. I feel like crying again in this kitchen, but for wildly different reasons than before.

That night, I look online for a wedding dress, sifting through dozens until I spot a simple A-line dress with a detachable train. I show it to Mike. At once he says, "That's it." The dress will be shipped to my mother's house a week before I arrive. If I don't like it, the seller will overnight another one.

One thing down, and seemingly a hundred other details to fix. But damn it, if I can master puff pastry, we can plan a wedding in another country in seven weeks.

Galette Feuilletée à la Ceviche de Thon

PUFF-PASTRY "CAKE" WITH TUNA CEVICHE

Eight to ten appetizer servings

This is not a cake but rather a flat pastry smothered with the flavorful Provençal tomato spread from chapter 13, then topped with the tuna ceviche, sort of like an elegant, savory pizza. If you feel compelled to make your own puff pastry, consider using Julia Child's recipe from *Mastering the Art of French Cooking, Volume II*. At school, we broiled the tuna in the oven. Here, it's "cooked" in lemon and lime juice *à la* ceviche. If desired, forgo the puff pastry and serve on toasted baguette slices. Directions for concassé—peeled, seeded, and finely chopped tomatoes—can be found in "Extra Recipes" at the back of the book. I serve this as a plated appetizer with a brut sparkling wine or a hearty Chablis.

CEVICHE

1 pound (500 g) ahi tuna, cut into small cubes

½ medium red onion, finely diced

2 medium tomatoes, *concassé* (1 cup)

1 or 2 cloves garlic, finely chopped

2 teaspoons coarse sea salt

Ground pepper, to taste

Tabasco, cayenne, or red pepper flakes to taste

Pinch of ground oregano

1 cup (30 g) fresh chopped basil

½ cup (125 ml) fresh squeezed lime juice

½ cup (125 ml) fresh squeezed lemon juice

1 sheet prepared puff pastry

1 recipe Provençal tomato spread (see page 133)

In a nonreactive casserole dish, preferably glass, or in a gallon-sized zipbag, combine the tuna, onion, tomatoes, garlic, salt, pepper, Tabasco, oregano, and ¾ cup of chopped basil. Cover with lime and lemon juice. Let sit covered in the refrigerator for an hour, and then stir to ensure all the fish comes into contact with the marinade. Let rest for about six hours. Fish should appear white and cooked.

When ready to prepare, preheat the oven to 350°F/180°C. Put the ceviche mix into a colander over a bowl, then return to the fridge for at least twenty minutes or the time it takes to bake the pastry. Roll out the puff pastry on a pastry sheet. Bake for about thirty minutes or until golden. When done, flatten slightly with a cooling rack, if available. Let cool slightly.

Spoon the Provençal tomato spread over the puff pastry, as on a pizza. Discard drained liquid from ceviche. Layer the tuna on top of the pastry. Add the remaining basil on top along with a few turns of fresh pepper on top.

CHAPTER 20

FINAL EXAM—INTERMEDIATE

LESSON HIGHLIGHTS: CASSOULET, CORSICAN STEW, AND A FINAL
BRUNCH WITH *LES FEMMES DU CORDON BLEU*

"In Southwest France, they eat the fat and foie gras, and you know
what? They have good, healthy hearts. No one can explain," Chef
Gaillard says via Anne, the translator. "Perhaps it is the red wine?"

Thus begins the lesson for cassoulet, one of our final recipes in Intermediate Cuisine. Chef Gaillard cranks the lid off an industrial-sized can of
La Marque de Roux brand duck confit. He plops its solid can-shaped mass
into a roasting pan, then shoves it into a low oven to melt the fat gently.
"And *voilà!*" the chef says, retrieving the pan later, nodding to the jumble
of beige legs settled atop an unholy pool of yellowish, oozing goo.

"The chef says that in Nice, he had a supplier who would deliver
whole ducks with the livers still intact," Anne tells us. The cooks rendered
the carcasses for fat and used it in cooking and to confit the legs, necks,
and wings. The breasts went into entrées, the bones into stocks. "They
used every bit of the duck. Nothing was wasted," she says.

Cassoulet derives its name from the use of the *casole,* an earthenware
pot typical of Castelnaudry, where the dish is thought to have originated
in the fifteenth century. "In France, there are strict rules about what can
go into cassoulet," Chef warns. Use anything other than white beans,

haricots, and it's no longer cassoulet. A gastronomical text of the 1960s decreed that the dish must contain at least 30 percent pork, lamb, goose, or duck; the addition of chicken or fish disqualified it as cassoulet.

A young British student in the front row raises his hand. "But I've had cassoulet with chicken," he says. "I had it at a French restaurant in London."

"You did not have cassoulet," retorts Anne, on the part of Chef Gaillard. The student doesn't argue.

Not surprisingly, Le Cordon Bleu's recipe for cassoulet adheres strictly to the classic requirements. Ours will be made from *haricots* and then packed with garlicky Toulouse sausage, braised lamb shank, salt pork, and duck confit. The only variation will be in the cooking time. "Really, it should cook for three or four hours," Chef says.

"Vous désirez une petite histoire?" he asks. *Do you want a little story? Oui, Chef,* we answer in unison.

"A few years ago, Chef Gaillard was head chef of one of the most famous restaurants in Paris," Anne translates. "He became a celebrity and was in magazines and on television. Then one day he asked his wife what she wanted for her birthday. 'To see you sometimes' she answered."

He nods at her translation. She continues, "Chef realized that he was spending too much time being a famous chef and not enough time with his wife. So he quit, and he joined Le Cordon Bleu." Joining the school meant more predictable hours, no 4:00 a.m. deliveries, and no more weekend nights overseeing busy dinner services.

"Je ne l'ai jamais regretté," says Chef Gaillard.

"Chef says that he's never regretted that decision," Anne translates.

"Maintenant, je peux vous transmettre tout ce que j'ai appris."

"Because now he has the chance to give back to you everything he's learned," Anne says, adding, "and I know that's more satisfying for him than running a famous kitchen."

It turns out to be the last story of Chef Gaillard's I will hear in a demonstration. He leaves the next day to teach at a Le Cordon Bleu school in Brazil. I used to fear him. Now, I miss him.

★ ★ ★

"So it's settled, we're coming to Paris," says the familiar posh accent. "Anna-Clare is going to stay with one of her friends, so can I stay with you? And, well, actually, can I bring a friend?" says LizKat.

Anna-Clare comes to one of our few Saturday demonstrations. "It's weird to be here," she whispers. She's the only one among us who isn't in a uniform. Instead, she's impeccably dressed in black, a Burberry scarf tied fashionably into a choker around her throat. "I feel like I'm going to get yelled at for wearing civilian clothes any minute now." It's a fairly standard class, featuring *cailles farcies aux raisins,* partially boned quail stuffed with a *farce* of foie gras, along with peeled grapes, one of several dishes we learn from the Vendée region, a sunny corner in western France.

The next day, we host a final brunch at our flat for LizKat and Anna-Clare. By popular demand, Sharon brings another round of her spaghetti bolognaise. Using a recipe from school, I make a wild mushroom tart. I toss an herb salad and whip up a strawberry vinaigrette. "Now don't give me a hard time about it being sweet," I instruct L.P., who is looking over my shoulder. "It's supposed to be sweet."

After lunch, we drink cold Chablis and from the kitchen window watch life down on the street. We talk about the details of the wedding, now mostly arranged thanks to Mike working nearly full-time to organize everything. In the last month, he's made accommodations for sixty guests, including his best friend's family. He spent days in London working with a jeweler to create my ring to his design. I shouldn't be surprised; he once oversaw the development of a worldwide Internet publishing platform, delivering it to thirty countries in just three months. I'm marrying a remarkable man.

"So when will you come back for Superior?" asks Sharon.

I shake my head. "Maybe this autumn, or in January," I say. It makes me sad to think of my friends in the kitchens without me. In the background, I hear the French radio station start to play the ubiquitous song "Those Were the Days."

> *. . . We thought they'd never end,*
> *We'd sing and dance forever and a day . . .*

As I look around the table, the scene fixes in my mind like a photo-graph. The pink sky of near sunset, the laughing faces of Sharon, Lely, LizKat, Anna-Clare, and L.P. All of us are from different countries, yet luck and circumstance brought us to this one moment, this slice of time sitting in a kitchen in Paris.

These *are* the days, I think. I wish they'd never end.

Sharon makes a toast. "As long as we can eat, let's always be friends."

"Yes, yes," agrees Lely. "Here's a toast to us, *les femmes du Cordon Bleu.*"

Of course, the moment we clink glasses, I think of all the people with whom I've promised to keep friendships yet haven't. I truly hope we will.

On the last day of Intermediate, the natives are restless. We are on the second floor for the demonstration again, with bright May sun cascading through the windows. There's an air of disorganization. John the stand-up comedian/translator is late. The lesson's slow to start. Few people take notes.

Chef Savard leads the demonstration on the cuisine of Corsica, the final region we'll study. As he begins the pork and chestnut stew, he admits that from a culinary standpoint Corsica isn't at the top of the pack.

"There's not much happening in Corsica in terms of French cuisine these days," John translates, adding, "but of course, it's basically Italy down there, so what do you expect? They're still getting over that Napoléon business."

Chef Savard says that during his reign, Napoléon helped the econ-omy of Corsica not only by sending money there but also by holding numerous banquets and receptions on a scale that's difficult to imagine now. "Très grandiose, énorme," Chef says. More than one hundred sheep roasted, thousands of pounds of beef and produce, and barrels of wine.

"Like the Cordon Bleus," John says.

At the end of class, *les femmes du Cordon Bleu* gather around the hand-some Chef Savard for a final photo.

"We're your fan club," says Lely. "And I'm the president!"

Later, we sit on the sidewalk drinking wine and sharpening our knives, chatting. No one wants to talk about good-bye. We want to pretend that we will come to school again tomorrow, all of us. Just then, the door swings open and a kitchen assistant leaks the two exam recipes: the lamb *navarin* or the complicated stuffed trout.

"Pray for the *navarin!*" advises Sharon, clasping her hands. "That trout was *impossible!*"

As I walk up to the assigned kitchen for the test, I slow to look closely at the picture of Julia Child on the wall. I think back to the promise I made myself about the short obituary—that my own would say that I graduated from Le Cordon Bleu, just like Julia. I do not want to break that promise to myself, but then, where will marriage lead me? Will Mike want to come back to Paris with me?

And then there's the one last major hurdle: in Superior Cuisine, there are *no* translators. Everything will be in French.

As it turns out, I get the trout. *Merde.*

Cassoulet

WHITE-BEAN CASSEROLE WITH PORK AND CONFIT

Serves eight

Adapted with permission from London-based chef Alex Mackay's excellent book, *Cooking in Provence,* this is a practical, one-dish version of cassoulet. You may substitute kielbasa or mild sweet Italian sausage for the garlicky Toulouse sausage. Prepared duck confit may be used, or make your own. (See "Extra Recipes" in the back of the book.) I use great northern or cannellini beans. In French homes, cassoulet is often served in its cooking pot, and guests cut or tear the meat off the bone. You can portion it into bowls, scraping the meat off the duck legs and lamb shanks before serving, if desired. Don't salt the dish until the end or your beans will stay tough. Splurge on a big French red such as Cahors, Languedoc, or even a Bordeaux.

10 ounces (300 g) thick slab bacon, cubed

1 pound (450 g) Toulouse sausages

Extra duck or bacon fat (as needed)

2 large lamb shanks

1 pound (450g) onions, chopped

2 medium carrots, peeled and chopped

1 pound (450 g) dried white beans, soaked overnight and drained

1 14-ounce can tomatoes, drained and chopped (2 cups)

1 tablespoon tomato paste

4 garlic cloves, minced

2 to 3 cups (680 ml) brown chicken stock

1 bouquet garni (bay leaf and thyme sprigs tied together)

2 duck confit legs

Salt, fresh cracked black pepper

1 cup (about 115 g) coarse fresh bread crumbs

Preheat oven to a low 225°F/110°C. In a large Dutch oven, slowly render the bacon until lightly browned. Remove meat from pot and set aside. Cook the sausages slowly in the fat until lightly browned. Remove, cut into bite-sized pieces, and set aside. Add or remove fat to get three tablespoons in the bottom of the pan; brown the lamb shanks on all sides in the fat over medium-high. Remove and set aside. Turn heat to medium-low, add the onions and carrots, and cook until softened and translucent. Add the beans, tomatoes, tomato paste, and garlic and bring to a boil, stirring, until the tomatoes start to caramelize, scraping the browned bits from the bottom. Add the lamb shanks, bacon, and sausages back to pot. Wet the beans with just enough stock to cover them, and add the bouquet garni. Bring just to the verge of a boil. Cover and cook in the oven for two hours, making sure the liquid doesn't get hot enough to boil.

Add the duck confit and cook for another hour or until the beans are soft but not breaking and the lamb-shank meat nearly falls off the bone. For a creamier texture, about a half hour after adding the confit remove about two cups of beans and puree with a bit of warm stock; return to the pan. Check the seasoning, adding hearty amounts of salt and pepper. Top with the bread crumbs and continue baking uncovered until lightly golden, about fifteen minutes.

PART III

❧

SUPERIOR CUISINE

"I am not young enough to know everything."

—Oscar Wilde

CLASS BREAK: NORMANDY, THEN AMERICA

My exam over, we have a week before our plane leaves France. We have no plans, but we do have a standing invitation to visit friends of Theo's, who run a chateau in Normandy.

"Let's just go," Mike says.

Picking up a car in central Paris is a unique experience, requiring a descent under L'Église de la Madeleine, the neoclassical church in the Eighth arrondissement designed as a temple to the glory of Napoléon's army. Under the monument, we wander through a labyrinth of garages until we find the Avis counter.

"That's not a car, it's a go-kart," I say to Mike when I see what he's rented. The Smart Roadster Coupe is a tiny sports car designed by Swatch but made by Mercedes-Benz. The roof comes only to the door handles of the Mini Cooper parked next to it. It has a trunk the size of most glove compartments. Somehow we squeeze our luggage in and get on the highway driving north. We are a speed bump to the trucks next to us.

Château de Saint-Paterne is a sixteenth-century estate owned by Charles-Henry and his wife, Ségolène. It's a massive structure, like a palace in the movies, carefully decorated in French country elegance. As they give us a tour, we run into their three-year-old boy drawing at the kitchen table. Charles-Henry reaches in the fridge and hands him a thick wedge of Camembert, and the little boy takes a big bite. "Eat your cheese. That's my good Norman boy!" says his father.

The tour finishes, and we settle down for some wine. Both Mike and I comment on the massive mirror above the medieval fireplace. It has hung there for more than a century, through two occupations, first by Nazi soldiers and later by Allied troops.

"We removed the mirror for the first time last year, to repair that wall," Charles-Henry says. Part of the "repair" was to fix leftover bullet holes. "It took several men to take it down! You know what we found? Signatures and messages from hundreds of Nazi soldiers. They had written notes in German to family, to loved ones."

They preserved the wall, left the writing intact, and hung the mirror back up.

"Are you heading up to the celebration?" Charles-Henry asks. The sixtieth anniversary of the D-Day landings will take place in a few days.

"Sure, why not?" Mike and I say in unison, nodding to each other.

Leaving Saint-Paterne with the top of our snazzy sports car down, we wind along the coastline. Finally, we stop for the night to take in the luster of the posh seaside resort at Deauville. Taking Charles-Henry's advice, we find a hotel in the less luxurious sister town of Trouville. Our room is high up in a 1960s-style hotel overlooking the casino. Done in old Vegas style, the casino's sign is emblazoned with American and French flags lit in colored incandescent bulbs.

The next morning, Mike pulls our zippy little black car to the door to pick me up.

"That's some car," says one of two aging gentlemen as we try to stuff our carry-on–sized bag into the trunk. An oxygen line runs under his nose. Mike asks if he wants to take it for a spin.

"Oh, no, with these old bones, I wouldn't be able to get out!" He's in town for the D-Day celebrations. Mike, the pilot, notices the wings and a Canadian flag pin on the man's jacket. On D-Day, this man had squeezed himself into the tiny cockpit of a Horsa glider full of British troops, on a one-way mission behind the German front line. He had been nineteen.

"He's getting an award from Prince Charles today," his friend brags. "You know, he was one of the men who took the Pegasus Bridge."

The man with the wings waves dismissively. "We all took that bridge," he says. "All the boys did. I wasn't the best pilot; I just did the best I could that day."

I think of Jovina and her fiancé in Iraq.

We arrive next at Mont St. Michel, the imposing gothic medieval castle of a monastery settled on a quasi-island off the northwest coast of France. When the tides come in, the Mont is cut off from the mainland and thus protected by a natural moat. The beauty of the place, thick with crowds of tourists, is compromised by the gauntlet of relentless kitsch that must be navigated through on the island's single, twisting lane to the top. Mike told me he'd originally planned to propose here. "I liked the proposal in Barcelona just fine," I tell him, eyeing a magnet that says, in English, "My cat loves Mont St. Michel."

On the morning of June 6, we make our way to Omaha Beach along the same route General George Patton used to lead his troops during the invasion. A mass of people walk alongside the road, thousands of men, women, and children, most of them French. Somehow, we end up in a convoy of vintage jeeps, their occupants all wearing wartime garb.

"These are the vehicles left behind from the landing," Mike tells me. "The locals keep them in shape to retrace the route each year, for the same reason people walk the road on the anniversary of the landings."

Driving along the hedgerows, we pass an ancient stone house where an old woman holds bunches of small American, English, and Canadian flags in her hands and waves them wildly. For a moment, surrounded by the jeeps, it feels as if we have been swept back in time. Sixty years ago, this was real. I wonder if that woman was here. She would have been just a child then. She may have seen real troops pass by, struggling and fighting in the places where she used to play. I think of Chef Gaillard, and how he was disappointed that the war changed the landscape and legacy of Normandy. How wonderful it would be to know it only for the cheese and Calvados. All those years ago, the jeeps around us carried men like the one we met in Deauville. So young, yet so many lie in graves here. They weren't just men who left home one day and never came back—they were sons, fathers, brothers, fiancés, and husbands.

Husbands. Mike will soon be mine. I say a small prayer. "I lost my father early, God. Isn't only fair that I should keep my husband for a long time?"

Finally, we arrive at Omaha Beach. It's dark, and we join the thousands who had been walking the route with us. We stand along the crescent beach with our feet in the cold waters of the English Channel as synchronized fireworks erupt over each of the landing points.

Just one month later, on the Fourth of July, we stand again on a crescent-shaped beach, this one in Florida. My mother stands beside me, Mike's father beside him, in our simple wedding ceremony. Under another set of fireworks, Mike and I dance in the powder-soft sand for the first time as man and wife. Our song drifts along the beach, echoing the word "forever" that once scared us both.

"*Amado Mio,* love me forever, and let forever begin tonight. . . ."

CHAPTER 21

BACK IN BLEU

LESSON HIGHLIGHTS: FISH WITH INDIAN SPICES, THE DANGERS
OF A BROKEN HEART, MOVING TO BELLEVILLE

As promised, I'm back in Paris. But I'm alone.

Mike and I planned to return to France together, move into the apartment on rue Étienne Marcel, and pick up where we left off. But of course, life doesn't always follow the recipe.

Not content with his other dangerous pastimes of driving motorcycles and flying small planes, Mike decided to take up paragliding, a sport where you fly off mountains with a high-tech parachute wing. A good friend of Mike's who has great passion for the sport took him on as one of his first students.

Two weeks before I am to leave for France, I get a call from Mike.

"How did the flying go today?" I ask.

"Well, I had a good flight, but the landing wasn't so great," he says. "Hakan is taking me to the hospital to get checked out. I'll see you tonight."

My heart dropped a bit, but the problem sounded minor.

I had no idea.

It had been a perfect day for flying, the blue sky dotted with paragliding wings resembling bright-colored jellyfish floating high above Tiger

Mountain, outside Seattle. Although many beginning paragliders learn there, it's a technically challenging place to fly.

"You're going to do fine," his instructor reassures Mike as he prepares for only his second flight off the launch. "Just do exactly what I say, and you'll soar."

Mike hooks into his red, white, and blue wing, checks his harness, then inflates the giant kite above him, his wing gently lifting him into the sky. In the air, it's quiet, with the mountain behind him and a forest of dense old-growth cedars below.

"Fly back toward the mountain," Mike hears on his radio, so he obediently makes a 180-degree turn. As he turns he sees he is perilously close to the mountain and struggles to turn away. But he finds himself caught up in what paragliders refer to as a "downwind demon," a ferocious tailwind that has caught his wing, hurling him toward the mountainside and a patch of dense 150-foot-high trees.

His wing catches the treetops, and he plummets through the tall cedars, grasping at branches as the sharp limbs rip his cloth wing to shreds. He lands hard on his back. Checking his legs and arms, he's amazed that nothing seems broken. As he lies stunned and breathless, his radio crackles.

"So are you on the ground?" he hears his instructor say. "Was the landing a thing of beauty?"

Mike answers, "Yeah, I'm on the ground, and it was something. . . ."

"Where are you?" asks his instructor.

Mike doesn't know. The sun is setting quickly, and he is deep under a canopy of dense forest in a state park with no roads or trails, just steep, treacherous hills. He stuffs the pieces of the wing into its bag and hikes down, keeping an eye out for bears, cougars, and other animals that lurk in the woods there, fully aware that it will soon be too dark for him to navigate, and he'll be left hopelessly lost with no way for anyone to find him. After two hours, he hears a dog bark and goes toward it, emerging in someone's backyard. As he waits for his friends to retrieve him, the surge of endorphins and adrenaline wears off, and Mike realizes something is wrong.

Soon, he's admitted to the cardiac care unit. I rush to the hospital.

"Mrs. Klozar?" the doctor asks. I almost don't respond—no one has ever called me that. "Your husband is lucky to be alive." He explains that the fall broke Mike's sternum, but, worse, he has a traumatic aortic injury caused by a contusion to the aorta wall. They need to keep him in the CCU for observation.

"His aorta is scraped, and if it ruptures he could bleed to death internally in minutes," the doctor says. "So we'll keep him here for seventy-two hours."

Just then, a counselor approaches me and touches my arm. "I'm sorry, Mrs. Klozar, does your husband have a living will? We need that." She hands me brochures about do-not-resuscitate orders and medical directives. I hide them in my purse.

I walk into the room in a daze, not knowing what to expect. I see his friend Hakan standing next to Mike's instructor, their faces white with worry. But Mike looks like himself, except he's accessorized by an IV and a host of monitoring machines.

"I guess my landings need a little work," he says to me, joking. It's so Mike. I sit on the bed and hold his hand. I'm trying to hold back tears again. "I'm sorry about this, Kat."

"Well, I did say I would stick around for better or for worse," I tell him.

But this is worse. It is the longest weekend of my life. When I go home that night, I don't have to search for his living will. The envelope from the lawyer with our updated man-and-wife documents arrived just a couple days earlier. I open it and look at his living will, signed with his neat signature. This is not supposed to happen to newlyweds.

When he finally arrives home, I don't want to go to Paris. He's in agony sitting up or lying down. But he insists that I go.

"I'll be there in three weeks," he assures me.

It's a sweltering day in late August when I return to Paris. Heat rises from the sidewalks in great waves of steam. Everywhere, the hot air presses my skin like in a sauna. I pull a mighty suitcase up the escalator at Les Halles train station and head down the familiar side street toward rue Étienne Marcel.

The Italians who own the apartment took up residence over the summer and plan to stay until the end of September, so it will not be ours again until then.

An elegant, thin man wearing a beautiful sage-green silk shirt and a well-kept goatee answers the door. "Buon giorno, bonjour, Kath-a-leen-uh!" he says. "I'm Niccolò," he adds, pronouncing it in a way that only Italian can. Then he looks around.

"Where is-a Mike?" he asks.

My throat still clenches at the question. I had second thoughts all the way up to the departure gate at the airport and beyond. When I landed at Charles de Gaulle, I debated getting on another plane and heading straight back to Seattle.

"Um, he had an accident," I say. "But he'll be all right. I know he will."

Niccolò looks genuinely concerned. He offers to tug my luggage up to the fourth floor.

Unlike horrible Arturo, the owners Alberto and Niccolò turn out be charming, thoughtful hosts who can't do enough for me. They ply me with fresh espresso and melon slices, and there's not a single mention of Nescafé. They smile constantly, almost beaming. Alberto has huge, expressive brown eyes and a propensity to talk with his hands. Yet everything about him is graceful, from his chic, fawn-colored silk shirt with brown linen trousers to the way he crosses his legs when he sits.

For the month of September, they've offered us rental of another apartment they've just acquired as an investment, a pied-à-terre in Belleville, on the eastern edge of Paris. It's about an hour-long commute to Le Cordon Bleu, one requiring three separate Métro lines. But if it means that eventually we'll be back on Étienne-Marcel, it's worth it.

The Italians help me pack my bags into a taxi and head to Belleville. I've never been to this part of town. As the taxi navigates onto its main drag, my impression is that this is an area that feels like it's willfully resisted gentrification.

The edges of the Nineteenth, Twentieth, Tenth, and Eleventh arrondissements come together at a point here. It's a notable metaphor, as Belleville is a mixed neighborhood, serving as home to mostly poor denizens of former French colonies in Africa, Asia, and the Caribbean. Their presence and poverty strike me as the unforeseen residue of France's flings with imperialism. When they were busy taking on colonies, they didn't consider the implications. Today the government struggles to cope with the offspring of the people they conquered, not in some faraway land but as a marginalized populace in their own country.

For now, all I can take in are the Chinese, Arabic, and Vietnamese signs hovering above a variety of shops, often next to boarded-up storefronts and in scruffy buildings, some of which have been hit with fits of graffiti. Once in Belleville, we turn down rue Rambuteau and get out of the taxi. The apartment is in a building that houses the local police station, now closed for renovation. The street itself is notable for ending at the *butte* of Parc de Belleville, the second-highest point in Paris, after Montmartre.

"You knowuh, Edith Piaf was a leetle girluh aroundhuh the corner from here-uh," Niccolò says as he tugs my suitcase up the five flights of stairs, the stairwell a patchwork of plaster in various states of repair. Then, he and Alberto open the door.

Like Étienne Marcel, this apartment carries their elegant stamp. Although small, no part of the 350 square feet has been wasted. Gilded paintings of the last emperor and empress of China flank a smart, slip-covered sofa. There's a gleaming antique desk, a deep-hued oriental rug, built-in bookcases, closets, and cabinets with exquisite molding. The bed is built into the wall under a shelf, making it appear more daybed than bed; it pulls out at night to reveal a full mattress. Four traditional French windows flank either side of the apartment, bathing it in light.

"It's beautiful," I say, and we exchange hugs before they leave.

There's no phone in the apartment. But I have my French mobile phone from our last trip and call Mike.

"Hi, handsome," I say. It is hard to keep my voice light.

"So there is one good thing about the accident," Mike says. "Now I'll be here to go to James and Amy's wedding." The friends who had gotten into that dreadful fight on Valentine's Day had made up and set their wedding date for two weeks after the beginning of Superior Cuisine. I'll miss it, but Mike and his broken heart will be there.

Diego is the only one of my classmates still in Paris. He's working two nights a week at a Michelin-starred restaurant, finding odd catering jobs, and asking his parents for occasional doses of cash. It's his birthday, so he comes over to pick me up and go out for a drink. We debate options and head to the Marais.

"This is sort of a tough neighborhood," he says as we walk toward the Belleville Métro. We pass the skeleton of a bike, obviously once set on fire. It's still chained to a metal signpost. "Are you sure you want to live here?"

As I turn onto rue Léon Delhomme, I feel a stab of nostalgia. I look at the stoop where the world's smartest homeless man used to sit and wonder about him. I enter the familiar doors and start to walk past the front desk. Then, I hear a voice.

"Kathleen! Well, hello!" Anne the translator smiles broadly and comes around the desk. "Back for Superior Cuisine? Did you get married?" I nod affirmatively to both questions. "Excellent," she says, "You're going to enjoy this part."

"Being married or Superior Cuisine?" I ask.

She laughs. "Both, I'd expect."

I think about those horrific seventy-two hours at the hospital but say nothing.

Since I've taken a break from school, Le Cordon Bleu requests that I attend orientation again. This time, the group is smaller, about sixty-five students packed into the upstairs demonstration room, the one with the windows. There's no Japanese translator. It feels less formal.

In such a short time, many things have changed. The previous administrator retired, soon to be replaced by the director of the Ottawa school. They've added a written test. Uniforms and equipment shifted, too. In my Basic class, the school distributed heavy-gauge Mundial brand blue-handled knives. Now, they use Le Cordon Bleu brand Wüsthof knives. Another assistant, this time a fragile-boned Taiwanese woman, is brought in to model the uniform. As with every *Star Trek* movie, the uniform has been updated. It now sports an attractive blue piping on the jackets, and the more traditional bib-style apron has been replaced with one that starts at the waist. I'll look out of place in my old gear, I think.

Halfway through, they ask everyone to introduce themselves, in either French or English, and state what they're studying. As I watch the introductions, I notice a thin woman with a bob of shoulder-length dyed-red hair leaning against the door, dressed in a simple yet expensive-looking blue linen dress. She says that her name is Margo and that's she's American and returning to study Superior Cuisine. Then, it's my turn.

"Je suis Kathleen, et j'habite à Seattle aux États-Unis," I say. If everything's going to be in French, I might as well start now. "Je retourne pour étudier la cuisine supérieure."

Anne smiles at me, nodding, and then translates into English for the class.

"Kathleen lives in Seattle in the United States, and she's returned to study Superior Cuisine." Oh, how ironic to have my French translated into English. As she does, I feel something curious. I can feel someone staring. I turn to see Margo's narrowed eyes on me.

We head downstairs to pick up our various course binders. After I grab mine, I head to République to a small Alsatian place, Chez Jenny, not far from the Métro. There is no point in going to the empty apartment. But as everywhere, there's a discomfort to dining alone. All around me, couples or groups laugh together. I've forgotten what this is like. When a single woman dines out by herself, she must have props. Thankfully, I have my binder from school. As I study, sipping a light Riesling and waiting for my parchment-wrapped trout with mushrooms, I marvel at the recipes in between interruptions from the solicitous waiter. Odd fusion dishes mingle with almost painfully correct French cuisine. Deep-fried grapes, shrimp with coconut and lemongrass, and terrines made from foie gras. Is this really the curriculum? When I don't find even one recipe with meat-stuffed meat, I can't wait to get started.

My first day begins in the dark, with a wake-up call from Mike.

"Time to wake up, sweetheart," he says gently. I ask about his recovery. He assures me that he's getting better every day. "Only a couple of weeks, and I'll be there."

My commute to Le Cordon Bleu from here is a different experience; coming in from the working-class neighborhoods on the city's outskirts this early in the morning offers a more intimate glimpse of Parisian humanity. Not all the women are thin, the men are not all well dressed, and they share a universal expression of fatigue. As we dip farther into the city, toward the more fashionable neighborhoods, the clothes improve; the women get thinner, with more stylish haircuts and impressive shoes.

By the time I get to the Vaugirard Métro, it's light outside. I stop at a small market for a crêpe. Lonely for Mike, I order his favorite, banana and Nutella.

Lesson one of Superior Cuisine meets on the second floor. My class comprises just twenty-eight students. Most of them are young and form a tight-knit clique – like *les femmes du Cordon Bleu* once were comrades, bonded in the trenches of culinary school. Now, I'm an outsider.

Four of us are wearing the last year's uniforms. Birds of a feather, we find one another. One is Margo, who has already commandeered the middle seat in the front row. Next, there's Jenny, another American, whose husband has been dispatched to Paris for two years with his company. The last is Isabella, a beautiful girl with soft brown eyes and long hair. Her accent sounds South American.

"Come sit with us," Margo says. She immediately starts a gentle interrogation, smiling and nodding at my answers. Had I worked as a professional cook? When did I study? Did I remember my class ranking?

Then, Chef Dominic DuPont begins. "La cuisine, c'est la sensibilité," he says. Cuisine is sensitivity, as opposed to pâtisserie, which is more about science.

No translator. Just me, my brain, and whatever I can muster in French. I have dreaded this moment. I'm surprised to find that it's not as difficult as I had feared.

Cooking has its own language, one that I've learned by osmosis via the recipes we've studied so far. Chefs require quick words to describe complex processes in the kitchen. When the chef says he'll *concassé* the tomatoes, that one word describes the entire process of peeling, seeding, and roughly chopping the tomatoes. *"Nappé"* means that I should reduce a sauce and cook it, thickening if necessary, until it can coat the back of a spoon. *"Mise en place"* means all the ingredients are prepared and ready to combine up to the point of cooking. Every culinary student understands mirepoix as the combination of diced carrots, onions, and celery. Most Americans grow up thinking *"gratiné"* means "topped with cheese," but it actually means "lightly browned." I've internalized common verbs, such as *"couper,"* to cut, *"bouillir,"* to boil and *"cuire,"* to cook.

As he pats red spices on the back of a fillet of fish, Chef holds up his spice-colored fingers. "Le garagiste, il travaille avec ses mains; le boulanger, il travaille avec ses mains," he says. "La cuisine c'est un métier manuel: on travaille avec ses mains."

It's OK to use your hands in the kitchen. A mechanic works with his hands; the baker works with his hands. In the kitchen, it's a manual trade, so it's all right to use your hands, as long as they're clean. I'm so pleased and proud that I follow him—until I lose him minutes later, when he wanders off on a tangent about fish markets.

I glance at my digital recorder and make a note of the time. Technically, we're not allowed to make audio- or videotapes of the class. (Fear that perhaps we'll sell copies on the black market?) But I notice that I am not alone; several students have some kind of audio recorder. If I miss some French, I can go back tonight, download it on my laptop, and listen to it over and over until I understand.

The list of ingredients seems long for *effeuillée de Saint-Pierre aux épices rouges,* or a fish known as John Dory with tandoori spices. Forget the simple chicken and cream sauce from Basic. This calls for filleting a fish and making a sauce, two side dishes, and three complicated garnishes.

I head up to our kitchen, the *grand salon,* on the second floor. I've worked in this kitchen, the largest of the cuisine kitchens at Le Cordon Bleu, only twice. With ten students in a kitchen meant for fourteen, it feels luxurious compared to the cramped kitchens I was used to earlier. I take one corner near the dishwashing station, graced by a small window. I can see people walking on rue Léon Delhomme below. I set out my gear, now bolstered by gifts from friends: a heavy eight-inch Wüsthof chef's knife, a fillet knife, and a quart-sized tub to hold a dozen spoons for tasting. Jenny sets up in the space across from me and Margo beside her. Isabella stands to my left. *"Dahrling,"* she purrs. "Do you mind if I work next to you?"

Then, in walks Chef Gaillard. His face lights with recognition.

"Ça va, mon amie?" he asks, wrapping an arm around my shoulder. I'm genuinely pleased to see him, too.

"Bien, Chef, et vous?"

"Comme ci, comme ça," he says. Not bad.

To start, we must fillet the John Dory, which the French refer to as a Saint Pierre, or St. Peter. The name derives from the dark blotches on either side of the fish, supposedly the imprint of St. Peter's thumb as he took a piece of money from its mouth. To me, the fish looks like a mean, grumpy old man. Not that I'm rebuking the biblical account, but I'm not clear just how St. Peter got around this thing's spiky fins. At the top, they look like a crazy man's hair, except they're razor sharp; on the bottom, the fins look like a ragged goatee, except far more lethal.

Chef Gaillard tells us that we're to split each fish between two people. I offer to fillet the fish. "Be my guest," says Jenny. "I don't want to go near that thing."

I cover my cutting board with parchment and set the fish on top. Carefully, I cut behind the gills with my new, ultra-sharp knife and then guide it along the backbone. It's a small battle, as I try to artfully tug and release the dense meat from the bones.

Chef Gaillard, prowling the kitchen, stops at my station. He peers over my shoulder, hands behind his back.

"Bien," he says, and moves on to another student. "Non, non. Vous perdez trop de poisson," he says, exasperated. *You're wasting too much fish.*

On to the sauce. I whack the hell out of the fish carcass with a cleaver. I've heated a fish fumet sent upstairs from the basement. The hot fumet smells slightly sour. "Yuck," I think before dropping my fish bones into the pot. When I taste the liquid, it is very fishy and . . . what is that? *Salt.* I dilute it with water, then add sliced mango and papaya. After a while, I taste again. The salt has diminished, and the fumet is now soft with the flavor of fruit.

Then, I remember the rice.

I opened my eyes wide in disbelief when I first saw the famous orange box of Uncle Ben's brand wild rice. I added water and slid the rice into the oven and forgot all about it. Now I rush to the oven and confirm I've cooked the hell out of it. *Merde.*

I'm a Superior student vying for a diploma from Le Cordon Bleu, and I can't cook rice? What will Chef say? I add a brick of butter and some water and set it aside, hoping it will soften.

I season the fish and sear it in hot oil. As it cooks, I finish the sauce, adding fresh cilantro. We've also had to sauté spinach, an odd addition, and candy limes by cooking them in water with sugar. I'm not crazy about the limes. They're fussy work, and in the end they still taste bitter to me.

Finally, I'm done. I contemplate the presentation. I know Chef Gaillard likes a simple plate. I know he also doesn't like too large a portion. On the other end of the table, I hear him say of Margo's plate: "Joli, mais c'est trop de poisson." *It's pretty, but too much fish.* I carefully taste everything again as I heat my plate. I take my rice—still hard and overcooked—and mold a small amount into a ring in the center. I ladle some sauce in two crescents on either side. As I start to top the rice with the spinach, I realize the spinach is too oily. I grab a sieve, throw the spinach into it, and press hard with a paper towel. Then, I assemble it on the plate atop the sauce and then gently add a piece of the reddened fish. I top it with minced cilantro and place the limes slices around the edge.

I present it to Chef Gaillard. "Bien," he says of the presentation. *Good.* He takes a small plastic spoon and tastes everything, digging under the fish to taste the rice. He hands me the small spoon. "Goûtez," he says, his face unchanged. *Taste.*

I taste it. "Trop sec, Chef," I say. It's too dry, and I know it. We banter for a couple of minutes. The sauce has good flavor, while other students' were too salty. The salty fumet, I think; in a week, the new basement team will know better. The spinach is good.

What's the most difficult part of the recipe, he asks? The fish, I say. He nods.

He deems my fish cooked perfectly. "Bien, bon travail," he says, and shakes my hand. "Re-bienvenue, ma petite amie." *Welcome back, my little friend.*

Something remarkable happened—I understood everything he said.

But no matter the critique, there's still a missing ingredient. I can't take my day's work home to Mike, to share with a bottle of wine. I never realized that for me, sharing with him has been an integral part of my education.

Filet de Bar au Lait de Coco et Épices Douces

SEA BASS WITH COCONUT MILK AND ORIENTAL SPICE SAUCE

Serves four

My Brazilian friend, Isabella, developed this using Colombo, a type of curry popular in the stews of West Indian islands such as Martinique. Instead of sea bass, you can also use another firm, sweet whitefish such as halibut, ocean perch, or grouper. Serve with basmati or jasmine rice. I'm partial to beer with Thai flavors, but a sharp, dry white, such as a Gewürztraminer, would work, too.

SPICE PASTE

2 cloves garlic, minced

¾ teaspoon curry powder

¼ teaspoon saffron (6 to 8 strands)

⅛ teaspoon cardamom (ground or seeds)

⅛ teaspoon cumin (ground or seeds)

SAUCE

2 teaspoons vegetable oil

1 tablespoon minced shallot

1 tablespoon minced ginger root or ½ teaspoon ground ginger

1 cup seeded and chopped tomatoes

½ finely sliced fresh red chili (or 1 teaspoon red pepper flakes)

2 teaspoons water

1 cup (250 ml) coconut milk

FISH

Coarse sea salt, ground pepper

1 lemon, juiced

4 sea-bass fillets (about 6 ounces each), skin intact

1 teaspoon butter

2 teaspoons olive oil

½ cup (125 ml) pineapple, diced

2 tablespoons chopped fresh cilantro

¼ cup roasted peanuts, coarsely chopped

Grind ingredients for the paste with the back of a spoon in a small bowl and set aside.

Heat the oil in a small saucepan over medium-high heat and add the shallots and ginger. Stir and cook for one minute; then add the tomatoes, chili, and spice paste. Cook and stir for a couple minutes until very fragrant. Add the water and coconut milk, stirring well. Add salt and pepper to taste. Bring to a boil, then reduce heat to a low simmer and allow sauce to thicken.

Rub the salt, pepper, and lemon juice into the fleshy side of the fish. Over medium-high heat, heat the butter and oil in a skillet until butter foams. Add the fish, flesh-side down, and fry for a few minutes, then carefully flip. Allow fish to cook for a couple minutes, then add coconut sauce and simmer, covered, until the fish is done. Uncover the pan and allow sauce to thicken. Add the pineapple and heat through. Using a spatula, remove fish to serving plate, leaving skin in the pan. Spoon the sauce over the fish, and garnish with cilantro and peanuts.

CHAPTER 22

GREAT EXPECTATIONS

"La sauce n'est pas chaude," says Chef DuPont. He holds his wrist to the plate and looks at me with alarm. "L'assiette n'est pas chaude."

He waves me away. "Nous sommes finis."

How could I be so stupid? I've forgotten to heat my plate—an utterly simple thing that I learned the first day in Basic Cuisine. "We're finished," he says, ending his critique abruptly. He doesn't taste anything. But for this, I can not blame him. In Basic Cuisine or even Intermediate, I might have gotten marked down for a cold plate. But in Superior Cuisine, it's inexcusable. Furious at myself, I shove my carefully nurtured lamb chops into a zipbag and separately bag up the wine-reduction sauce that I'd crafted so lovingly for more than an hour.

I have made myself look incompetent in front of Chef Dominique DuPont. He is the executive head chef of the school, not to mention the head chef for Superior Cuisine.

At six-foot-three, Chef DuPont towers over the other chefs. His smile reveals an endearing gap between his teeth, while his glasses seem always perched on the edge of his nose.

Like most of the chefs, Chef DuPont began his career in his teens. After he had worked in some of Paris's most famous restaurants, a Tokyo hotel recruited him to head up a famously expensive French restaurant frequented by Japanese businessmen. Randomly, I'd been to that hotel on a business trip to Japan in 2002. Always the Francophile, when I heard there was a hotel in Tokyo with an Eiffel Tower on top of it, I had to seek it out. In its day, it was a place of obvious splendor. When I visited, it looked dated, like a 1960s venture on the edge of decline. By then, Chef DuPont was long gone, having joined Le Cordon Bleu in Paris in 1992.

This morning, Margo has once again taken the middle seat in the front row in the demonstration room. She waves me over, along with Jenny, with whom I've just split another banana-and-Nutella crêpe.

Jenny and I opt to sit with Isabella in the third row. I prefer a more inconspicuous seat. I want more than anything to impress Chef DuPont. Now he knows me only as the dumb American woman who doesn't heat her plate.

Today, he's running through the recipe for *petit bar en croûte façon coulibiac*. Coulibiac is the French version of a traditional Russian loaf made of a mélange of fish, boiled eggs, parsley, and other flavorings, encased in pastry. For this, he begins with a "mock brioche," banging it onto the marble counter and rolling it a few times before letting it rest for an hour.

"Pour la vraie brioche, vous la travaillez pour au moins une demi-heure," he says. For real brioche, we'd keep working it for another half an hour.

Next, he fillets the sea bass. Curiously, he takes the skin and puts it onto a piece of parchment with salt and pepper and then into the oven. You can't waste anything, he says of fish. He makes quick work of the other elements, cubing fresh salmon to sauté with a generous dose of onions. The salmon is mixed with bread crumbs, mushrooms, and rice for a stuffing. This gets set aside while he works on what sounds like a very American dish: a raspberry crumble.

"Vous pouvez employer cette même recette avec quelque chose de savoureux," he says. We could choose to use it as a savory dish instead, he says, perhaps adding a tomato confit. Jenny turns to me. "Huh, how interesting," she says.

Chef looks up. "Quoi?" he asks. *What?*

"De rien, Chef," says Jenny. *It's nothing.*

In Basic, people talked through the demonstrations—a bit less in Intermediate. When Chef DuPont leads a class, respectful silence blankets the room. Yet Chef DuPont is also at times the most jovial of the chefs, with a standard group of gags to keep our attention. He bangs pots goodnaturedly, whistles, sings, and jokes. Today, he offers a couple of comic episodes. He noisily crumples a plastic cup hidden behind his back as he twists his neck, physical comedy reminiscent of Jerry Lewis's.

"Ah, that's bet-ur," he says in English with a heavy French accent.

When the male assistant returns to the room, Chef offers him the fish guts. A treat, he says. The Chinese assistant shakes his head. Chef pretends hurt feelings. Then he snaps the assistant with a towel.

Back to business. He rolls the mock brioche into a rectangle, places the filleted sea bass in the center, and then tops it with the salmon stuffing. He places a single line of hard-boiled eggs along the top. He then folds the dough over.

"A cocoon," Chef says. The edges are turned into a decorative pattern like those on a fancy pie crust. After the fish bakes for about a half hour, we are to tell if it's done by using this trick: insert a trussing needle, then pull it out, touch it with your finger, and then put to your lips. If it's hot, then it's done. The finger test is crucial, to avoid burning the lips.

Once the coulibiac comes out of the oven, Chef does just that. He nods at the heat. Then, he gasps at the beauty of his pastry. Isn't it beautiful? He *oohs* and *ahhs.*

"It's gre-at," he says in a fake American accent.

He coos lovingly to his sauce, too. "Ah, c'est beau. . . ."

As we taste it, he's right. It *is* great. I never would have thought fish in pastry with eggs would appeal. Then, he pulls the bits of fish skin out of the oven. I'd forgotten about them. He offers them up to us as a possible garnish for some dish we might invent. The dried fish skin didn't taste bad, either.

My mother has an alter ego she calls Gerta. If she can't move a piece of furniture, for instance, she steels her will and says, "Gerta can do it."

I try to muster my inner Gerta. "Now *Meeze* Gerta, do your best, you can do it."

Suki from Japan works at the other end of the table, but she's impossible not to notice. She speaks little English or French, so she communicates via a series of high-pitched, emotive wails. *"Ahhhhhhh!"* she cries brightly when she's happy. *"Ohhhhhhhh noooooo,"* she wails when things don't go well. A piercing *"Eeeeeeek!"* comes forth when things go especially wrong.

Next to her is Marcus, a tall, lanky Canadian. A veteran of restaurant kitchens, he's already an accomplished chef. His workstation is immaculate; his vegetable cuts are things of beauty. He came to Paris with a goal: to intern with famed French chef Joël Robuchon.

This time, Meeze Gerta and I present the Chef a very warm plate. He touches it and smiles his gapped-tooth grin. Chef looks over my fish and then tastes my sauce. My fish is fine. The sauce? "Very nice," he says. Victory! And yet. . . .

"Désolée pour l'assiette froide," I start to say, trying to apologize for yesterday's unwarmed plate episode.

He shakes his head and waves me off with a smile.

It's too early to call Mike. I head back to my old neighborhood. I drop some of my fish off with the Italian landlords, who are enjoying the fringe benefits of renting their apartment to a Le Cordon Bleu student. Then I head to the wine store and its curious proprietor with the long, gray hair. "Ah, ma chérie!" cries Marc when I walk into the store. "How are you? Why have you not come to see me sooner?"

"Je suis à Paris depuis quatre jours seulement, et maintenant j'habite à Belleville," I say. *I've been here only four days, plus I'm living in Belleville.*

"Come, *chérie,* let's talk." We sit on his plush leather seats in the orderly store. I tell him about Mike's accident. He raises his eyebrows. "But he is all right, yes?"

He goes down into his cellar to get me a special bottle of wine. While I linger near his register, I see a photo of Marc with someone else—a famous person whom I can't place.

"Who is this?" I ask when he returns.

"Oh, that was my old friend Frank. He died several years ago," he says. I look more closely. It's Frank Zappa. "That was another life," he says.

I am still unemployed and can't afford retail, yet I long for the whole de-signer-shopping-in-Paris experience. A coworker in London told me she used to go to Paris to shop at the thrift stores, picking up what she referred to as "the stuff French women had edited from their wardrobes." She'd come back to London with Prada sweaters, Chanel skirts, and Ferragamo shoes. Once, she showed off a genuine Hermès scarf she'd picked up for fifty euros, a little more than sixty dollars. I always meant to get the names of the stores from her but never got around to it. So, guidebook in hand, I set out to see what I can find.

First, I stop at what turns out to be a sort of Goodwill store with racks of dingy clothes under harsh fluorescent lighting. A strong smell of moth-balls and body odor hovers over the place. I pick out a couple of items on the long rack at random: €1.50 for a button-down pink shirt, €1.75 for a battered sweater. Just then, I hear an odd falsetto voice behind me. "Par-don moi, chérie."

I turn to face an aging, rail-thin transvestite wearing a sequin-studded denim jacket and leopard miniskirt. His platinum blond wig is brushed and hooked on one side with a rhinestone barrette. Lopsided falsies push out from under a white camisole. In one hand, heavy with fake red nails, he holds a half-dozen items on hangers, in the other, a cigarette. A singsong of *"Mer-ci, maaaa-dame,"* trails behind as he teeters by in his black heels.

The odds of finding a Prada sweater seem low, even if the entertain-ment value is high. I leave and get on the Métro to the Seventeenth.

It's a posh neighborhood. I see nannies pushing toddlers in expensive strollers. My destination is a store decorated in muted tones with track lighting and the hushed air of a moneyed boutique. Immediately, I feel underdressed and outclassed. I go to the organized racks and look for a price tag. A white silk shirt is €150, a pale cream sweater €175. Around the corner sit two rows of beautiful shoes. The cheapest pair is €200. The women here look not unlike the transvestite: taut skin, virtually all blond, and excruciatingly thin. I leave without buying anything and head back to Belleville, a long trip across Paris.

★ ★ ★

Jeff, my former neighbor from London, arrives to spend the weekend. We've signed up for a one-day course on *viennoiserie,* or Danish pastry. Croissants and brioche are the main events, and the butter-to-flour ratio is alarming. The day is overseen by Chef Colville, who is in good form, mugging it up for the group, a motley collection of American tourists, French residents, and expatriates from various countries.

We learn to make real brioche, rather than the mock variety we used on the coulibiac. The word "brioche" has been in use for centuries, derived from *"broyer,"* meaning "to break." I understand where it comes from when Chef demonstrates the proper technique.

The dough gets slammed hard onto a lightly dusted counter. *Wham!* Then, it's rolled with the palm of the hand into a ball. Then, *wham!* Roll. *Wham!* Roll. *Wham!* Roll. A half hour of this. It's a great way to release frustration.

Afterward, Jeff and I start to wrap up our dozen croissants and two loaves of brioche. Then there's the matter of the prepared dough that still needs another twenty hours to rise.

"Does anyone want to take it home?" Janine asks. There are surprisingly few takers. So we collect up several batches of dough. We're delighted until we burst into the Belleville apartment and try to cram it into the tiny fridge.

Jeff makes an observation. "Um, Kat, where's your oven?" he asks.

Oh. I sort of forgot. I don't *have* an oven in this apartment.

We get the dough into the fridge overnight while we try to figure out what to do with it. The next morning, we awake to find the door open. The dough quadrupled in size and spilled out onto the floor like a postnuclear monster from a 1950s horror film.

"It came from the refrigerator!" Jeff shouts, mimicking a B-movie trailer. "You can run, but you can't hide from . . . the Deadly Blob of Brioche!"

A few days later, Superior Group 3 is breading grapes for a bizarre combination of red mullet with guacamole and fried grapes. I'm late to start breading, and I notice we're low on bread crumbs. I eye the room. Suki and Isabella still need to bread their grapes as well. Although the recipe calls for twelve, they're used only for garnish. I choose to make five, leaving some bread crumbs.

Suki goes next, and makes three. *"Oooooooooh!"* she wails. "Noooo bed-cumbs!"

Isabella is the last to start her grapes. Suki was right. There are no bread crumbs left.

"Are there more bread crumbs?" Isabella asks Margo, class assistant today.

"No, there are no more in the whole school," Margo says. I look at her side pan. She's rolled out and deep-fried fourteen grapes.

"Margo, you should give some of yours to Isabella," Jenny says.

Margo acts as if she doesn't hear her. Isabella, Jenny, and I all look at one another. Jenny has nine grapes. "I'll give you three of mine," she says. I contribute two of mine. At least she'll have enough to plate. Margo watches peripherally but never offers.

"That Margo, why would she do it?" Isabella laments later after class. "It's as if she wants me to fail."

It makes me think of the thrift stores. The price of the clothes in one place was one hundred times more expensive than in the other. But were the women paying the higher price that much happier?

For Margo, it is not about doing her best, it's about doing better than *everyone else.* Frankly, I don't care about my class ranking. I just want to learn and to graduate. But for Margo, I wonder if graduating higher in the class rankings is worth the price she may ultimately pay.

Crêpes à la Banane et au Nutella

BANANA AND NUTELLA CRÊPES

Makes eight

Like so many things in cooking, crêpes are a blank canvas—you can fill them with anything. Try a bit of jam, some applesauce, some slow-cooked pears and cream. They also freeze well. I slip each crêpe in between layers of parchment, then into a gallon-sized zipbag, which I lay flat in the freezer. While crêpe pans work best, a good, heavy flat skillet or omelet pan will work. One note: it's important to let the crêpe batter rest once it's mixed.

CRÊPE BATTER

¾ cup (80 g) all-purpose flour

⅛ teaspoon salt

2 tablespoons sugar

1 cup (250 ml) milk

½ teaspoon vanilla extract

2 eggs

3 tablespoons unsalted butter, melted and cooled slightly

Extra butter for coating pan

FILLING PER CREPE

1 tablespoon Nutella

½ banana, sliced

¼ teaspoon brown sugar *(optional)*

Prepare the crêpe batter by sifting the dry ingredients together in a bowl. Make a well in the center. In a separate bowl, stir together the milk and vanilla. Add one third of the milk mixture and the eggs to the well and beat with a whisk, slowly incorporating the flour. Then whisk in the remaining milk mixture and the melted butter. Allow batter to rest for at least thirty minutes. The batter should have the consistency of heavy cream.

Heat a crêpe skillet or a six-inch nonstick skillet over medium heat. Brush with a bit of butter. The butter should melt and bubble but not brown rapidly. Adjust heat if necessary. Scoop about ¼ cup of the batter and pour into the heated pan. Tilt pan to allow the batter to completely cover the bottom. If the batter is too thick or the pan too hot, the crêpe will have holes or burn. Add milk to batter or adjust heat. The crêpe is ready to flip when the bottom is golden brown, the edges look dry, and the crêpe slides easily when you give the pan a good shake. This may take thirty seconds or three minutes. Be patient.

Flip the crêpe and quickly dollop the Nutella onto it and gently spread it around a bit. Precision is not important. Add the sliced bananas, and sprinkle with the brown sugar, if using. Remove from the pan, and fold in half like an omelet. Serve on a plate or Parisian street food–style: wrapped in a paper towel or foil.

If preparing crêpes to freeze for future use, do not fill but set aside to cool. Stack crêpes with alternating layers of parchment or wax paper. Store in a gallon-size plastic bag, or wrap well with plastic wrap, and freeze for up to one month.

CHAPTER 23

GODS, MONSTERS, AND SLAVES

My cutting board is covered with gristle and flesh, my apron drenched in blood. Somehow, I hit a blood line in my quail as I was deboning it. Who would have thought that such a small bird could contain so much blood? I've experienced blood and guts before, especially with fish, but the feel of hacking into such a fragile body unnerves me. I could crush this skeleton with one hand, as if it had bones made of toothpicks. Chef Bouveret asks what's wrong.

I hold up my still bloodied hands as I tell him. "Je suis un monstre."

He laughs and replies, "C'est pourquoi les femmes font de mauvais bouchers." *That's why women make poor butchers.*

Today, we're making quail and veal sweetbread pastries with shiitake mushrooms. I must bone the bird's tiny legs and slice the slivers of breast off its delicate carcass. Then I move on to the sweetbreads.

"Sweetbread" has always struck me as a vastly euphemistic term for a gland. A lot of people think the term refers to brains, but sweetbreads actually come from the thymus gland or the pancreas of calves or piglets under a year old. (In some countries, llama thymus is a delicacy, but there aren't many llamas in France.) It's a curious expression, as they taste neither sweet nor like bread. To me, they're a velvety and mild version of liver, although I'm hardly a connoisseur. Ever since experiencing food poisoning from undercooked pig kidneys in China a few years ago, I've been reluctant to eat much organ meat.

The grayish-white lumpy mass of sweetbreads is soaked to eliminate any impurities. Nestled in water, like the caul fat, they look remarkably like withered human brains. Then we remove any excess sinew. We slice, season with salt and pepper, then sauté in butter for two minutes before setting aside.

Quickly, I dice carrots, onion, and celery. For the sauce, Chef DuPont instructed us to add only enough vegetables to equal 10 percent of the volume of bones, a much smaller percentage than we'd use for stock. So for ten ounces of bones, we use just one ounce of mirepoix. The reason, he says, is to allow the meat flavor to be enhanced, not overwhelmed by the vegetables.

I recall my past struggles with puff pastry. No more. I give my pastry a final two turns, roll it out into a decent rectangle, and then slice it in half lengthwise with a paring knife. A slip of parchment goes under one piece, and I begin layering the stuffing with pieces of sweetbreads and quail breast. I repeat this until I've used everything and then place the other piece of puff pastry on top. Instead of meat-stuffed meat, it's meat-stuffed pastry, a more difficult and elegant variation. Swathed in egg wash, the pastry goes into the oven to cook for about thirty to forty minutes.

With that, we wait. As we usually do, we chat.

A dark beauty in her late twenties, Isabella was born to a Brazilian father and Italian mother in the United States and lived there as a child before her parents moved back to São Paulo. She speaks Spanish, Portuguese, English, and Italian fluently. Her French is very good, too. Even looking at her in her kitchen whites, you can tell that in another era Isabella would have been a glamorous movie queen. *"Dahrling,"* she purrs to begin each sentence in her Brazilian/Italian accent. *"Dahrling,* could you pass me an onion? *Grazie, dahrling."*

By contrast, Margo exudes a get-out-of-my-way kind of ambition that seems very American. After a lucrative legal career for a couple of big corporations, she retired at age fifty. My guess is that she's spent her life sitting front-row center. It turns out she ranked first in her Intermediate Class. She doesn't say, but it's obvious her burning desire is to place first in Superior, too. She has no apparent plans to use her degree. This is recreation.

"So I bought €70 of food magazines yesterday," Margo says while we wait. "The woman at the newsstand thought I was a little crazy."

Isabella and I exchange quiet glances. That's $95 on food magazines.

"I just want to get great ideas for how to present my plates," she continues.

Jenny listens to all of this intently. She's the lovely, blond ex-pat wife of an American executive. They live in the swank Passy neighborhood in the Sixteenth arrondissement. We've had only six lessons, but I've watched her as she's cooked across from me. She's confident, sometimes doing things her own way. She's been gifted with marvelous taste buds; her food is always delicious. Invariably, her plates look unique, different from the chefs', yet alluring. She doesn't need magazines.

"May I borrow a couple of your magazines?" asks Isabella. Margo's face takes on friendly false smile, and her voice goes up a notch.

"Sure, I'll bring them in," she says. It sounds hollow. Margo turns back to her stove. Forget comrades, I realize. To Margo, we are competition.

The next day, I meet up with Isabella at a bookstore devoted to cookbooks on rue Dante, near Saint-Michel. She's lusting over a massive oversized book about the work of Ferran Adrià, the chef of El Bulli in Spain, considered by some the best restaurant in the world. The book shows off his experimental cuisine, which features the likes of culinary foam made of beet and melon, foie-gras ice cream, and pasta made of seafood. The unwieldy book costs €165.

"It's even more than Margo's magazines," Isabella laments. Together, we flip through the pages. His work looks not like haute cuisine but small nuggets of Modern art. Some of it reminds me of science-fiction food. Small red squares that taste like cherry? Is the future of food a variation on *Soylent Green*? Will it leave deglazing and sautéing in the dust?

But I like the ethos. In his twenty-three-point "synthesis of El Bulli cuisine" are some remarkable comments, one of which explains the look of the food: "A culinary language is being created which is becoming more and more ordered, that on some occasions establishes a relationship with the world and language of art."

This statement catches my attention, too: "The barriers between the sweet and savoury world are being broken down."

Who decides what is quality cuisine anyway? Some of the sauces we learned in Basic were once thought daring, revolutionary. The unusual combinations we're learning in Superior are trendy; unconventional pairings with classic technique are common on haute-cuisine menus. But it makes me wonder more about the general nature of evolution. We can reinvent anything, even ourselves, and some things will change, but in the end, something familiar always remains. Mike might enjoy chocolate foam, but he'd probably never crave it the way he would chocolate-chip cookies. Why? The chefs at El Bulli can never compete with the memory of his mother pulling them hot out of the oven when he came home in his Little League baseball uniform.

Ultimately, Isabella leaves the store without her book. We head to the St.-Germain-des-Prés outlet of the teahouse chain Mariage Frères. In Paris, it's chic to drink expensive tea. We each order a pot.

"My parents are both psychiatrists, very successful," she says. "So they say to me, 'Isabella, you must get a degree in psychology.' So I did. I worked at it for a while. I didn't like it. Always in my heart, I wanted to be a chef. I was deceiving myself trying to be something else. I gave in to my passion and came to Europe to study cooking. First, I went to Italy. I studied in a beautiful castle for three months, learning to make Italian food."

"Why Italian?" I ask.

"My grandfather," she says. "I loved him, and he loved food. As a little girl, I helped him make fresh pasta each Sunday. He grew up in Brazil, but he was Italian. When he got old enough, he went to Italy to study violin professionally. It didn't work out. He sold his violin, filled the case with prosciutto, and headed back to Brazil."

After the Italian cooking course, she went to work in a one-star Michelin restaurant as an intern. "I was the only woman in the kitchen, and they kept teasing me, calling me 'samba' and asking what I looked like in my bathing suit," she said. "They treated me like a slave. They made me do all these awful jobs, but that's what you do when you start out. It's always the way." After three months, she confronted the chef who teased her most: "I don't want trouble; neither do you. The others listen to you. If you stop the teasing, they'll quit, and I won't have to say anything to the owner." He stopped. They let her start filleting fish. But it was too late. She left and went to Paris.

"I chose Le Cordon Bleu because it's famous, so when I went to find a job, people would know I was serious. People hear your name, they know nothing of your cooking. They hear Le Cordon Bleu, they know that name."

But the name will get you only so far. "It is very hard work in a kitchen," she begins. "I mean, you are a slave when you start a career, even if you go to a place like Le Cordon Bleu. It is hot, you're on your feet, the hours are long, you smell not so good at the end of the shift. You work weekends, holidays. You lift heavy things, you get dirty. Always, there is stress and yelling when there is a service. You need a lot of passion, or you will burn out in the kitchen. This I know. But I don't want to use my passion for anything else. Cooking, that's all I want to do now."

The next day, Isabella and I go to school on our day off to represent Superior Cuisine at a sort of welcome party for Basic students.

As I wander with a glass of cheap white wine in my hand, I chat and meet a dozen of the students in the Basic class. I am struck that the makeup of the incoming class always seems so similar: many Asians, a handful of Americans, some serious students, some young women learning to cook and speak French, and some students like me and Isabella, refugees from other careers finally coming to terms with what they want.

One guy from Israel finds the classes are too easy. "Wait a couple of months," I tell him. "You'll feel differently."

Another student from America was sure she was going to flunk. "The chefs hate me," she says. I feel a stab of nostalgia. Everyone thinks that sometimes, I tell her. It's normal. "Just cook from your heart and you'll be fine."

Among them are a pack of Brazilians. Amazingly, Isabella went to high school with one of them, a heavyset guy named Renato who wears black wraparound glasses. Somehow, I end up with them at an old Belle Époque bar not far from Les Halles. Renato's wife, a pleasant woman with a musical accent, is there, as is their friend, a thin guy named Marcos, who speaks French and Portuguese but no English. Then there's Esteban from Spain.

Esteban is an assistant in the basement. I've seen him before, but then he's hard to miss. He's handsome, with a shaved head and pierced nose, lower lip, and tongue—an uncommon look among Cordon Bleu students. His eyes are hard and blue. His job at school makes him privy to all the gossip, and this seems to empower an already strong rebellious streak in him.

"These chefs, I won't call them 'Chef So-and-so,' " Esteban tells us over bottle of wine number one. "I call them Monsieur Savard, Monsieur Gaillard, but never 'Chef.' " Calling them "Chef" has been so pounded into me that to call them "monsieur" seems like heresy. It's about respect; Esteban thought it should be mutual. He remains unimpressed by the chefs who seem to worship at the feet of Escoffier.

Over bottles number two and three, he tells us all in great detail about the massive, beautiful meal he plans to prepare for his father and his brother when he returns to Spain.

By bottle number four, he's on to the restaurant he plans to open, probably in Madrid. I tell him about the conversation with Isabella.

"It's true, when you are in the kitchen, most of the time you are a slave, a slave to the customers," he says. "But then they eat their meal, and if they like it, then I am a god!" He puffs up his chest and points to himself.

Such is the religion of Esteban.

"Is that what keeps you from calling the teachers 'Chef'?" I ask.

"Exactly," he says, flicking an ash off his cigarette. "I've already been a mechanic, a salesperson, and now I'll be a chef. I am as important as they are, you see? I have the same power. We all do."

By this time, we were all drunk. No one had ordered food, save a plate of charcuterie and some bread. Everyone got tired of translating for Marcos, so we all just speak French.

Wine has a powerful effect on the ability to speak a foreign language. In my current state, I'm certain I speak fluently.

★ ★ ★

I wake up the next morning thinking in French. I decide to keep on speaking it, regardless of whether someone asks me something in English. I want to stay in this immersion, as if I'm on the precipice of speaking French and won't be able to come back if I stop. It's like being a child. You understand, but you can't speak much beyond simple phrases. But one day you know you will because everyone else can.

The wine might have helped my French, but the hangover does nothing for more wrestling with my least favorite fish, the dreaded hake. This time, the fish is to be wrapped in prosciutto. Isabella and I joke about her grandfather's violin case.

Once we've filleted the fish, we place a large sheet of heat-resistant plastic wrap on the counter and lay out slices of prosciutto. On top of this, we lay a slice of fish and spread a dense mixture of fresh herbs, garlic, black olives, and olive oil. Another fillet of hake tops that, and it all gets rolled up tight in the plastic, like a hard candy. We put it into the freezer to firm up and then cut one-inch slices from it, sautéing them in hot olive oil. Voilà! Each is a perfect little ham-wrapped parcel. Chef DuPont tastes everything and approves. "Bon travail," he says.

Today, the sous-sol has been generous; I have about six portions of fish. I call the Italian landlords to see if they want some for dinner. "Ah, Kath-a-leen, we cannot take-uh de fish," he explains. "We head to Rouen-a for de night."

I look for the world's smartest homeless man, but I've not seen him since my return. So I head home on the Métro. At the Montparnasse station, I see a heavily disfigured young woman. She sits quietly, jean jacket buttoned up, a hand-lettered sign in front of her. "J'ai faim," it begins. *I'm hungry.* Anything, please.

I walk past her, caught in the throng of Parisians anxious to get home. On the platform, a train stops. The hake weighs heavily in my hand.

I turn around and walk against the tide of people.

She looks up expectantly, surprised to see someone coming the wrong way. "Vous *désirez* du poisson?" I ask, bending down to her.

I can see a map of deep scars around her bald head. Burns, I think, horrible to experience and maybe worse to live with. Her green eyes glow against her purple, discolored skin. She adds something about her *"petit garçon,"* her little boy.

I'm a culinary student, I tell her. I often have food, and I'll look for her. I walk away but turn to see her looking through the various zipbags, the fish for once served with a generous side of vegetables. Happy and almost hugging herself, she looks at me. She smiles and, like Chef Bouveret, gives me a thumbs-up.

Maybe Esteban is right, I think, as I walk back down to the platform. In the kitchen, I might be a slave to the chefs. But now, feeding this woman made me something remarkable. At first, it feels godlike.

But once off the Métro at Belleville, I walk home through the poor streets. Some local kids around eight or nine years old follow me down my street. At first, they're asking for something. Then, realizing I don't comprehend, they start tossing out taunts in French that I don't understand.

How quick the fall can be from godliness to humility.

Rouget Farci aux Olives et aux Tomates, Enrobé de Prosciutto, Citron Beurre Blanc au Citron

RED SNAPPER STUFFED WITH PROVENÇAL TOMATO SPREAD, WRAPPED IN PROSCIUTTO, WITH LEMON BUTTER SAUCE

Serves four

This is an easy recipe that can be used with any firm whitefish, such as cod, grouper, sea bass, or halibut. This uses the Provençal tomato spread from page 133. The spread can be made a day or two ahead and stowed in the fridge until needed. The spread and prosciutto are salty, so don't add extra salt to the fish before baking it.

4 slices (about 2 ounces) prosciutto
4 fillets (about 5 ounces each) red snapper
Fresh ground pepper
½ cup Provençal tomato spread (see page 133)

LEMON BEURRE BLANC

1½ cups (350 ml) white wine

½ shallot finely chopped, (about 2 tablespoons)

1 tablespoon champagne or other white-wine vinegar

6 peppercorns

1 cup (2 sticks) butter, cut into small pieces and chilled

1 tablespoon lemon juice

Coarse salt, ground pepper

Preheat oven to 350°F/180°C. On four sheets of parchment paper or foil, lay the slices of prosciutto. Lay a fillet of fish atop each slice. Top with a piece of plastic wrap and flatten by lightly banging the fish with the bottom of a pan. Flatten just enough to make the fish roughly the same size as the prosciutto and an even thickness. Season generously with pepper. Spread on a tablespoon of the tomato mixture and roll each up like a pinwheel. Wrap parchment paper or foil around the rolled-up fish, and crimp or twist the ends like a hard candy to tightly seal. Place seam-side down atop foil in a casserole or roasting pan. Place in oven and bake for at least twenty minutes until the flesh is firm and cooked through. Make sure minimal juices are escaping package during cooking time.

As the fish cooks, make the sauce: Combine wine, shallots, vinegar, and peppercorns in a small saucepan and boil to reduce to about ⅓ cup of liquid. Lower heat until the liquid stops bubbling. Do not allow liquid to keep boiling or sauce will separate when butter is added. Add butter, one or two pieces at a time, whisking constantly to incorporate completely before adding more. If the sauce bubbles, remove pan from heat, whisking constantly to cool it before resuming. When all the butter is incorporated, add the lemon juice. Check seasonings, adding salt and pepper to taste. Strain in a mesh sieve before serving.

Remove fish from the oven, checking doneness by gently squeezing sides of the package. The fish should feel firm, not mushy. Cut open parchment and remove fish. Slice each into two or three pieces per person and put on a plate with the lemon beurre blanc.

CHAPTER 24

LA DANSE

LESSON HIGHLIGHTS: MIKE COMES TO PARIS, DINNER AT
LE DOYEN, AND A TOUR OF RUNGIS

The next morning, I dress, shaking, giddy as a teenager on her way to a first date. I change my clothes four times, settling on new black boots and a short black skirt so ancient I can't remember where I bought it, but at least it makes me feel thin.

It takes three trains and more than an hour to get to Charles de Gaulle airport. I wait, nervously perched at the small bar near the exit from customs. It's only noon, but I order a glass of white wine. I check my watch. I know he made the plane; he'd called me from the gate.

And then, suddenly, Mike was there again.

I tug him to the side of the stream of passengers, and we press hard in a hug in a small vestibule near an ATM. The ferocity of it surprises us both, as if we needed to be sure that the other was not an apparition.

"Hey, I've got a broken chest, remember?" he says softly.

What does absence do to a heart? In Mike's case, it allowed his to heal. Yet his absence made mine ache. Our romance has been a verbal one—we talk for hours at a time—yet on the train rides into town we barely speak, holding hands and nuzzling each other.

I am acutely aware that he might never have come home that afternoon from paragliding. Living here by myself in Paris, I've had a preview of how empty my life would feel without him. How quickly I became used to being part of a couple.

We crawl in bed together, and we both fall into luxurious napping in each other's arms. I wake up a few minutes before he does. As the afternoon sun slants into the room, I watch him sleep. The same thought comes to me as it did that morning in the castle house.

I could wake up next to this man every day for the rest of my life— and his.

At twilight, we take the Métro down to St. Michel and walk along the river. We kiss in the same place we came to when he joined me in Paris the first time. On the horizon, the thousands of strobes on the Eiffel Tower explode in sychronized bursts. We hold each other close, and although there's no music, we dance.

For me, Paris is complete.

Mike's arrival is just in time for our class dinner at Le Doyen. Established in 1792 by Pierre Ledoyen, the three-star restaurant just off the Champs-Élysées is considered among the best in Paris. We are greeted at the door by the elegant Madame Madeleine Bisset. Whenever I see her, she invariably wears a chignon and beautiful clothes, and tonight is no different. Chef DuPont is beside her, too. I've never seen him out of his kitchen whites. In his stylish beige sport coat, he looks shorter, although he still towers over me. He kisses me on both cheeks.

"Bonsoir, Kathleen, est-ce que c'est votre mari?" he says, nodding to Mike.

Yes, this is my husband, I answer, and make introductions.

"Enchanté," he says, gripping Mike's hand in a firm handshake. "Vous désirez du champagne?" *You want some champagne?*

"Bien sûr," says Mike, and the chef leaves to retrieve glasses of champagne. When he returns, we chitchat a bit in French. Somehow, we end up on the subject of fast food.

"Ah, j'aime McDo!" he says. Chef loves McDonald's? He goes into a rhapsody about Big Macs, but he eats them only in America. They taste more American in the U.S. and that's part of the appeal. The things you learn about people.

Dinner begins with an *amuse-bouche,* "something to entertain the palate," of beet sorbet atop a small chunk of fish that tastes of smoky bacon. The first bite explodes with an unexpected sensation of savory and sweet. A universal "wow" hums through the room.

This balancing act continues through dinner, from the appetizer of foie gras with fried porcini mushrooms and truffle ravioli to a main dish of duck breast seasoned with Chinese five-spice in pastry with a veal-stock-based cream sauce.

The desserts arrive. The first is a glass of sorbet that smacks of marvelous lemon-meringue pie. Then come nests of spun caramel with hints of hazelnuts and chocolate; none of us could figure out how it was made.

The chef appears, to make his rounds. A native of Brittany, Chef Christian Le Squer is a handsome, trim man in his late thirties. He's followed the traditional route, starting at age fourteen, then passing through some of the top kitchens in Paris, including Taillevent, Lucas Carton, and L'Espadon in the Ritz.

Now when a chef who has three Michelin stars walks into a room filled with culinary students, it's a big deal. Everyone pays attention. Some students attend Le Cordon Bleu for one major reason: they want to intern at a restaurant in Paris. On the night of our dinner, two Le Cordon Bleu students are working away in the restaurant's pristine kitchens. Le Doyen would look good on any aspiring chef's résumé. So, as he walks from table to table offering pleasantries, more than a few are eager to get in a word.

He comes to our table, stands behind me, and asks how we liked the dinner. Everyone nods fervently.

I think of the book about El Bulli and the breakdown of barriers between savory and sweet. In my awkward French, I try to explain that I thought each plate seem to do that yet keep a balance of the two. "Une danse," I say of each plate.

He responds excitedly. "Oui! Oui! C'est mon intention," he begins, then asks which course I liked best.

"L'amuse-bouche," I decide, the beet sorbet with the fish.

That's it. By dumb luck, I've hit some nerve and named his favorite dish, one that he's been working on for months. He kneels down, and for twenty minutes we talk. Well, mostly he talks and I try to figure out what he's saying. Lately, he's been thinking about the idea of masculine and feminine foods. Do I agree that some foods are masculine or feminine? Before I answer, he tells me how he thinks about making them "dance" together. Sometimes, at night, after the kitchen has closed, he takes ingredients that he thinks will not work together and figures out how they could. Beets alone didn't work with fish, but beet *sorbet* was sweet enough to offset the salt of the fish, for instance. He has many thoughts about sauce, which I miss entirely when he begins talking too fast for me to follow.

Eventually, he asks about me. Do I want to be a chef? What are my plans?

No, I'm a writer, I say.

He sees my menu and a small notebook nearby, both covered with tasting notes. I explain that I sometimes review restaurants. Taking notes is a habit. He feigns fear, and we both laugh. I'm only a student now, I assure him.

Then he asks me if I am planning a *stage*. Was I interested in an internship at Le Doyen? I hadn't planned to intern anywhere, so I had not done the paperwork before I left the United States. He prods me, urging me to reconsider. Eventually, a member of his staff pulls him away. "Bonsoir, madame," he says rising to his feet. "La conversation a été un plaisir." *The conversation was a pleasure.*

Margo is fuming. I feel bad. She never got a chance to talk with him. Who would have guessed he'd spend so much time talking to me, a student without Michelin ambitions and so-so French?

After dinner, I take my menu around the room to have students and chefs sign it. Suki signs it in Japanese symbols, and others follow her lead, signing in Korean, Chinese, Greek, Spanish, Portugese, or whatever their native language is. A few sign in French, a couple in English. Chefs Savard and DuPont sign sweet notes in French.

Rebels always seem to make great poets. My favorite comment is this one from Esteban: "How easily a dinner can be a feast of friends, those pleasures you enjoy breath by breath."

★ ★ ★

The night after our dinner, I reluctantly leave Mike, if only for one night, to gather with the other students near the school at 4:15 a.m., to catch a bus to Rungis, generally considered the largest wholesale food market in the world.

The Métro begins around five in the morning. Trying to catch a cab in Belleville or Montmartre at that hour? Forget it. So Isabella and I find a €26-a-night room in a dilapidated tourist hotel around the corner from school. For our money, we get sagging twin beds, a sink, and a bidet. Our room is adjacent to the communal bathroom in the hallway. The toilet echoes noisily each time other guests flush. We get little sleep before the alarm rings at 3:45 a.m.

"This better be worth it, *dahrling*," Isabella says, navigating the dark, winding stairs.

We arrive at Rungis in the dark at 5:40 a.m. A stern man hands each of us a white coat made of tough, papery fabric, paper booties to cover our shoes, and a hairnet. For sanitation, it is de rigueur to wear all this in the food stalls, says our tour guide, Claude, a tall man clad in a knee-length white butcher's coat. He has a white mustache and wears a baseball cap emblazoned with the spirited Rungis logo.

Rungis replaced Les Halles, the maze of covered markets that used to occupy a vast swath of choice Parisian real estate just down the street from the apartment on rue Étienne Marcel. The Les Halles markets prompted the development of dozens of all-night eateries and stores to supply the restaurant trade, as well as a strong prostitution trade on seedy side streets, such as rue St.-Denis.

A market had existed on the site of Les Halles since 1100, when the monarchy agreed to let peasant women sell fish there. In 1183, Philippe Auguste ordered the first covered building there, which was added to and expanded, rebuilt and upgraded, until the city erected metal and glass pavilions in the 1860s, they were considered the architectural feat of day, surpassed only when the Eiffel Tower was built twenty years later. By then, Les Halles had evolved into France's central clearinghouse for food and flowers, with a festive air referred to as burlesque or carnival-like. Frenetic bargaining ended in deals agreed on with a handshake. Around dawn, sellers, buyers, and night owls would flock to the dozens of restaurants nearby, often opting for steaming bowls of French onion soup, eager for its famed restorative powers.

By the 1950s, pressure mounted for Les Halles to move. The crush of trucks paralyzed traffic in central Paris, pickpockets roamed the area, and rumors abounded of a major rat infestation. Officials bought a property about eight miles east of the city. On March 3, 1969, the flowers, vegetables, and fruits shifted, later joined by the meat purveyors on January 15, 1973.

"One night, they were at Les Halles, and then next night they were doing business here," Claude tells us, as we walk from the bus into the new fish pavilion, an airplane-style hangar so long and symmetrical that it resembles an infinity mirror: it's difficult to tell where it ends.

But it's empty. We've missed the fish—the reason we got here so early. A slippery floor, remnant ice, and an acrid, salty smell are all that are left of the fish and seafood. Workers with snaking hoses begin to wash and sanitize the hangar.

"Quel dommage," *a pity*, says Claude.

"The suppliers for the Japanese restaurants, they are here at midnight, waiting until the doors are open at 1:00 a.m. so they can be the very first to buy," Janine translates for Claude—this tour is one of the few times translation is offered in Superior Cuisine.

"*Dahrling*, it's just a bunch of fish," Isabella says as we get on the bus.

"I know, I just really wanted to see it in action," I say, disappointed. On a business trip to Japan a couple of years ago, I got up in the middle of the night to watch the famous tuna auction at the Central Wholesale Market in Tokyo. Massive gray tuna were lined up in rows, a flap of skin cut away to reveal the density of each fish's pink, fleshy interior. Tails cut off, marked with bright red numbers, and their mouths agape, the tuna appeared surprised to find themselves in such a state. For a half hour, a sweaty, spitting auctioneer managed feverish bidding until about two hundred fish had been sold, roughly one every ten seconds. Some weighed as much as one thousand pounds and fetched the price of a car. It was a breathless, ruthlessly efficient sight. I didn't expect the fish market at Rungis to have the same vigor, but I wanted to at least see it.

On the bus, we're treated to a bit of warmth and a series of dazzling statistics. At 570 acres, Rungis is several times the size of Les Halles and larger than the principality of Monaco. Some 12,000 people work here, and another 20,000 come regularly to buy; about 26,000 vehicles come in and out of here daily.

Claude rattles off what's sold each year:

- 500,000 tons of fruit
- 67,000 tons of fish
- 430,000 tons of vegetables
- 26 tons of cheese
- 5,000 tons of French butter
- 76,000 tons of poultry
- 32,000 pounds of tripe
- 34,000 tons of cut flowers.

Isabella and I just stare at each other blankly. We didn't sleep enough for this.

"Who knew tripe would be so popular?" is all I can muster. The jaunty Claude stops and bounces off the bus. Esteban shuffles in front of me as our crowd files out as if sleepwalking. Shivering despite a heavy wool cap, he stops at the door and holds out his hand. "It's hailing," he informs us dully.

Next, we visit the beef hangar. The building itself is so ultramodern, it could double as a spaceship set in a science-fiction movie. The peach-colored industrial floors give way to individual purveyor areas, each flagged with stainless-steel markers with letters in glowing red that could pass for signage at Tomorrowland at Walt Disney World. The temperature of this building is kept just above freezing, and hundreds of heavy carcasses dangle by one foot in orderly rows, each attached to a track in the ceiling by a frightening spike. The butchers in their traditional long white coats carry around clipboards, consulting with buyers and one another, making verbal deals. They strike me as resembling a group of doctors tending to an alien race. A few steers hanging with one leg extended remind me of ballet dancers posing in an arabesque. Fully intact baby pigs hang like prizes at a carnival game. Horses strung up by their ankles hang in one area, the meat a dark purplish color. Some of the animals have photos attached, showing what they looked like before they'd been slaughtered.

"About two hundred million tons of meat moves through this hangar each year," Janine translates. Although most of it's from within the country, some of the meat is flown into nearby Orly Airport from all over the world. "Here you'll find Kobe beef from Japan, beef from Argentina." Only two countries are not allowed to sell any meat here: the United States and the United Kingdom. "Due to problems with hormones," she translates for Claude.

There's no mention of BSE, or mad-cow disease.

As a young reporter, I once visited a county morgue. The technicians wore the same kind of long white coats, and they pushed the dead bodies around on trolleys with the same indifference with which the men here maneuver the meat. The morgue was quiet, just like in the cliché. Here, Claude goes on with his tour, yelling over the noise of the vendors, whose voices compete with the thunderous hum of the air conditioners.

Back on the bus, we pass by the poultry pavilion. All sorts of chicken, ducks, geese, and their various products are kept separate from all other meats, Claude says. Everyone notices this, as the avian flu is front-page news. More than 270 tons of foie gras pass through that hangar every year, he tells us. Then he stops abruptly and takes a deep breath.

"Ah, can you smell it?" asks Janine.

A pungent scent penetrates the bus. Once inside the dairy pavilion, the smell is overwhelming. We've stepped into the world's largest cheese shop, where nearly one hundred thousand pounds of cheese are stacked in virtually every corner of the stalls. Some merchants advertise their wares with names such as La Maison du Gruyère. Our group moves slowly among crates of Camembert, racks of hard cheese, and massive round, yellow wheels, some as wide as three feet across and weighing more than one hundred pounds, as people take photos.

"Suki just took thirty photos of that wheel of cheese, darling," Isabella says.

The two-hundred-meter-long fresh-produce area strikes me as a vast version of Costco. We dodge sellers who cruise through on bicycles, the common way to get around the Rungis campus. The fruit and vegetable sellers' area takes up eight airplane hangars. As we wander through a full acre of vibrant fresh flowers, Claude offers a final tidbit. "He says that Holland is the largest exporter of flowers in Europe, if not the world," says Janine.

It's past 8:00 a.m. I'm fatigued by the numbers, the lack of sleep, the sheer volume of everything. In some way, vast quantities render themselves meaningless. It reminds me of a folktale: An emperor walks with his court through many fields of roses until they come to a barren spot. There, he sees one rose. "It's the most beautiful rose I've ever seen!" the emperor cries. Those walking with him point out that he'd just been through a field of similar roses. "Yes, but *this* one I can see."

We pile on the bus. On the trip back, we talk about the old Les Halles tradition of capping off the workday with steaming bowls of French onion soup. A group of us head to a local brasserie, and as we cradle our bowls of soup for warmth, we all agree we wish we had been around to see the old Les Halles in action.

Three days later, Mike and I move back into the apartment on rue Étienne Marcel. We trade keys, kisses, and good-byes with Niccolò and Alberto, who pack up their bags and rush for the airport. We open a bottle of wine, and for the rest of the evening Mike and I sit at our kitchen table. We dine on a simple roast chicken and marvel at the view overlooking the busy five-way intersection. We love watching Paris in action: the stream of people coming and going through the curved art-deco entrance of the Métro; tourists dragging wheeled luggage toward the train station at Les Halles; and the comedy and high drama of French driving. We watch the color of the sky change above the gray tin roofs, so solid with time, and the limestone walls graced by delicate etchings. In some buildings, the white French windows open outward onto their wrought-iron balconies, revealing interiors or inhabitants. A few others play the same game, watching the street. Sometimes, we catch them watching us.

It's been a good week. No, it's been a good month. Although I was alone, I learned a lot. I met new people, and I saw sides of Paris that I hadn't expected.

I think of the chef from Le Doyen, trying to find a balance with every-thing, even things that would not seem to work together. As a girl, I studied ballet. I remember the times that learning all those techniques seemed like just repetitive, boring work. But the point of it all was that in the end, the work should appear effortless. It takes time and patience to make *la danse* work. But when it does, it is marvelous.

Soupe à l'Oignon Gratinée

ONION SOUP GRATINÉED WITH CHEESE

Serves four

In a recipe with few ingredients such as this one, it's essential that all are of the highest possible quality. For best results, give the onions a careful, slow cooking to properly caramelize, and then simmer them in a broth that itself is rich with flavor. Be sure to use bowls that can stand up under a broiler or the whole exercise may end in tears. For good stock, see pages 44–45.

2 medium (1 pound) yellow onions, sliced thin
1 tablespoon unsalted butter
2 tablespoons flour
½ cup (125 ml) dry white wine or dry vermouth
1 tablespoon cognac
2 quarts (2 l) beef stock, boiled
½ teaspoon dried thyme
1 bay leaf
¼ French baguette, sliced thin
6 ounces (180 g) Gruyère cheese, grated
1 ounce (30 g) Parmesan cheese, grated *(optional)*

In a heavy saucepan over medium heat, slowly brown the onions in butter until caramelized. Be patient; this will take at least a half hour. Sprinkle the onions with flour and stir thoroughly. Add the wine and cognac, cook long enough to evaporate the alcohol. Then add the hot stock, thyme, and bay leaf. Simmer for one hour, uncovered.

Preheat oven to 350°F/180°C. Meanwhile, toast the baguette slices. Just before serving, top one side of the bread slices with some of the Gruyère cheese and broil lightly until cheese melts slightly. Remove the bay leaf and ladle soup into four broiler-safe bowls, such as heavy crockware. Put the toasts into the soup, cheese side down. Top with a layer of Gruyère, and then a bit of Parmesan. Bake for fifteen minutes and then put under a broiler for a couple minutes until the cheese bubbles and browns.

CHAPTER 25

BYE-BYE, LOBSTER

LESSON HIGHLIGHTS: ROASTED LOBSTER, SHRIMP-STUFFED CHICKEN,
RUINED GUINEA FOWL, AND PROBLEMATIC HOUSEGUESTS

"So sar-ry, lob-sta, so sar-ry!" wails Suki at the other end of the worktable. She begins to sing a Japanese bedtime song to her lobster, trying
to soothe it as she attempts to ram her trussing needle up its backside before
placing it in boiling water. Chef Bouveret advised us on this cooking
technique to keep its tail straight for proper presentation.

But the lobster will not go silently into the pot. The creature fights
back, snapping its tail frantically. Suki jumps away, letting go just long
enough for the lobster to escape. In seconds, it scurries off the marble
counter and drops to the floor. One of the bands on its claws breaks in the
fall, and it starts snapping frantically in self-defense.

"*Eeeeeeeeeeek!*" Suki cries. She grabs her tongs and gives chase, clacking
at the crustacean. "Come on, lob-sta! Come on, lob-sta!"

Suki can't get a good grip with the tongs. She tosses her side towel
over it, then swoops down and picks it up with an oven mitt. "Soooo
sorry, lob-sta!" Tossing it in the boiling water, she bangs the lid on top.
"Bye-ee-bye-ee, lob-sta!" she sings. With a sigh, she turns to see all of us
watching and is immediately embarrassed.

But in truth, we've all fallen in love with sweet Suki. Everyone in the room starts singing in high falsettos "Bye-ee-bye-ee, lobsta! Bye-ee-bye-ee!"

The *tournedos de homard rôti,* or sliced roasted lobster, offers a busy practical. After we dispatch our poor crustaceans, we make risotto, dry zucchini flowers, and craft a complex puree from fennel. In the end, Chef Bouveret gives me a thumbs-up, and I tuck all the food into zipbags. Isabella offers me her extra risotto.

"*Dahrling,* take this for your visitors," she says.

It's only our second night back in the apartment, and we already have houseguests.

Now it's only a twenty-five-minute or so commute home, compared to the hour to Belleville. Emerging from the Métro near the apartment, I walk over to rue Montorgueil to our usual *boulangerie.* It's a crisp autumn day. By the end of Intermediate Cuisine, I learned that the friendly blond woman who works here is named Lydie.

"Bonjour!" she says enthusiastically. "Ça va?" *How are you?*

"Ça va, Lydie. Et vous?" My French is good enough for these brief pleasantries. She's all right, bit of a cold, but nice weather, yes? I agree, pushing two baguettes down in my black bag. "À demain," *see you tomorrow,* I tell her. We've exchanged gracious dialogue, baguettes, and euros in fewer than thirty seconds—efficient yet genuine, unlike the artificial friendliness that pervades so much of retail America.

At the corner florist, I pick up a bouquet of red lilies. I've gotten to know this friendly merchant, too, a hulking man whom I'd more likely expect to see in the World Wrestling Federation than managing in a flower shop in Paris.

On rue Étienne Marcel, I pass a gaggle of women stopped dead in their tracks by a window filled with expensive shoes. Crossing rue Turbigo, through a window I first spot his waist-length gray hair. "Bonjour!" I sing out, entering the well-ordered wineshop.

"Ma chérie!" Marc says. "What have you made today?" He suggests a sauvignon blanc from the Loîre Valley to pair with the lobster. He comes around the register to hand me the chilled wine and kisses both my cheeks. "It's so good to have you both back in the neighborhood. *À bientôt.*"

As I head up the stairs to our apartment, I think that I'm finally back into the rhythm of our life here, the way I envisioned it would be when we returned. Well, almost. We're newlyweds, Mike's almost died, and we'd just moved back into the apartment. I would have preferred a few days to ourselves before Belinda and Amanda arrived.

I'd met Amanda, a lean thirty-something with short black hair, through a running club in Seattle. Mike and I barely knew her partner, Belinda, a tax attorney and a self-described "wine snob." Arriving for a party to celebrate Mike's birthday, Belinda had surveyed the crowd. "We thought it would just be us," she said as her face clouded with genuine dismay. The rest of the evening, Belinda huddled near the refrigerator, doling out the moderately expensive wine she'd brought to a few select guests, as if it were a priceless elixir.

"I've been thinking of taking Amanda to Paris," Belinda said, cornering me in the kitchen that night, dribbling a bit of her wine into my glass before refilling her own. "When will you be there again?"

Then, the notion of houseguests in France in October seemed pleasantly far away. *It's only for a couple of days,* I think now, pushing open the door. We did invite them, sort of.

Belinda and Amanda sit in the kitchen sipping cups of café au lait that Mike made for them. Mike gives me a kiss. They both get up to give me a hug and sit telling us about their trip as I reheat the food. It's not overwhelming; one lobster doesn't yield that much meat. Even with Isabella's portion, there's not much risotto, either. It's only 4:00 p.m., so it will make a nice snack anyway.

Belinda grabs Amanda's hand as they gaze out the kitchen window. "Baby, isn't this nice?" Belinda is cooing to Amanda. "We're in Paris! See, I told you I'd bring you here." She nuzzles her ear. "What baby wants, baby gets."

Amanda grimaces. "You know, I *hate* it when you call me 'baby.' "

Mike opens the wine. He sets out four glasses. Belinda eyes it. "Do you have any red?" she asks. "I don't drink white wine. Everyone knows that white wine isn't real wine."

I lay the table with some baguettes, chèvre, and the bit of food from class. We toast, Belinda with a red that Mike opened, the rest of us with the white. Belinda eyes the plates. "What is this, haute cuisine where they just serve you little bits of food?" Belinda says. "I need more to eat than this. Where can we get a burger?"

Mike and I take them on a brief walking tour down to the Seine and then to dinner at a small bistro around the corner from our apartment. I order a glass of white wine. Mike orders a beer. Amanda does the same.

"Baby, if you're going to drink beer, then you can pay for it yourself," Belinda says. Amanda leans over and hisses whispers into Belinda ear. Belinda hisses whispers back.

"Amanda is going to pay for her share, and I'm going to pay for mine," says Belinda. "I think she should have to start paying her own way, don't you, Mike?"

At this, Amanda calmly picks up her menu and puts it front of her face. Belinda picks up hers and does the same. Behind their menus, they argue angrily. Other diners stare at the scene; our waiter stops in his tracks at the sight. After a few moments, they place their menus on the table, Amanda's face red yet placid.

When the bill comes, neither of them motion for it. Finally, Mike picks it up and calculates. "It comes to about twenty euros each."

"I didn't have any wine, and I only had a salad," Belinda insists. She slaps €11 onto the table and stands up abruptly. "I'm exhausted. Take us to our bed."

Since they are here only a couple days, we insist they take our bedroom. I have to get up at 7:00 a.m. the next day, so this way we don't have to worry about waking them up. At school, I tell Isabella, Jenny, and Margo about their argument behind the menus.

"*Dahrling*, they sound awful," Isabella says. "I'd tell them to get a hotel."

I shrug. "They leave for Belgium in two days. Mike and I can be alone together then."

Today, we're making *blancs de volaille aux langoustines au parfum de curry*, or chicken stuffed with shrimp in a curry sauce. In the tasting, it had a nice, slightly fruity flavor.

I slice off the breasts and hack the carcass to bits for sauce. We get four langoustines each. I shell them and pull out the threads of veins. The shells get seared with the chicken bones as the base for the sauce. To this, we add curry, onions, and celery and get them hot, to release the flavor. As the smell of burning curry drifts over the kitchen, I'm reminded of a London curry house. We deglaze the pan with white wine, add coconut milk, mashed bananas, mangoes, and other fruit, and let it simmer.

Chef Gaillard oversees the practical. As extra practice today, he wants us to demonstrate our ability to *brunoise,* a fine precise cut. I get lost in the Zen of fine dicing. I look up to discover that everyone else has moved on. I've spent half an hour just cutting vegetables.

I rush to butterfly the two breasts, line each with a row of langoustines, roll them up in foil, and put them into a roasting pan before slamming them into the oven. I glance at the clock. It's 2:36. Class ends at 3:00 p.m. In demonstration, Chef cooked his chicken for twelve minutes. I should still finish on time. I finish my sauce, prep everything else, and then slide my plate into the oven to heat.

That's when I notice something. My oven's not hot.

I touch the roll of foil. *Merde.* It's still soft, not firm as it would be if it were cooked. I cut off a small slice from one end. It's 2:51, and my chicken is almost raw.

People are presenting their plates. Chef declares Jenny's plate "magnificent." While she's talking to the chef, I shove my pan into Jenny's still-hot oven.

Chef moves on to Suki. Her sauce is too sweet, her chicken is undercooked, her *brunoise* is poor, her spinach is cold, and everything needs salt. Chef asks her, "Do you think this is good work for a Superior student?"

"Nooooooo, Chef," Suki says softly, gulping down tears.

Memories of that too sweet orange sauce come flooding back. I taste my sauce. While it has a good flavor, it's overwhelmed by the sweet coconut milk.

"Can I taste your sauce?" I ask Isabella. Hers has a stronger curry flavor. I need to rework my sauce, fast. But checking for a clean small saucepan, I find no clean pans or pots anywhere. Just then, Jules the dishwasher arrives in the kitchen. *Great.* As Jules yells at me, I wash out a small saucepan in his sink. Back at my stove, I combine two spoonfuls of Isabella's sauce and two spoonfuls of mine in the saucepan.

"Attention à l'heure!" Chef yells. It's 3:01. We're late.

At 3:05, Margo presents her dish. She went against the recipe and made some extra tomato concasseé to add color for presentation. "C'est mauvais!" he yells at her. I'm shocked to hear him tell Margo her plate is *bad*. Chef is full into a gray mood now.

At 3:08, I check my chicken. Hmmm. A few more minutes will do it. Should I wait? The chef roars again. I take it out, slice it, and finish my plate.

Chef scoops up a bit of sauce. It's fine. The spinach is good, and my *brunoise* looks excellent. He pokes at the chicken, pushing through the slice with a small spoon. "This side is cooked fine, but this side isn't," he says in French.

"Deux, trois minutes," he says. Why didn't I wait? I wouldn't serve this, would I? Of course not.

"Merci, Chef," I say. At least he didn't yell at me.

Isbabella is not so lucky. He begins to nag her at 3:12.

"Mon four ne marche pas," she says. Her oven isn't working, either.

A Superior student should know to check her oven, and if it isn't working find another way to cook it, he bellows. Would she give that excuse to Alain Ducasse?

Chef Gaillard bangs some pans together and takes them into the dishwashing station. Isabella rushes over to me. "Darling, my chicken is still almost raw, what am I going to do?" she laments. I have just pulled my other, now-cooked piece from the oven. I drop it, still wrapped in foil, like a hot potato onto Isabella's cutting board.

When Chef returns, she presents her plate with my chicken.

He decrees that one cooked just right. If only I had waited. But then he tells Isabella that since it's late, it doesn't matter that it's perfect.

When I return that afternoon, I notice a stack of new fluffy white towels in the bathroom. When we moved into the apartment originally, we had bought some light-blue towels. Over time, they'd become streaked with white, the result of accidentally washing them in the intense stain-busting solution I used for my uniforms. I wash my face and go into the kitchen. Mike, Belinda, and Amanda are sitting around the table, drinking wine. Mike looks pained.

"Hey, we bought some great wine today!" Belinda says, offering me a glass. Six wine bottles sit on the counter, still wrapped. "Oh, that's ours. I had better put that away," she says. They promptly leave to stash those bottles in the bedroom.

During the day, Mike had learned that all of Belinda's knowledge of wine comes from a single Dorling Kindersley book. Mike took her to see our wine merchant, Marc. There, she shopped book in hand, rejecting any bottle of wine not listed and chastising him for failing to carry others mentioned.

Once at our apartment, they opened wine Mike had purchased.

"At least they bought us towels," I say.

"No, *I* bought the towels," Mike says, exasperated. "They complained about the others, and I took them to BHV. I thought they were going to buy them, a sort of host gift, but when we were in the cashier line, Belinda dumped them into my arms, saying she didn't want to have to speak French to the cashier."

Amanda and Belinda refused to go forth into Paris alone, they constantly argued, and they didn't want to pay any of the bill at lunch. "It's exhausting. They expect us to be their personal tour guides all the time," Mike says. "Can you deal with them for a while?"

"Thank God they're leaving the day after tomorrow," I say. "All right, I'll take over. I just need a shower."

Wearily, I walk into the bathroom. The towels are gone.

Amanda walks out of the bedroom.

"Hey, have you seen the new towels?" I ask.

She winces, without responding, and turns back into the bedroom. I hear bitter whispering. Instead of Amanda, Belinda surfaces.

"Here you go, use one of ours," she says. "Oh, by the way, we're enjoying Paris so much that we're not going to Belgium. It's going to save us so much money to stay here for another week. Isn't that great?" She heads out into the kitchen for more wine, leaving me with a single towel.

★ ★ ★

Days later, I develop a cough, then a fever. Every day, I am a little worse. I'm not alone. Several students have *la grippe,* the French term for the flu.

"Ah, it's probably from the early-morning trip to Rungis," says Anne the translator when I show up wheezing at school. "It's those cold buildings, especially when combined with lack of sleep. What you need is a lot of rest."

But I can't rest. We're trying to figure out how to evict our house-guests from our bedroom. I bring home pigeon stuffed with foie gras and quail in a red-wine-reduction sauce, yet they never offer to treat us to dinner or offer to chip in for groceries. Worse, they never say thank you.

Mike has some friends who are expecting him to join them in the south of France. Now that I'm not feeling well, he and I both convince Belinda and Amanda to leave for Amsterdam.

The morning after Mike boards the TGV for the Côte d'Azur, I wake up with a pounding head, a fever, and a deep cough. *La grippe* has taken hold with a vengeance.

I feel miserable. I hobble to school. The weather's turned especially cold. I can't smell anything. I ache everywhere. We have only a morning practical. *Meeze Gerta* can do it, I think.

The recipe calls for seared breasts of guinea fowl. We're greeted by a half bird, still on the bone. Someone is out sick, so there's one extra. Arriving early as usual, Margo takes the extra half bird and shoves it in her fridge.

Isabella grabs my arm as I unpack my knives.

"Darling, you look terrible," she says. "Are you sure you should be here?"

I assure her that I'm OK. But halfway through class, I'm not. I'm feverish and dizzy with cold medicine. Shaking with chills, I bone the guinea fowl and season the tender meat.

When I start to brown the birds, my pan is too hot. I burn one side black immediately. Worse, I put the breasts into the oven and then forget them. When I pull them out they are charred, black lumps.

I glance at the clock. There is time—I could start them over.

"Margo, wasn't there an extra guinea fowl?" I ask.

She continues stirring, her back to me at her stove.

"Margo?"

Nothing.

"Margo?!"

Jenny shakes her head. "It's in her fridge," she says quietly. "But forget it."

Fine. I need to go home anyway. I drop the hard, black breasts onto the plate. Next, I plop a spoonful of mashed cauliflower alongside. The sauce goes into an unpleasant, oily pool next to that. I add a bit of parsley, for color.

Chef Savard frowns when he sees my plate. He prods the edge of my *pintade* with a fork. He seems concerned.

"Are you feeling OK?" he asks.

"No, I'm sick, Chef. I have the flu."

He goes over my work, trying to be nice. "Well, the puree has a nice consistency. But the *pintade* is not . . ."—he tries to finds a tender word—"it is not good. There's not really any flavor to the rest."

"I can't taste anything," I say flatly. "Is that all?" He nods.

"Merci, Chef," I say.

I turn, stomp on the lever, and scrape the plate's contents into the trash can. I walk back to my station, past Margo.

"Thanks for sharing, Margo," I say, grabbing my knives and turning to leave.

"Oh, I'm sorry, did you need something?" she asks.

In France, doctors still make house calls. An hour after I phone, a charming, handsome doctor arrives, carrying a smart leather bag. He resembles François Truffaut, circa *Close Encounters of the Third Kind*. He's chatty, to the point of flirting.

It's wasted on me. I feel horrible, plus I'm married. He listens to my chest, checks my ears. He tests my blood pressure and then takes my temperature.

"What is it?" I ask.

"A bit high, 39.5," he says.

Celsius means little to me. "What's that in Fahrenheit?"

"About 103. You are very sick," he says, starting to write on a pad. "Infected everywhere, your head and your chest." He rips a piece of paper. "You'll need to fill these two prescriptions. Take a double dose of the antibiotic now, and go to bed for seventy-two hours. No nightclubs, yes?" He winks at me. "If your fever is not better in twenty-four hours, call me." He gives me his mobile-phone number and a bill. His house call costs just sixty euros.

I hobble down the stairs to the store. I buy some chicken and some orange juice. I make some soup and collapse in bed.

"We brought you something from Amsterdam," Belinda tells me when they return, carefully balancing a new, heavy parcel in her hand. Ah! A gift! Maybe they weren't so bad after all.

"Hold on, I just need to put this into the bedroom," Belinda says. She returns, confused. "Where is our stuff?"

"Well, I'm sick. We moved back into the bedroom since you were gone," I say. Almost apologetically, I add, "The doctor told me to stay in bed."

"Oh." Belinda seems disturbed. Then she smiles. "Come in the kitchen, I'll give you your gifts!"

At the table, she digs into her purse. She produces an unused plastic-wrapped loofah from their hotel room and a couple of battered, free guides to Holland. Then she makes me close my eyes and hold out my hands for the real treat: a lacy wine "tux" designed to go over a bottle to provide the illusion of a formally clad waiter. She bought a dozen as stocking stuffers.

"We were going to ask you to come out to dinner with us, our treat," she says. "But I can see you are not feeling well."

I see them only once more the next day, as they head out the door to the airport. Belinda wishes me a speedy recovery. Amanda is sweet, and for the first time thanks me for the hospitality.

"Come on, baby, we're going to be late for the plane," Belinda yells up the stairs.

"STOP calling me 'baby'!" Amanda hollers back. The echoes of their argument drift up the staircase until the front door crashes closed. I shut the door to the apartment.

Bye-bye, lobsters. I think. *Au revoir.*

Potage de Poulet aux Nouilles, avec de l'Ail et des Herbes

CHICKEN NOODLE SOUP WITH GARLIC AND HERBS

Garlic is thought to have an array of medicinal qualities, including the ability to kill bacteria. I use a mix of dark and white meat for this soup, but you can use all-white meat, if you prefer. Bone-in chicken is very important; it adds significant flavor. Keep the bones for stock if desired. (See the recipe on pages 44–45.) I use whole-wheat yolkless wide noodles, but use your favorite. If you don't have herbes de Provence, thyme or mixed Italian herbes will work just fine. If you don't have all the fresh herbs for the bouquet garni, use whatever you've got on hand. This also freezes well.

Serves eight

1½ pounds (750 g) chicken pieces, skin removed

2 tablespoons olive oil

½ chopped onion

2 large chopped carrots

2 stalks chopped celery

½ cup (125 ml) white wine

5 quarts chicken stock (may substitute water for half)

1 teaspoon herbes de Provence

½ bunch parsley, ½ bunch thyme, 3 bay leaves, tied together

4 cloves garlic, minced

2 ounces (50 g) wide noodles

½ teaspoon salt, a few cranks pepper

2 teaspoons minced fresh parsley *(optional)*

Rinse the chicken under cold water; pat dry. Trim any excess fat. Set aside. In a large Dutch oven, heat the olive oil over medium heat. Add the onions, carrots, and celery and cook, stirring regularly, until softened. Add the white wine and stir the bottom to loosen any brown bits as it reduces by one half. Add the stock and/or water. Heat through. Add the chicken. Bring to a low boil, skimming fat and foam from the surface. When it appears that no more skimming is necessary, drop the heat to a simmer and add the herbs. Simmer partially covered for a half hour. Add the garlic. Simmer another half hour. Remove the chicken from the soup with tongs. Continue to simmer the liquid for a few moments while the chicken cools. Remove the meat from the chicken and shred it into pieces and return to the pot. Add the noodles and increase the heat to a gentle boil, then cook until soft. Skim off any foam and check seasonings, adding salt and pepper as needed. Remove tied herbs. Stir in the parsley. Makes enough for a couple days with the flu.

CHAPTER 26

I DIDN'T ALWAYS HATE MY JOB

LESSON HIGHLIGHTS: BEEF WITH A RED-WINE-REDUCTION SAUCE
AND THE SEDUCTION OF CORPORATE LIFE

The bottle shatters as it hits the floor. Margo stands motionless, her hand frozen in the air, her apron splattered with droplets of red wine, as in a bloody scene from a TV crime show.

Jenny, Isabella, Suki, and I rush in to help, along with a gentle woman from Israel named Samara.

"Ooooooohh, nooooo!" cries Suki in her high-pitched wail. "I find . . ." and leaves it unanswered, clearly unable to think of the word in English.

The rest of the practical group continues chopping, unmoved.

Jenny grabs the kitchen's massive paper-towel roll and begins to mop up the wine. Samara puts on silicon oven gloves and begins to pick up pieces of glass. Suki returns with the janitor's mop and starts to earnestly clean up.

"Aw clean! Seeeeeee!?" Suki sings. "Awwww clean . . . ."

Through all this, Margo stands like a statue, staring at the floor, aghast. Isabella touches her arm.

"It's only a bottle of wine, darling," Isabella tells her. "It could happen to anyone."

Margo, white-faced, slowly turns her gaze from the floor to Isabella.

"No, it doesn't. It doesn't happen *to me.*" With that, she turns on her heel and heads out of the room, leaving the rest of us to clean up.

Later, she returns with a new bottle of wine and puts it on the table. Her mood has shifted. She must have had a Tony Robbins pep talk with herself.

"Thank you everyone for helping me," she singsongs across the table, then repeats it in French. Acting as if nothing occurred, she starts to trim her piece of beef tenderloin.

But something has happened. Unwittingly, she's given us a glimpse into her true self. Perhaps she competes so hard because if she fails she can't forgive herself. I feel sorry for her, but then I know how she feels.

She's a corporate woman. She's been programmed not just to please but to achieve. It's a subtle thing, really, the shift that renders a normal person into someone who thinks it's all right to succeed at any cost. If you go to enough sales meetings or product rallies, after a while you begin to think that "you must do whatever it takes."

If you don't catch yourself, you can be stuck there.

I was originally hired by my company as the restaurant "producer" for a prototype of a network of online city guides. It was like working for a well-funded start-up and perfect for me, combining my geeky tendencies with my passion for food. My evenings were spent eating in restaurants, research for reviews.

After three years, listening to National Public Radio one morning as I got ready for work, I learned that my company had sold the city guides to our competitor. Like other employees at our offices around the country, I discovered I lost my job via the news. Later that day, the head of our division sent out a long self-congratulatory email detailing the sale. Near the end, in a masterstroke of understatement, he noted that "some of you might be worried about your employment status." Full-time workers had ten weeks to find another job within the company; after that, the networks would officially merge, and our jobs would go away. We could apply to the new company.

"That bastard," one of my contract employees yelled at his computer. "He just got rid of all of us, and he doesn't even care."

Research shows that children who lose a parent early in life show remarkable flexibility in the face of adversity. While other people stormed around my office, I got on the phone and started asking friends if they knew someone in London.

That's when I talked to my three friends, and they all led me to Mike.

In London, I worked in editorial as senior content manager. I helped design "channels" of content, oversaw the home page and news coverage, and managed online events. I had a great flat above a French wine bar. The owners gave me free wine since I never complained about the music, which shook my floors until midnight. I threw dinner parties out of my kitchen, the size of a walk-in closet. It was glamorous, exciting, and I loved it.

But after a couple years, things changed. At work our small group of twenty-four exploded to a crew of almost eighty. I respected my initial boss. Max switched our job titles to "network programmers" with the hope that software higher-ups unfamiliar with content jobs would think twice before they cut "programmers." Max kept getting promoted. I got upgraded on his coattails until finally he left to run editorial back in the United States. I got a new boss and a management team united around a single idea: that a major website didn't need "content."

"Let's have the advertisers provide the content," says Tim, a senior sales director. "Who knows what these network programmers do all day anyway? Oh, I mean, except you, Kathleen. . . ."

In this elevated role, my new boss required that I discipline my best friend at work—a person I adored and with whom I'd bonded while working eighty-hour weeks to produce the webcast of Madonna's comeback concert in London's rough Brixton neighborhood. The event made the *Guinness Book of World Records* as the largest webcast ever, with ten million viewers.

"It doesn't matter if he's your friend," I was counseled. "You've got to show you've got what it takes. To be an executive, you have to be ruthless."

So I chastised my best friend as ordered. That started a tense standoff which lasted until one day he cleared out his desk and left the building. He never spoke to me again.

This was when I started hating my job.

I got lucky. While I was on vacation, I was laid off, fired, or whatever they want to call it. (Technically, in UK employment-speak, I was "in threat of a redundancy due to reorganization.") Thank God. I don't know if I had it in me to quit. A gilded cage is still a cage, just the same, but I might still be there, putting up with it.

That's why I understand Margo. She just hasn't shaken that corporate expectation yet.

"The constant desire to win is a very American kind of trouble," writes William Zinsser in his book *On Writing Well*. "Less glamorous gains made along the way—learning, wisdom, growth, and confidence, dealing with failure—aren't given the same respect because they can't be given a grade."

Or a paycheck, I might add.

Two days after the wine incident, we hear about the one thing that will be given a grade that matters to me: our final exam.

Chef DuPont hands out the ingredient lists and explains the rules. The exam will be graded by a jury of three chefs, and each of us must present exactly on time. Each student will present ten minutes after the previous one. Each minute we're late, we lose points. The time is crucial, Chef explains, to demonstrate that we've learned how to prioritize, organize, and work quickly yet with precision.

We must prepare a main dish—in this case, using a fillet of veal. There's a list of other items we must use: endives, *mousse de foie gras*, salsify, cauliflower, and chanterelle mushrooms. We have another list of optional ingredients, all of which will be available in our baskets, that includes standards such as garlic, shallots, onions, flour, yeast, wines, oils, and so on. We must come up with three side dishes.

"It's like *Iron Chef*," Jenny observes.

A good plate demonstrates multiple techniques, Chef says. One item should be simple—say, sautéed vegetables. The others should be complex. Also, we must provide our recipes to the chef—written out in French— before we begin.

Chef comes around the front of the workstation. It feels intimate.

"Écoutez, c'est très important," he says. *Listen, thi*
Keep plates simple, he says. The judges are classic
or unusual concoctions will turn them off. 7
by well-seasoned and properly cooked meat and a fin
make a menu too complex to complete. Avoid puff pastry,
takes a long time. If you can't turn vegetables well, don't do them. 1
can do what you want, but whatever it is, it better be good, and it must
be hot.

The final exam is worth 45 percent of our grade. He doesn't need to
say it. To fail the exam means you don't get a diploma.

Boeuf en Croûte Champignons avec Sauce Vin Rouge

MUSHROOM-CRUSTED STEAKS WITH RED-WINE SAUCE

Serves four

A classic red-wine sauce can accompany any kind of red meat. Trim extra
fat or sinew off the meat to use as the basis of the sauce or use a few
pieces of stew meat. I use a mix of seasoned bread crumbs and panko,
Japanese bread crumbs. Serve with mashed potatoes and an earthy red
wine such as a Cabernet Sauvignon.

RED-WINE SAUCE
1 cup (250 ml) dry red wine
2 to 3 ounces stew meat or beef trimmings
1 tablespoon olive oil
¼ cup chopped onions
¼ cup chopped celery
¼ cup chopped carrots
Parsley stems
½ teaspoon dried thyme
1 tablespoon flour
1 cup (250 ml) brown beef stock
1 tablespoon butter
Salt, pepper

SHROOM-CRUSTED STEAKS

8 ounces mushrooms, sliced

2 tablespoons butter

¼ cup bread crumbs or panko

1 tablespoon parsley stems, chopped

Coarse salt, ground pepper

4 beef-tenderloin fillets (6 to 8 ounces each)

1 tablespoon olive oil

For the sauce: Reduce the wine by half in a small saucepan over medium-high heat. As it reduces, in a separate saucepan sear the beef trimmings in oil over high heat. Degrease by pouring out any leftover fat. Add the onions, celery, and carrots and stir until softened. Add the parsley stems, and thyme. Top with the flour and stir to coat. Add the reduced red wine and the beef stock. Bring to a boil, skim any foam off the top, and then reduce heat. Let simmer for a half hour while you finish the recipe.

Sauté the mushrooms in the butter over medium heat until browned. Strain, then chop finely together with bread crumbs, parsley, a teaspoon of salt, and several grinds of black pepper (or blend in a food processor).

Preheat the oven to 400°F/200°C. Season the meat with salt and pepper on both sides. Heat the oil over high heat in a skillet. Sear each side about two to three minutes. Remove from the pan to a cookie sheet lined with foil or parchment. Press the mushroom mixture on top of each steak. Turn on the broiler. Broil until the mushroom coating browns and the meat firms to medium-rare, about six minutes.

To finish the sauce, strain it through a mesh sieve or a colander lined with cheesecloth. Check seasoning and add salt and pepper to taste. Return it to the saucepan and stir in the knob of butter to finish. Serve the sauce alongside the meat.

CHAPTER 27

AN AMERICAN HOSPITAL IN PARIS

LESSON HIGHLIGHTS: PREPARING FOR THE FINAL EXAM,
VEAL, PIGEONS, AND TROUBLESOME KIDNEYS

The pain is blinding. It feels like someone stabbed me in my right side.

I let out a gasp. I lose my balance and grab the edge of the worktable during our afternoon practical, right in the middle of *pigeon rôtis sur crème de céleri*. Despite the heat in the kitchen, a chill runs through me.

From across the table, Jenny's maternal instincts kick in. "What's wrong?"

"I don't know. . . . It's nothing," I say, trying to stand upright in a sudden wave of exhaustion.

"Bullshit," she says. "You're hunched over like an old lady, and your face is as white as a sheet."

I can sense that I'm beginning to sweat, and a lot—Nixon-in-his-second-term kind of sweat. I've had a nagging pain in my side for the last few days, but now it has shifted around to my back. I had hoped it would just go away. Now, it feels as if something is attacking me inside with daggers and a vengeance.

Please don't let me be sick, I pray silently.

The sharp pain eases into a dull, throbbing ache. I try to pretend nothing is wrong, even smiling and humming as I finish my chestnut-and-truffle garnish. Chef Bouveret gives my plate a thumbs-up. Margo, Jenny, and Isabella give me worried looks as I walk out the kitchen door. "I'm fine," I assure them.

Two hours later, I am in the emergency room at the American Hospital in Paris.

It's a quiet evening at the hospital, housed behind a handsome brick façade nestled on a leafy, broad side street in the plush Neuilly-sur-Seine neighborhood on the western edge of Paris. Founded in 1906 as a nonprofit endeavor to serve the burgeoning American expat community, it's now recognized as one of the top private hospitals in Europe.

Mike insisted I go. And now he steadies me as we walk through the main lobby toward the emergency room. I notice black-and-white photos lining the wall. Several show old Red Cross vehicles, from the hospital's days serving Allied troops during the world wars. In French, I give my name and address; but I can't remember the French word for "pain" when asked for my symptoms.

"It's *douleur*," prompts the receptionist, a pretty young French woman. "You're American? You are not well. We will speak your language. You have enough trouble being sick." She leads us into a massive exam room, big enough for perhaps four beds but holding just one on the right side of the room and a large desk to the left.

Mike and I appear to be the only visitors to the ER tonight. In walks the nurse, looking at my chart. She's got a wide smile and a mess of curly black hair.

"Yes, Mrs. Klozar?" she asks. Why are people in hospitals always confusing me with Mike's mother? Oh, right, that's me now, according to my passport.

"Sit up here," she says, slapping the bed. I crawl on top. "You'll need to get into a gown. You want this handsome guy to leave?" She winks at Mike.

"I think I've seen everything she's got to hide," he says. Without asking, he comes to the bed, unzips my boots, and gingerly removes the first one.

Perhaps fresh from his own injury, he's figured that it's hard for me to bend down to do it myself. The nurse watches.

"So nice, maybe I would like one of those," she says, nodding toward Mike.

"These boots?" Mike asks.

"No, a husband," she adds, as she pulls up the cart of blood-sample needles. "You are married long, yes?" I start to explain how we were friends, and then we started dating. She interrupts with a rehearsed singsong phrase, "I don't know what you're saying, my English is not so good! I know only a little!"

Then the doctor enters the examining room in a whirlwind.

"Hello, hello, hello!" he says, smiling broadly as he offers us each his hand to shake. "Please, please, sit down over here." He skirts the desk and looks over the nurse's notes. He runs a hand through his salt-and-pepper mound of hair. Then, he settles his gaze on me. "Tell me about your symptoms," he says. I give him the list: chronic abdominal pain, sweating, fever, chills, and overall lethargy. "When did this start?" A few days ago, I say.

"Any back pain?" Maybe a little, I tell him. He gets up and walks around the desk. Without comment, he pokes me in the back, near the waist. I screech and nearly jump out of the chair in pain. Mike lurches back in his seat at my reaction.

"I thought so," the doctor says. "We'll do some tests."

Within an hour, they draw my blood, take a sample of my urine, and put me through both a CAT scan and an X ray. This is all too familiar. Three months ago, I was the one holding Mike's hand while he was tied up to an IV and stuck with needles. Now, he's holding mine. I know the vow says "in sickness and in health," but is it necessary to test this so early into our marriage?

Results in hand, the doctor sits down with me and patiently goes through every one of my results, something a doctor has never done with me before.

"You have a kidney infection, and a fairly serious one," the doctor explains. He'll give me a shot of antibiotics tonight. I can go home, but I'll need to return for two more shots and take some other medications. I'm to stay off my feet for a week. But it will take another six weeks to re-cover, and it will be possibly six months before my kidneys return to normal.

"But Mrs. Klozar, if you don't respond to the antibiotics within three days or you get any worse, we will have to admit you," he says. "A kidney infection is nothing to fool around with. Why did you wait so long to come in?"

They give us the CAT-scan negatives ("You paid for them," the doc-tor says) and a bill for six hundred euros for everything. We never cease to be amazed by the economics of medicine outside the United States. Mike's CAT scans had cost around two thousand dollars each.

On the taxi ride home, the shot of antibiotics takes effect. The scenery whizzing by melts into a haze. I don't remember how I get there, but I wake up in bed the next day. As I awake, reality hits me.

I'm allowed four absences, and I've had two. I have four more classes plus the final exam one week from now. Then there's the written test, being held this afternoon. To miss that would be an absence, too. I decide I can manage sitting at a desk. Over Mike's protests, I get dressed for school. "It's ten percent of my grade," I keep telling him. Tomorrow is the five-hour practice, working in a kitchen for the final exam. It's been years since a student missed it. If I miss that, how will I be able to graduate?

After years of resisting, the Paris school begrudgingly agreed to provide a written test. We've been advised there's "no way to prepare for it." Rumor has it that it's the same written test as in the London school. However, our curriculum isn't identical. As I ease into a chair, I'm presented questions in both English and French.

Immediately, I know I'm going to fail.

"Where does Sarawak pepper come from?" Have we ever used it?

"What is *vergeoise*?" I learn later from a Google search that it's a type of brown sugar. It was used once in an early Intermediate demonstration.

So it continues. Some are fair, such as, "When should you salt vegeta-bles?" Others are debatable, such as, "What is the proper temperature for roasting beef?"

For the next hour, most students squirm around in their seats. My side nags with pain. Afterward, I gingerly make it down the stairs. Every step hurts.

A Canadian student named Margaret finished well ahead of everyone else. I ask how she knew everything. "I realized I didn't know any of it," she says. "It made me so angry that I just guessed at random and went down for a smoke."

The ever-competitive Margo was apoplectic. She'd tried to study, reviewing tomes by Escoffier and our French/English cooking definitions. "Wasn't that test a little slice of heaven?" she asks sarcastically. I don't answer. "Are you worried about the final?" Margo asks.

"All I want to do is go home and lie down," I say.

That night, we go back to the hospital for my second shot of antibiotics. "At least we can cross this part of town off the map," Mike says.

After another hazy drive home, I'm back in bed. I sleep for eleven hours.

The next day is the five-hour practice for the exam. I am as shaky as a newborn calf. Just getting ready to go to school exhausts me. "I can't do it," I tell Mike.

He's relieved. "You're not supposed to be on your feet, remember? Why don't you go back to bed?" I fall into a troubled sleep punctuated by a series of anxiety dreams.

In the first dream, my planned celery and salsify flan melts into a creamy heap of mush. Next, my *en croûte* pastry burns, turning black. In the last, I keep plating my food but somehow never get done, like the famous Lucille Ball scene in which she tries to keep up with the chocolates in the factory.

I wake up in a cold sweat, hearing my phone ringing.

"Darling, it's Isabella, I'm here with Chef DuPont. I told him you were sick. He wants to know how you're doing. Here, he wants to talk to you."

Oh, shit. "Bonjour, Chef," I say.

"Bonjour, ma petite amie," he starts and goes on in rapid French. I don't understand.

"Pardon, répétez, Chef?" I ask.

More rapid-fire French, then "Au revoir, ma chérie."

Isabella comes back on.

"What did he say?" I ask.

"He was saying it's a disadvantage that you couldn't be at the practice, so he will look over your recipes and plans and advise you personally," she says. "He said to bring them to school, and he'll talk to you about them after class." I'm amazed—that's so nice of him to offer.

"Oh, *dahrling,* it's so sweet. He's genuinely concerned about you."

That evening, before heading to the hospital for my shot, we decide to get some dinner in the Seventeenth. Mike's found a beautiful little bistro. We toast to my health—the doctor said that I can drink some wine even on antibiotics—and then share a slab of chateaubriand. After our final visit to the emergency room, I take a last hazy ride home.

Another round of anxiety dreams haunts me all night. The one I remember the most: a call from the school, saying that I failed my exam. "I'm sorry, *Meeze Fleen,*" I imagine the chief administrator, Madame Sofia Rousseau, saying in her charming accent. "But theeze eeze going to be a very difficult conversation. . . ."

A few days later, I am back at school. I meet with Chef DuPont and give him my menu and sketches of my planned final plate. His advice is concise. I'd planned a flan; he advises against it. I had two white or beige side dishes; he says to avoid that, too. Color, think of how the colors interact on the plate, he says. He told us not to do puff pastry, but I'm pretty good at it now.

"C'est tentant," he says. *It's tempting,* but don't do puff pastry.

Then he asks about my health. I'm all right, I say. After a few more minutes, he gives me a quick hug around the shoulder. "You're gre-at," he says in his exaggerated American accent, usually reserved for class. It's funny, but it hurts to laugh.

Antibiotics are remarkable. Only a couple of days after that, I'm in our kitchen. It's filled with produce from a shopping trip with Isabella on rue

Montorgueil. Mike lugged it all upstairs. I've bought enough stuff to practice my exam menu at least twice.

I decide on a Normandy-style approach. My final menu:

> *Fillet of veal in pastry, stuffed with apples, celery,*
> *and mousse de fois gras with Calvados sauce*
>
> *Endive flowers with marinara sauce*
>
> *Whipped cauliflower with salsify and roasted garlic*
>
> *Chanterelle mushrooms sautéed with parsley*

For a special garnish, I'll finish the plates off with tomato roses to lend each more color. Heeding the chef's words, I decide on a mock brioche for the pastry, the light puffy number that requires only five minutes of hard kneading and an hour to rise.

But making anything *en croûte* is tricky. The ovens have been acting up in some kitchens and won't be serviced until after the break. It could be problematic to rely on them. The dish will take longer to cook in pastry, and once it's cut, that's it. There's no going back into the oven. I know some students will likely cut the veal into medallions and sauté. I stick with my plan anyway.

To stuff the veal, I make a fine dice of the golden apples, celery, and onions and sauté gently, deglazing with the Calvados. Once cooled, this mixes with the required *mousse de foie gras*.

"Hmmm, I like it better without the foie gras," Mike says, tasting it.

"Sorry, it's required," I tell him.

This mixture gets smeared onto the trimmed veal fillet, now sliced open for easy stuffing. I tie it off with kitchen string into a squat roll and then sear it to get it browned. Once cooled, this gets wrapped in a rolled-out rectangle of mock brioche, brushed with egg wash, and baked.

The salsify and cauliflower will be cooked in milk and then put through a food mill with roasted garlic. The chanterelles get a quick sauté in butter and are then tossed with parsley.

The endive flowers take me a while to figure out. Braised endive has been a household favorite since it was first demonstrated back in Intermediate. After simmering endive in butter, lemon, and chicken stock, I make a cup of the leaves with a marinara sauce to offset their slightly bitter flavor, nestled into a carved carrot stem.

The plan is for my plate to show off several techniques: pan-braising, sautéing, pureeing, making pastry, searing, and roasting. It's not the most original plate, but I think I can get it done in four hours without seriously screwing anything up, and that's what counts.

On round one, it takes me six hours. Mike, Isabella, and a few gathered friends happily eat up the results.

Round two, the next day, takes me five. Mike eats it, but with less enthusiasm. I notice that he loads up on the endives.

I set a plate from round three in front of him. He just eyes it. "Just how offended would you be if I went out and got a slice of pizza?" he asks, then eats it anyway.

Chef DuPont leads us through the final demonstration. But we are weary now. Some of us don't even takes notes. All we're waiting for is the exam.

I realize that I am sitting in exactly the same spot where I sat during the first demonstration in Basic, the one that L.P. saved for me next to LizKat.

What a different person sits here now. I'm following the chef in French. What I learned those first few days at school now seems like second nature. He takes an onion, cuts it in half, and starts to dice it the way we've been taught.

A Venezuelan TV crew bursts into the room unannounced. A woman producer leads them, her head a solid helmet of glossy hair. She asks Chef DuPont if he speaks English.

"Very good," he says and then laughs. The class laughs, in on his joke.

"Great!" she says. "What are you making?"

"Yes," he says. The class roars its approval. After a few minutes, the crew leaves. "Bah-bye," the chef says, waving.

After a show of pan-cooked Saint Pierre and pasta made of vegetables, we're done. In addition to our usual taste, the assistant hands out plastic tumblers filled with champagne. There are some hugs and a few photos. I have mine taken with Chef DuPont.

The night before the exam, stressed out and worried, I decide to do yet another four-hour practice. I time myself on how long each step takes. Using my training in project management, I stay up until 1:00 a.m. writing out a full time line:

9:00 Arrive, unpack, set up. Boil two pans of water and milk
9:10 Cut up cauliflower and salsify for puree, put in water/milk
9:15 Trim the veal
9:25 Brown the veal trimmings for sauce, cut mirepoix for sauce
9:40 *Brunoise* apple, celery, and onion for stuffing

And so on. Four hours of this. I even set myself a couple of key "milestones." For instance, I know that I have to start my brioche dough by 11:15 a.m., or I won't finish on time. The veal has to go into the oven no later than 12:15 to give it enough time to cook and, crucially, enough time to rest before I slice it.

Mike goes to sleep before I get done, thereby escaping a late-night plate of stuffed veal. I finally sit down to write out all the recipes—in French—finishing at 2:00 a.m.

"That's all I can do," I say, putting everything by the door. Tomorrow, I'll take the exam, and with that pass or fail Le Cordon Bleu.

If I don't pass, have I truly failed? I had thought I wanted my obituary to note that I had graduated from Le Cordon Bleu. Maybe I sold Gladys Smith short, like her obituary. Maybe she lived a very rich life, one that couldn't easily be measured or graded. I've learned a great deal and met so many people here. But as Julia Child told me, I'll never know everything about anything, especially cooking, which is something I love. Mike says the more you learn, the more you realize how much you don't know.

I have so much more to learn about everything.

Chicorées Frisées Classique

CLASSIC BELGIAN ENDIVES

About six servings as a side dish

In France, endives are a common yet cherished commodity, and this is a classic, simple preparation. Don't skimp on the butter, and be sure you serve extra bread to sop up the sauce. For my final exam, I wrapped the endives around a sort of marinara sauce to form small packets. I've since used the same combination on slices of toasted French bread as an appetizer. You can use the tomato sauce from the grilled-pizza recipe on pages 156–157.

8 Belgian endives, sliced in half lengthwise
3 tablespoons butter
1½ cups (125 ml) chicken stock
1 tablespoon brown sugar
¼ cup lemon juice (juice of ½ lemon)
Salt, pepper to taste

Slice off discolored portion of the hard root end of each endive. With a paring knife, remove the tough triangular core.

Melt butter in a large, heavy skillet over medium-high heat. Add the endives, cut-side down, and cook for two minutes or until endives are very browned but not burned, then turn over carefully. Cook a further four or five minutes, until butter gets very brown but not burned. Adjust heat if necessary. Add stock, brown sugar, lemon juice, salt, and pepper. Bring to a simmer, lower heat, and cover. Cook about twenty minutes, until tender and browned.

CHAPTER 28

FINAL EXAM—SUPERIOR

LESSON HIGHLIGHTS: KEEP IT SIMPLE

As usual in the mornings, a musician boards my Métro train at Châte-let, pulling a heavy amplifier on a luggage cart behind him.

As he plays, I sing along in my head:

Those were the days my friend,
We thought they'd never end.
We'd sing and dance forever and a day.

By the time I get off the Métro at Vaugirard, my heart is beating wildly. I get to school at 8:00 a.m., a full hour before my exam starts. The school is almost empty—all the exams are over except for that of Superior Group 3. In the deserted locker room, my hands shake as I put on my uniform one last time. I've heard we are graded on everything today, even our uniforms. I washed and ironed the one I'm wearing so thoroughly that it almost looks new. I head to the Winter Garden, carrying my gear and the thermos of hot tea Mike made me. Others begin to arrive. I spot Jenny; she looks tired.

"Did you sleep?" I ask. I hadn't slept. My anxiety dreams plagued me again.

She shakes her head. "No, I was too wound up. I gave up at four."

"And away we go," I tell myself softly. I am to start ten minutes before her, so I head up to the kitchen on the first floor. Chef DuPont assigns me to the corner, the same spot where I spent most of Basic Cuisine.

For the final exam, we are assigned five to a kitchen. In mine are Isabella, Jenny, Marcus, and Demetrius, a student from another group whom I don't know. The other half of Superior Group 3, including Margo and Suki, is in another kitchen.

On this spot, I first chopped mirepoix and filleted a fish. Here, Anna-Clare watched in horror as I dropped our shared duck. I almost expect L.P. or LizKat to walk in. Those days feel like yesterday and a hundred years ago all at once. I pull out my knives, and I start to hum.

When I asked L.P. about her own exam, she told me, "The final exam happens only once. I wanted to experience it, not rush through it." As usual, she's right. Like her, I do not want to hurry through this once-in-a-lifetime event.

I hear a voice behind me. *"Meeze Fleen!"* I turn to see Chef Gaillard at the door. Beside him stands one of the chefs on the jury for the exam, an older, gray-haired gentleman with thick glasses who is dressed for the occasion in a Cordon Bleu jacket over elegant gray trousers.

"Chef!" I walk over and shake Chef Gaillard's hand. This final exam is a test not just of the students but also of the chefs and their ability to teach. "J'espère que je fais bien, pour vous," I say to Chef Gaillard. *I hope I do well, for you.*

Chef Gaillard assures me that I'll do fine. He wags a finger and says, "Goûtez, goûtez, goûtez," taste, taste, taste, as if I need to be reminded to taste my food as I cook. "Bonne chance, mon amie," and he waves goodbye. I can't believe that I was once afraid of him.

I set out my recipes and my time line on the marble counter. I pull my *filet de veau* from the ingredient basket assembled by the *sous-sol,* trimming and shaping it until I end up with an eight-inch by four-inch oblong piece of tenderloin. As if by habit, I sear the trimmings in hot oil until they're dark brown. To make the mirepoix once took me twenty minutes; it now takes me under five. I sauté the vegetables, taste the veal stock, and then add it to the saucepan. I taste again, and I know that this sauce will be fine.

I move on to the *farce*. As I chop the apples and celery, I toss the remnants into the sauce. I look across at Isabella. Like everyone else, she's working intently, barely talking. The tension on the part of the other students is palpable, but I'm striving for Zen.

That is, until 11:00 a.m., when I panic.

Yeast, yeast, yeast . . . where's the yeast? I search all the fridges, all the baskets.

No yeast.

I confer with Nicholas, a fellow student who has volunteered to work as assistant for our exam. A cousin of Demetrius's, Nicholas is an affable Greek chap with a perpetual five-o'clock shadow and both ears pierced like a pirate. We both search again, with no luck. *Merde,* I think. I have to finish my pastry no later than 11:15 a.m. It needs at least forty-five minutes for the initial rise, then another fifteen minutes after I wrap it around the veal.

While he leaves the room to search, I measure everything else and dust the counter with flour. Minutes later, breathless, he returns with packets of the fresh yeast.

"Ah, merci bien, Nicholas!" I exclaim.

I crumble the yeast into lukewarm water to proof, taste my sauce, check the apples, and put the onions on to start my tomato sauce. I make the dough, then begin banging and slapping it against the counter. I finish it into a ball, lightly dust it with flour, and set it in a bowl above the stove to rise. It's exactly 11:15.

I realize that, preoccupied with the brioche, I've burned my onions. *Merde.* But I planned ahead and chopped twice as many as I thought I'd need. I start them over.

At noon, I roll out the dough. All my vegetables are done or nearly finished cooking. All that's left is to wrap my pastry carefully around the veal, now stuffed, seared, and cooled.

In one hour, my training at Le Cordon Bleu will be over.

I've gone through more than three hundred recipes, ninety lessons, my entire savings, and an incalculable number of calories from fat, cream, and butter. I look at my hands, scarred from a motley assortment of cuts and burns. I recall the woman from next-door-to-Cartier and think how appalled she would be at this sight. I notice my wedding ring, a simple platinum band with a nearly flawless diamond set flush in it. Mike designed it so that I would never have to take it off, especially in the kitchen. I scan the room, so familiar now yet soon to be a part of my life that I will forever refer to in the past tense. Everyone is working intently, the pulse quickening as the deadlines loom.

Soon, all of these people will go back to their lives or, more likely, go on to start new ones. I wonder how they will remember their times at Le Cordon Bleu. I start humming and then sing softly to myself.

Those were the days my friend,
We thought they'd never end.

Across the worktable from me, a drama unfolds.

Demetrius made the classic mistake, the one that Chef DuPont warned against. His menu is too complex to complete in four hours. Due to plate at 12:40 p.m. exactly, he starts rushing, making mistakes, dropping things, and even cutting himself. He's burned a sauce for a side dish and must restart it. He starts to yell in Greek at Nicholas, who tries to calm him down.

Everything from my anxiety dreams happens to poor Demetrius. His puff pastry burns thoroughly, rendering the golden dough into a hard, black crust. When he turns over his chanterelle-mushroom flan, it collapses on the plate into an unrecognizable yellow glob. In this exam, as in any real kitchen, it's all about timing. His is dangerously off. I wish there was something that I could do, but we're not allowed to help each other in exams.

The drama does not end there.

Isabella pulls her veal wrapped in caul fat from the oven and slices into it. It's almost raw. Chef DuPont snaps, "Ça n'est pas cuit!" *It's not cooked.* It's 12:42 p.m., eight minutes before she is due to present her plates.

It's obvious what's happened. Her oven isn't working properly. *Merde.* I should have insisted she take the oven thermometer that I'd brought in. Panicked, Isabella throws the stuffed veal back into her oven and cranks the heat. She's behind already anyway; she spent much of her exam on a complicated potato-and-mushroom galette derived from a dish by Charlie Trotter, a chef in Chicago—beautiful result, but her other vegetables suffer.

"My purée is too soft to pipe, *dahrling*," she says, almost in tears as she starts to plate. She resorts to plopping a blob next to her semicooked veal.

Demeterius finishes at 12:52—twelve minutes late. Technically, after ten minutes he should have lost his chance. But Isabella is behind as well. Chef DuPont gives Demetrius an ultimatum: "Either give us your plates, or give up."

Demetrius drops the last pieces of parsley as garnish, and Nicholas takes them away. Then Demetrius collapses, cradling his head in his arms on the worktable. He won't let anyone near him.

The chef clucks at Isabella that she's now five minutes late, as Nicholas takes her first plates into the jury. Then, he turns to me.

"Kathleen, *cinq minutes,*" and holds up five fingers.

Showtime.

I put my four plates in the oven to warm them. I hold my breath as I slice into my veal. The night before, I cut the veal wrongly, and the crust fell apart. I noticed that Marcus, the experienced chef from Canada, had cut the veal into medallions and pan-seared them instead. Why did I do meat in a crust? I knew it was risky.

The veal is reassuringly pink. I breathe again. My vegetables are fine. I pull the tomato roses from the fridge and gently place one on each plate. They're close to perfect, but then I'd obsessively made at least thirty in the past ten days. The endives prove tricky, slipping around in my hand, which starts to shake as I spoon the bit of glistening marinara sauce into each one.

Finally, I add a last strand of chive to each of my quickly cooling plates. Nicholas takes the last one away. It is exactly one o'clock.

With that, it's over. No more classes, no more uniforms to wash, no more Tupperware or zipbags filled with food from school. I turn to my fellow American, Jenny, raise my arms in victory over my head. "I'm finished!"

"Hold that thought for ten minutes," she says, plotting little carrot balls around the edge of her plates. "I'll be done, too. Right now, I'm so stressed I might pass out."

I am happy but almost cry on the spot in a fit of stress relief and melancholy. Demetrius still has his head on his arms. I start to pack up my knives.

Students *do* fail final exams at Le Cordon Bleu, and they do not get diplomas. We're reminded of this at the beginning of the test, when we verify our phone numbers. If we fail, the school promises to call within twenty-four hours to let us know. If you don't hear anything, then you can assume you have passed.

So it is a surprise when Chef DuPont comes into the kitchen and gives me a quick hug around the shoulders. "Kathleen, c'est bien," he says. So it was fine. It appears that I've passed. A few minutes later, he returns with a laminated tag. "Comme souvenir," he says. *"Souvenir"* means "to remember" in French. From photos of past exams posted on the walls, I recognize it as the card that accompanies the official photo of my final-exam dish. It reads: "Kathleen Flinn, États-Unis, Août–Novembre 2005." I put it in my bag and look up in time to see Isabella talking to the chef.

Visibly shaken, she asks whether he thinks she's passed the exam.

"I hope so," Chef replies curtly in French. This is too much for her. She cut her hand slicing potatoes, her veal wasn't cooked, and she finished five minutes late. To fail puts in jeopardy not only her diploma but also an internship she's set up at Le Doyen. Thinking of Anna-Clare, I tell her I'll clean up her station so that she can leave quickly. I give her a hug. Steeped in depression, Isabella heads home to prepare for a houseguest from Finland.

"There's nothing I can do about the exam now," she says, on the brink of tears. "I'm in a bad mood, which is sad for my guest, but she's going to have to deal with it." I make her promise to call me. "Of course, darling, I will. Thank you." She leaves, and I tend to both our stations. Chef DuPont returns to the kitchen as I prepare to leave. We are on our own.

"C'est bien, Kathleen. Merci pour votre travail aujourd'hui," he says, a gentle smile on his face. *You did well. Thank you for your work today.* I put down my bags and knives and go to the chef.

I tell him in French, "Thank you for everything, Chef. And thank you for your kindness." I give him a quick peck on the cheek.

"Vous êtes très gentille," he says, smiling. *You're very kind.* "Comment va votre santé?" I assure him my health is fine. "Bonne chance, ma petite," he says, and gives me a chaste kiss on my forehead.

I go to the empty locker room and change out of my uniform for the last time. I turn out the light and gently shut the door.

Jenny, Margo, and I head to the Auvergne brasserie near school, joined by Samara. We split a bottle of champagne and two huge plates of *frites* and laugh and talk about the exam. Margo, the consummate competitor, finished five minutes late. Still, she was smiling and happy.

"I've been taking it all too seriously, I think," she says. Yesterday, she practiced her wine-reduction sauce three times. She burned it twice. "I was so upset. I mean, I *never* burn my sauce. But something in me clicked. When I came in today, I decided to forget the burned sauces. I would just do my best because really, that's all I can do." She took a sip of champagne.

This was a shocking statement from the woman who once spent seventy euros on food-styling magazines to try to impress the chefs, and she knew it.

"Everyone learns something different at Le Cordon Bleu, and maybe this is my lesson," she says. "Sometimes, I can't be the best. Like today. My sauce was fine. It wasn't the greatest sauce the judges saw, but it was what I could do today. I have to be happy with that."

Everyone learns a different lesson. I mull it over. I wasn't alone. The table went quiet. Then, soft-spoken Samara cleared her throat.

"You know, Le Cordon Bleu was hard for me," she started. "I had never really done anything with my hands before. Always I studied philosophy and history, and that was my life. But it was only with my head. So here, I used my hands and my heart, because it is hard for me to separate my heart from cooking. It is so . . . ." she stops, trying to find the right word.

"Personal," I offer, and she nods.

What is my lesson, I wonder?

Jenny and I stop by the school to pick up her stuff from the office. As we are about to leave, Madeleine Bisset, the woman I met the first day, asks me what I am going to do next.

"I might do an internship in the U.S. or London, but what I really need to do is get back to work and make some money," I reply.

"Ah, doing your journalism writing?" she says brightly, her words flowing in her singsong accent. I nod. She pulls out a business card from her desk drawer. "Maybe you should write about going to school here, don't you think? If you need anything, old documents, schedules, or interviews with anyone, just let me know. It's an interesting story, Le Cordon Bleu, a lot of history here, many lessons."

I might have to take her up on that. As I push open the door of 8 rue Léon Delhomme, I put on my Audrey Hepburn sunglasses, pull my sack of knives around my shoulders, and head out into the bright November day.

In the week between the exam and graduation, I seem to hear from everyone by phone or email. L.P. is back in England, starting a career as a chef-for-hire. Anna-Clare is moving back to Canada to be closer to her family; she's still throwing ambitious dinner parties and happy with her corporate life yet not ruling out making a change. Sharon is married, cooking in a small restaurant in Israel. Lely sends me congrats, plus the business plan for ChezLely, her cooking school in Jakarta. LizKat is living a glamorous life in London, marketing doughnuts. I hear Amit is back at work in his father's restaurant.

For the ceremony, we gather in the Eighth arrondissement at Cercle de l'Union Interalliée, a private club set in a massive mansion of more than twenty-one thousand square feet and formal gardens. It's decorated in Old World decor, antiques everywhere, plush Persian rugs, walls covered with oil paintings or massive tapestries—even the ceilings are gilded with gold. In the ballroom, a motley collection of Louis-the-something chairs are set up to accommodate a temporary audience. Out of our kitchen whites now, this is our last step before heading back to the real world again.

Demetrius is there to get his diploma. Despite the ruinous exam, his daily work was strong enough to make the grade. Isabella is absent, traveling with her houseguest, but she passed, too; her excellent potato galette must have made up for the delay and the undercooked veal.

"Lobster, you look gorgeous," I tell Suki when I see her shuffle into the room. Like several other Japanese women present, Suki is in a full ceremonial kimono, hers a lovely light blue. Her swept-up black hair looks lacquered, with an ornate spray of flowers cascading around her face. She looks like a geisha doll. She plans to return to Japan to start a cooking school for children, an oddly popular plan for the female Japanese graduates.

The main speaker is Jean Harzic, the former head of Alliance Française, an elegant man who speaks with a proper British accent. "You are entering a new life, and for many of you a life that will be greatly enriched by the fact that you are following your passions," he begins.

"Every culture has it own approach and thought about food. The chefs hope you will take the discipline from French cuisine, the techniques and the ideas behind them, back to your own culture and country. I encourage you to mix what you've learned with the cuisine of your own region. Experiment, be bold, create."

Afterward, each chef spoke, starting with Chef Gaillard.

"Voulez-vous une petite histoire?" he asks and the students roar with laughter and claps. He beams, proud of his joke.

Chef DuPont appears on the verge of tears. "You may have noticed that I am very sentimental," he begins in French. "It will be very difficult for me to let go of you."

Finally, it's time for us to walk onstage to gather our diplomas from the chefs.

Janine the translator announces, "Kathleen Flinn is a journalist from the United States," as I walk across and greet the chefs.

Chef DuPont smiles broadly and kisses me on both cheeks as he hands me the diploma, printed on an enormous piece of stiff white paper. Chef Savard places a tall, white paper toque on my head. "Bon travail," Chef DuPont says.

I look out over the audience, the students, their families and friends. Then I spot Mike, who has slipped to the side of the stage to snap a picture of the moment.

I turn for the official cameraman and walk off the stage. Mike looks proud.

"Thank you for this," I say, and kiss him softly. "I couldn't . . . no, I *wouldn't* have done this without you."

After the ceremony, we retreat to a set of beautiful rooms for cocktails and flutes of champagne. For her determination, Margo ranked in the top ten of our graduating class. I congratulate her. She just laughs.

"I was surprised about that, since I finished late on my exam. But it doesn't matter, does it?" She smiles and invites me and Mike to join her and her husband on their last night in Paris at the Café Trocadéro. "We'll be sitting there, drinking wine, and watching the Eiffel Tower light up in strobes every hour," she says. "We'd love you to join us." We agree we will.

Afterward, I seek out Chef Gaillard. I thank him for being tough on me. It made me work that much harder, I tell him. He smiles, and we hug, but then he holds me back by my shoulders and looks me in the eye as he says, in French:

"Don't forget, taste, taste, taste."

Veau en Croûte avec Farce de Pommes et Céleri, Sauce Calvados

VEAL IN PASTRY STUFFED WITH APPLES AND CELERY, CALVADOS SAUCE

Serves four

I prepared this for my final exam. Pork or turkey breast would work with the same flavorings; ask the butcher to butterfly the meat and give you the trimmings. The "mock brioche" recipe can be found in the "Extra Recipes" section at the end of the book (see pages 276–277), or use prepared pastry.

Prepared puff pastry or mock brioche
1 egg beaten with water (for egg wash)

1½ pounds (600 g) boneless veal, butterflied
Salt and pepper
Vegetable oil, for searing

SAUCE
Veal trimmings
1 tablespoon olive oil
1 medium onion, chopped
1 carrot, peeled and chopped

1 celery rib, chopped

1 quart (1 l) beef or veal stock

1 tablespoon butter

Cognac or Calvados to taste

STUFFING

½ medium onion, finely chopped

1 celery rib, finely chopped

1 large apple, peeled, cored, and finely chopped

1 tablespoon butter

2 tablespoons Calvados or cognac

¼ pound (115 g) ground pork, cooked

3 ounces (90 g) mousse of duck foie gras with truffles *(optional)*

Salt, pepper, nutmeg to taste

If making dough, start it first and allow it to rise. If using prepared dough, be sure to allow time for it to thaw. Trim the veal of any excess fat and season with salt and pepper. If not a uniform thickness, bang with the bottom of a pan to flatten thick areas. Set aside.

For the sauce, brown the meat trimmings in the oil. Add the onions, carrots, and celery and cook until softened, then add the stock. As you prepare the vegetables for the stuffing, toss in any trimmings, such as the apple peels. Simmer as you prepare the rest of the recipe, or until it is reduced by half.

For the stuffing, cook the onions, celery, and apples in butter over medium heat until soft. Add one tablespoon cognac or Calvados and let evaporate, scraping up the brown bits. Set aside and cool completely. Add the ground pork and the foie-gras mousse if using, the rest of the cognac or Calvados, and salt, pepper, and nutmeg.

Spread the stuffing in the center of the veal fillet and roll into a rectangular bundle. Tie with kitchen string. Sear the veal package in hot oil until brown on all sides. Remove and let cool. Pour three tablespoons of the sauce into the pan, scrape the browned bits off the bottom, and pour back into the sauce.

Preheat oven to 350°F/180°C. On a floured surface, roll out the dough into a thin circle, about ⅛ inch thick. Be sure to remove the string from the cooled meat. Wrap the veal in the dough like a present, seam sides on the bottom. Brush the pastry with egg wash. Bake for forty to fifty minutes, until a thermometer registers 150°F/65°C. (If substituting turkey for the veal, the internal temperature should read 160°F/74°C.) Let the veal rest for at least ten minutes before cutting into slices. Strain the sauce through a mesh sieve. Check seasonings. Stir in butter and cognac and whisk well. Serve the sauce alongside the meat.

THANKSGIVING IN PARIS

I stare at the turkey, feet attached, neck lamely hanging to the side on the kitchen counter. It's a fine specimen, weighing in at more than twenty pounds, with a few feathers still clinging to its dry skin. I've taken the chefs' advice and befriended a butcher, one who saved this bird just for me.

"Je sais, vous les Américains, vous aimez votre Thanksgiving," he said when he handed over the awkward bundle. *I know you Americans love your Thanksgiving.*

Now I slide my eyes over to our Euro-sized oven. The bird will never fit. About to panic, I explain the dilemma to Mike.

"Do what you learned at school: bone it and stuff it with something," he says. So, I bone the whole turkey, hacking the carcass down to make stock to use for the sauces today and gumbo later. I make a *farce* of sautéed wild mushrooms fresh from the markets. I roll it up and, using my trussing needle, sew a seam down one side; it looks as if it's wearing a complicated Victorian corset.

The legs I treat like a *jambonette*—keeping a bit of bone at the end and then filling the cavity with stuffing until it appears the leg is intact. I use a version of my stuffing from my final exam, blending diced apples, celery, and onion with a slather of *mousse de foie gras*. Bound up with caul fat, the legs hold their shape beautifully.

Among our guests from London are Marietta and her French husband, Emmanuel, who follows haute cuisine the way others follow baseball. He's been reading the Michelin *Red Guide* to Marietta's pregnant belly. "You know, the way some parents play Mozart," he starts to explain. My phone rings.

"Darling, can I bring a guest?" Isabella asks. She now works as an intern, or *stagière,* at Le Doyen. "I want to bring along someone who works with me at the restaurant." Absolutely, no problem, I say.

I go back to cooking and talking with Emmanuel. My cutting board stays clear, but otherwise the kitchen's chaos. The chefs would not approve.

As people arrive, Mike greets them with champagne. He spent the morning with Marc at the wine store, splurging on some great wines. Isabella arrives and comes into the kitchen.

"This is Olivier," she says, introducing a tall, handsome Frenchman with round wire-framed glasses. Olivier stays with me by the stove, watching intently and asking questions while Isabella laughs and jokes with Jeff and some other guests camped out in the kitchen.

"So are you an intern, too?" I ask Olivier, tasting the sauces. He shakes his head.

"No, I work in the kitchen," he says.

"Oh, in what area do you work?" I ask.

"I do banquets and private events," he says.

Oh, shit, he's a *chef,* I think.

I'm horrified to realize that there's a chef from a three-star Michelin restaurant watching me make Thanksgiving dinner. It turns out that last week he cooked for Prince Charles.

"Um, could everyone leave the kitchen now?" I ask. Mike picks up my cue. Without question, he gracefully escorts everyone into the other room for more champagne and shuts the door behind him.

Alone, I take a deep breath. The counter is strewn with pots, pans, wine bottles, stacks of produce everywhere. I walk to our window; it's so fogged from steam that I can't see outside. I throw it open for a moment and look at Paris in twilight. The crisp November air hits my face. I think of the glider pilot we met in Normandy and also of Margo's comment after the exam. I can only do my best, and today that will have to be good enough. I shut the window and go back to the stove.

Half an hour later, we sit down to dinner. We start with a gingerbread velouté soup ladled over small pieces of seared foie gras—something I learned in a Superior lesson. Jeff helps me serve the turkey off two platters, separate sauces for the white and dark meat. Among the side dishes are French beans sautéed in pancetta and mashed potatoes smoothed with chèvre. For the heck of it, I've even turned some carrots to simmer in Vichy water.

Everyone fills their plates and begins to eat heartily—except Olivier. He examines everything on his plate carefully, samples the fare, and then sits with a thoughtful look. In the middle of a raucous discussion, he takes his spoon and rings out a single, strong note against his wineglass. The table goes quiet.

"I want to make a toast to the chef," he says, and stands up. Everyone raises their glasses. "I apologize, my English is not so good. But this is a serious toast. No one but a chef knows how much work goes into a meal like this or appreciates it as much. Boning a whole turkey? It is not an easy task. Her sauces are well constructed. And the soup was good enough to serve at Le Doyen." He turns to me. "So *merci,* Chef, thank you." Everyone cheers in a toast, and he sits down. I look around the table.

This is truly a time for thanks.

This is a meal that I could not have made before I attended Le Cordon Bleu. More than half the people here are friends that I made in Paris.

My grandmother had a saying: "Every woman should get herself two things: a good husband and a good set of knives." Bad husbands aren't worth the trouble, and cheap knives aren't worth the purchase.

I amassed a great set of knives attending Le Cordon Bleu. I married the man who encouraged me to follow my dream to come here, even when it meant putting his own life on hold. We never completely filled in the map of Paris, but on my journey here I've found places within myself where I'd never been. From my romance with Mike, I've come to realize I'd never explored the streets of my emotions enough to learn the geography of my own heart.

From the chefs, I learned lessons that extend well beyond the kitchen.

As in cooking, living requires that you taste, taste, taste as you go along—you can't wait until the dish of life is done. In my career, I always looked ahead to the place I wanted to go, the next rung on the ladder. It reminds me of "The Station" by Robert Hastings, a parable read at our wedding. The message is that while on a journey, we are sure the answer lies at the destination. But in reality, there is no station, no "place to arrive at once and for all. The joy of life is the trip, and the station is a dream that constantly outdistances us."

How many tears did I cry because I didn't know what I wanted? "The sharper your knife," as Chef Savard had said, "the less you cry." For me, it also means to cut those things that get in the way of your passion and of living your life the way it's meant to be lived.

Of course, I also learned to make a mean reduction sauce and to bone an entire chicken without removing the skin, which is nice, too.

EXTRA RECIPES

The following are a few basics utilized in recipes throughout this book.

Pâte Brisée

This is the standard dough used for savory tarts and quiches. It can be made up to a day in advance.

2 cups (300 g) all-purpose flour
½ teaspoon salt
1 stick (113 g) butter, cut into pieces and chilled
2 tablespoons water

To make with a food processor: Add flour and salt to a processor fitted with a steel blade. Process a few seconds. Add butter. Pulse until it appears crumbly and coarse. Add water a bit at a time, pulsing just until the dough forms into a ball and sticks together.

To make by hand: Sift flour and salt into a bowl or on a clean surface. Rub the butter in with your fingertips until the combination appears crumbly and coarse. Make a well in the center. Add in one tablespoon of water to start. Stir it in by making circles with your index finger, adding more water until it forms a soft dough.

Form into a disk, dust with flour, and wrap in plastic. Let rest in the fridge for at least a half hour or up to one day. Roll out as directed in the recipe.

Tomato Concassé

Concassé refers to peeled, seeded, and finely chopped tomatoes, and is a staple in French cuisine. This recipe yields about two cups, depending on the size of your tomatoes.

2 pounds (900 g) fresh tomatoes

Slice an "x" on the bottom of each tomato. Drop into boiling water for a few seconds, then plunge into a bowl of ice water. Tear the flaps on the "x" to remove skin. Cut out the core and then cut the tomatoes into quarters. Using a small knife, carefully cut out the seeds and core from each piece so that only the red outer edge of the tomato is left. Chop into small pieces.

Mock Brioche

This is used in the recipe for veal *en croûte* from my final exam. Fresh yeast can be found in many supermarkets and results in a more pliable dough.

2 tablespoon fresh yeast, or 1 package active dry yeast
1½ cups (120 ml) lukewarm water
4 cups (500 g) all-purpose flour
1 teaspoon salt
½ teaspoon sugar

4 tablespoons vegetable oil

2 eggs

Egg wash

Start the pastry by adding the fresh yeast to lukewarm water and setting it aside for fifteen minutes. In a mixer with a dough hook on medium-high, blend the dry ingredients, and then add the oil and eggs. Add the yeast, water and continue mixing until it forms a dough, adding extra flour if needed to form a ball. When removed from the mixer, it should feel fairly tacky. Roll the dough onto a floured surface, then put into a large, oiled bowl. Cover with plastic and let rise for about forty-five minutes, until it's doubled in size. Use around meats or fish as a pastry crust as directed in the recipe.

Duck Confit

You can substitute four duck legs and purchased duck fat in place of whole ducks. Fresh ducks can usually be found in Asian markets. Save the breasts for another recipe. Remove the skin and roast the bones and wings for stock. The leftover fat may be kept for future confit or used in sautés. Duck confit is traditionally used in cassoulet, but pan-fried duck confit makes an excellent main dish on its own, paired with green beans. Its meat can also be shredded and added to salads.

2 large (around 5 pounds [2 kg]) whole fresh ducks

3 tablespoons coarse salt

½ teaspoon freshly ground black pepper

1 teaspoon herbes de Provence or thyme

4 cloves garlic, crushed

Cut each duck into six pieces (breasts, legs/thighs, and wings). Put the duck legs and thighs in a bowl and mix in the salt, pepper, herbs, and garlic. Reserve the remaining duck pieces for other uses. Cover and refrigerate for twelve to twenty-four hours.

Remove the fat and fatty skin from the interior of the duck and cut into small pieces. Simmer over low heat to slowly render (melt) the fat. Cool slightly. Store the fat in a sealed container.

The next day, preheat oven to a low 225°F/110°C. Gently rinse off remaining salt and herbs from duck pieces and blot dry with paper towels. Arrange snugly together in a single layer in a baking dish just large enough to hold them. Cover with the duck fat made the previous day. Bake slowly for about two to three hours until they're firm and slightly brown. Cool. Store fully covered in fat for up to three weeks in the refrigerator.

ACKNOWLEDGMENTS

This is too long. But a lot of people helped to get this book into your hands.

I'd like to thank everyone at Viking Penguin, notably Carolyn Coleburn, Lindsay Prevette, Stephen Morrison, Nancy Sheppard, Paul Slovak, Patti Pirooz, Beena Kamlani, and my wonderful editor, David Cashion. My amazing agent, Larry Weissman, and his clever wife, Sascha Alper, offered remarkable patience, advice, and feedback. They also fed us great scallops at their home in Brooklyn. A nod goes to my friend Cyrus Krohn for hooking us up.

My assistant, Lisa Simpson, has as astute a palate for words as she does for food, and for that I'm grateful. My sister, Sandra Klim, let me share her unrequited dreams of attending the Sorbonne and gave great editing advice. My mother, Irene Flinn, nurtured me through anxious phone calls and shared memories of life on the farm.

I have a lot of talented friends, and many read drafts, offered advice, gave feedback, and came to early readings. Chief among them: Deirdre Timmons, Laura Evelev, Kevin O'Halloran, Jane O'Halloran, David John Anderson, Cherie Jacobs, Kim Thompson, and Jeff Manness. My chef friend Ted Lawrence did all this, plus evaluated and edited recipes and gave me his two-thousand-word missive on stock. My pal Bill Radke didn't complain that his sole appearance involves food poisoning.

Food-studies major Jamaica Jones and chef Richard J. Lawson fact-checked culinary history and details. Elizabeth Prot cheerfully corrected my French. Several avid home cooks tested recipes, among them Lee Mohr, Diana Wisen, Barry Foy, Liz Herrin, and Marie Claire Dole. Staff at the Richard Hugo House in Seattle offered an encouraging environment; I wrote much of the book in my office there.

Gillian Kent eliminated my job in London, and I'd like to thank her for that. It's one of the best things that ever happened to me.

At Le Cordon Bleu, many fellow students had a major impact on my experience. Among them: Katherine Ferguson, Karina Ferrari, Juliana Garcia-Uribe, Julie Hinson, Tzay Pyng Hong, Anne-Catherine Kruger, Dennis Herrera Lozano, Susan Luter, Shanaz Rauff, Jose Riutort Canovas, Shelly-Anne Scott, Lely Simatupang, and Sharon Yahalom.

Of the many gracious people at Le Cordon Bleu in Paris, I'm indebted to André J Cointreau, Catherine Baschet, Sandra Messier, Sylvie Sofi Alarcon, and Patricia Gastaud-Gallagher. More thanks go to Margaret Warren of Le Cordon Bleu, Inc. and Tony Garcia of Le Cordon Bleu Ottawa.

I owe much to the talented chefs who unwittingly became major characters in this book, notably Chefs Didier Chantefort, Bruno Stril, Patrick Terrien, Marc Thivet, and Claude Boucheret. I will never forget them or what they taught me.

Finally, thanks deeper than the Pacific go to Mike Klozar. I knew he was remarkable, but he turned out to be an inspiring editor on top of his many other talents. I couldn't have done this—any of it—without him.

SELECTED BIBLIOGRAPHY

Adria, Ferran, and Juli Soler. *El Bulli: 1998–2002*. New York: Ecco Press, 2005.

Bourdain, Anthony. *Kitchen Confidential*. New York: Bloomsbury, 2000.

Brown, Dan. *The Da Vinci Code*. New York: Doubleday, 2003.

Child, Julia, Simone Beck, and Louise Bertholle. *Mastering the Art of French Cooking*. New York: Knopf, 1961.

Child, Julia, and Simone Beck. *Mastering the Art of French Cooking,* vol. 2. New York: Knopf, 1970.

Child, Julia, with Alex Prud'homme. *My Life in France*. New York: Knopf, 2006.

Davidson, Alan. *The Penguin Companion to Food*. Harmondsworth, England: Penguin Books Ltd., 2002.

Dominé, André, ed. *Culinaria France*. Köln, Germany: Könemann, 2004.

Escoffier, Auguste. *The Escoffer Cookbook* (trans. of *Le guide Culinaire*). New York: Crown, 1969.

Fisher, M. F. K. *The Art of Eating: The Collected Gastronomical Works of M. F. K. Fisher*. New York: World, 1954

Fitch, Noël Riley. *Appetite for Life*. New York: Anchor, 1999.

Herbst, Sharon Tyler. *Food Lover's Companion*. 2nd ed. Hauppage, N.Y.: Barron's Educational Series, 2000.

Jacob, Dianne. *Will Write for Food*. New York: Marlowe and Company, 2005.

Jones, Colin. *Paris: The Biography of a City*. New York: Viking Penguin, 2005.

Joseph, Robert. *French Wines: The Essential Guide to the Wines and Wine Growing Regions of France.* London: Dorling Kindersley Adult, 1999.

Le Cordon Bleu. *Le Cordon Bleu at Home.* New York: Morrow Cookbooks, 1991.

Le Cordon Bleu. *Le Cordon Bleu's Complete Cooking Techniques.* New York: Morrow Cookbooks, 1997.

Levinson, Frances. "First Peel an Eel," *Life,* November 19, 1951, pp. 83–90.

Lucas, Dione. *The Cordon Bleu Cook Book.* Boston: Little, Brown, 1947.

Mackay, Alex, and Peter Knab. *Cooking in Provence.* London: Headline, 2003.

Mayle, Peter. *A Year in Provence.* New York: Knopf, 1990.

Montagne, Prosper. *Larousse Gastronomique.* New York: Clarkson Potter, 2001.

Ostmann, Barbara Gibbs, and Jane L. Baker. *The Recipe Writer's Handbook.* New York: John Wiley and Sons, 2001.

Ruhlman, Michael. *The Making of a Chef: Mastering the Heat at the Culinary Institute of America.* New York: Henry Holt, 1997.

Sedaris, David. *Me Talk Pretty One Day.* Boston: Little, Brown, 2000.

Sokolov, Raymond A. *The Saucier's Apprentice.* New York: Knopf, 1976.

Zinsser, William Knowlton. *On Writing Well: The Classic Guide to Writing Non-Fiction.* Twenty-fifth anniversary ed. New York: Collins Resource, 2001.

INDEX OF RECIPES

MENU GUIDE FOR BOOK CLUBS

I've been a member of book clubs most of my adult life. In all of them, we consumed food and wine as well as words as part of our gatherings. This history combined with an odd affinity for antiquated "entertaining guides" prompted me to put together a menu guide for clubs reading *The Sharper Your Knife, the Less You Cry.*

Serving notes

For appetizers, consider a grazing selection of cheese, olives, prepared paté and baguettes, and perhaps Provençal spread (page 133). One main course that says it serves from six to ten, a cheese selection, a side, and a salad should be plenty for most gatherings of twelve or less. If you have more than twelve guests, solicit a member to bring a second dish. Of course, if it's a portioned thing, such as the steaks with red wine sauce (page 247), then you'll need one per person.

Allow about a half ounce of greens per person, and about two ounces of cheese (see the "elusive cheese tray" below). For dessert, persuade a member or two to bring a fruit tart, an assortment of chocolates, or a cheesecake (invoking the cheesecake disaster from chapter 18), either homemade or purchased.

Most popular book club recipes

Often it's hard to know exactly who will show up, so main dishes without specific portions serve admirable function. *Poulet à la Moutarde* (page 80) is straightforward enough for a weeknight, and inexpensive to prepare for a group. Other than the long cooking time involved, Sharon's spaghetti bolognaise (page 141) is undemanding yet satisfying. The *coq au vin* (page 162) can be time consuming, but made a day ahead (see notes below), it needs only to be reheated. Ditto for beef bourguignon (page 63).

Don't let the idea of making a leg of lamb scare you from the olive-marinated grilled lamb with white beans (page 147). Elegant and easy, the bulk of the recipe can be done ahead of time and serves a crowd. It's my favorite recipe in the book.

With all these main dishes, you can serve braised endives (page 258) as a side dish, although you need only a simple salad to round out the meal. Try arugula drizzled with fresh lemon juice, olive oil, coarse salt, and freshly ground pepper, which is Mike's favorite.

Make-ahead/potluck

These are recipes that lend themselves to being brought to or served at a club as the bulk of the work can be done ahead; I've included some tips on how to make each work

- Quiche (page 53): This reheats well in a low oven (225 degrees)
- Provençal spread (page 133): Make up to two days in advance; used in recipe below.
- Puff pastry with tuna ceviche (page 175): The ceviche needs to marinate at least six hours but not more than twenty hours. Then just bake the pastry, layer the spread, and top with the ceviche. Or you can always serve the ceviche on its own.
- Gumbo (page 100): The roux can be made up to a month in advance and frozen. The gumbo can be made a day ahead up to the point of adding the shrimp, cool and refrigerated, or even frozen for up to a

month. Thaw if necessary, and then reheat slowly to near boiling before add the shrimp.

- Spaghetti Bolognese (page 141): Make sauce up to two days in advance.
- Chicken cordon bleu (page 72): Prepare bundles a day ahead except for breading; store in airtight container in the fridge until just before cooking; bread packages and continue with recipe.
- French onion soup (page 229): Prepare onions and broth the day prior and prepare croutons. (Don't grate the cheese though; it may dry out.) Before serving, reheat soup, add to bowls, and continue recipe. Note: Make sure you have enough ovenproof bowls for all your guests.
- Crêpes (page 208): Prepare crêpes, cool and separate with pieces of parchment paper, then place in sealable plastic bags. Keep up to three days in the fridge or frozen for about a month.

THESE DISHES ARE BETTER THE SECOND DAY:
- Cassoulet (page 181): Make up to point of adding bread crumbs, cover and refrigerate. Add bread crumbs when reheating and continue.
- Grilled lamb, white beans with artichokes, and tomatoes (page 147): The beans can be made up to two days in advance and reheated. The marinated lamb can be grilled before guests arrive and kept warm in a low oven covered with foil. (Or it can be roasted in the oven, 14 minutes per pound at 450 degrees; let rest before carving.)
- Coq au vin (page 162): Make the whole dish except parsley a day prior, cover and reheat in the oven at 275 degrees until hot, about 20 to 30 minutes.
- Beef bourguignon (page 63): Same as the coq au vin above. Always a crowd pleaser.
- Minestrone soup (page 33): Make up to two days in advance, also freezes well; check seasonings before serving.

Hands-on approach

In London, I belonged to a club that liked to make dinner together. We'd talk and sip wine as we cooked, then discuss the book as we ate. The grilled pizza (page 156) is a fun option in good weather. The crêpes recipe (page 208) can be used with both savory fillings such as chicken in cream sauce, or simple ham, cheese, mushrooms as well as sweet stuff. The chicken cordon bleu (page 72), the mushroom-crusted steaks with red wine sauce (page 247), and the red snapper stuffed with Provençal spread wrapped in prosciutto (page 218) are all elegant anchors for a dinner. Pair with sautéed or mashed potatoes and braised endives (page 258), and end with chocolate soufflé (page 89) for dessert.

Virtually no cooking method

Too busy to cook? Call a local French bistro and see what they have to offer. A lot of restaurants will do takeout even if they don't advertise it. Otherwise, make a calculated stop at a deli or quality supermarket. Prepared duck confit makes its own entrée when paired with mixed greens. (If you can't find it locally, it can be ordered from dartagnan.com.) Many cheese shops also have collections of pâté and spreads, an easy appetizer when paired with sliced baguette. Roasted chicken makes an easy main course when paired with simply prepared green beans.

Vegetarians unite

These recipes can be prepared sans meat: Golden onion quiche (page 53), Provençal spread, grilled pizzas (page 156), Crepes with bananas and Nutella or jam (page 208). The white beans with artichokes and tomatoes (page 147) are good even without the salt pork.

Mastering the elusive cheese tray

Once, I suggested "bring some cheese" to my book club. All seven brought brie.

Select three or four from the groups below for a group up to eight people, and four or five for larger groups. Allow about two ounces per person. Round out a cheese platter with a baguette, sliced apples, pears, quince paste, figs, baguettes, and crackers. There's no science to it, just go for an interesting mix—say a goat, sheep, and cow's milk mix—or focus on all French or American artisanal.

- Goat or sheep's milk cheese: Chevre, Montrachet, and feta, among others.
- "Monastery" cheese: Typically semisoft and mild, these include Port Salut, Chaumes, and Belgian Chimay. Look for a monk on the label.
- Cheddar-ish: Mostly English or American made. Cantal is a French version.
- Soft-ripened cheese: Camembert and brie are easy to find. Consider St. Albany, Sainte Andre, or even a flavored Boursin.
- Swiss-style: Emmathaler is the Swiss version, Gruyere and Comte are French varieties. Gouda is a distant cousin.
- Something blue: Roquefort, Stilton, gorgonzola, et al.

You'll find more suggestions for book club menus, including additional recipes, discussion points, and more at kathleenflinn.com . . . or share your own.

Best,

Kathleen Flinn
Anna Maria Island, Florida
March 2008